I0814444

TATIANA POPOVA

Tatiana Popova is a Ukrainian embroiderer. She learnt to stitch at an early age and for a time pursued her passion for stitching by studying a huge variety of embroidery styles and techniques, both at school and in her own time.

Flowers have always had a special appeal to her. Having trained as a floristry designer, Tatiana continues making flower arrangements, now worked in silk ribbon and thread. She started her own business, Owl Crafts Company, producing kits for silk ribbon and crewel embroidery. Tatiana teaches at a number of craft shows and Embroidery Guilds all around the world, including the UK, USA, Japan, and Australia.

You can find out more about Tatiana and her work on her website www.owl-crafts.com

Also by Tatiana

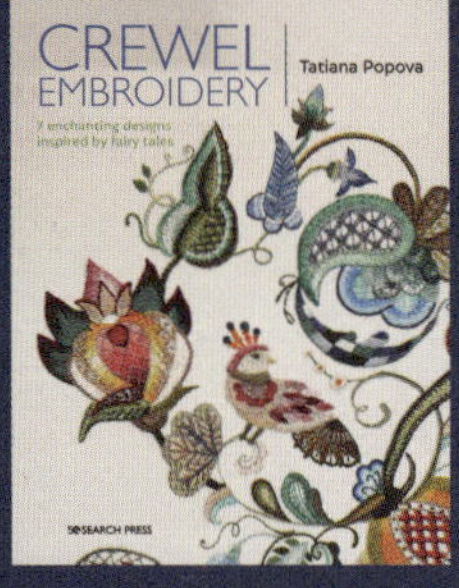

978-1-78221-722-0

978-1-78221-655-1

Contrast in CREWEL EMBROIDERY

Your eyes are not in possession of all the facts!

– Sir Terry Pratchett, *A Hat Full of Sky*

Contrast in CREWEL EMBROIDERY

Modern designs on light and dark

TATIANA
POPOVA

SEARCH PRESS

CONTENTS

INTRODUCTION

Besides being complicated, reality, in my experience, is usually odd. It is not neat, not obvious, not what you expect.

– Professor C. S. Lewis

These words of the celebrated Professor were meant to describe reality – but for me they reflect exactly what I feel about the shape of traditional crewel patterns. In my childhood, the seeming absence of rhyme or reason in their designs confused me a good deal. 'What strange people those artists must have been not to see the obvious things – there are no flowers with petals attached to the stem in such an odd way! A tendril is never that stripy, either. And those leaves – they look attached to the branches sideways!' The more I looked, the more questions arose. 'Whoever heard of a fruit placed inside... a leaf? Why is the tree trunk that thin?'

As time passed, however, it was this very feature of crewel designs that became its principal attraction for me, because I began to find a new harmony there. In Professor Lewis' words again: 'It has just that queer twist about it that real things have'.

Have a Nice Day ***(opposite) and*** **Good Night** ***(above)***
Each of the designs is worked in two versions: one on light fabric, and one on dark.

Irresistible colour

When I began to work embroidery on a regular basis, I was convinced that textures and new stitches were the things I was, and would always be, after. Later I realized that the appeal for me was really more about colour – and it is colour that we are going to explore in this book. It is an attempt to answer a question one of my students posed: 'Do people do crewel on coloured fabric?'

Besides exploring this, in this book I will share my experience of the process when creating an embroidery and choosing which stitches to include in a new design. Enjoy your adventure and let your artworks be impressive!

Details of the Light ...

What is in this book?

There are eight designs altogether, and they are of two different kinds. Four doodle designs will allow you to master the embroidery techniques while also giving you beautiful finished pieces as you learn.

The other four are the light and night designs, so-called because each of them is worked in two versions: upon light and upon dark fabric backgrounds. I flatter myself that these light and night designs will give you plenty of enjoyable challenges and new techniques to master – even for a skilful embroiderer.

Details of the doodle designs

The doodle designs (shown in circles here) allow you to practise the stitching for the main projects shown opposite. From the top:

- **Happy Birthday** which has all the stitches you need for the *Queen Rose Light* design
- **Tiny the Snail** which shows the stitches for *Green Brougham*
- **Goldfish** which contains the *Jewels of November* stitches
- **Columbine** which incorporates the stitches for *Have a Nice Day*.

Queen Rose Light See page 52.
Captured by Flora See page 72.
Jewel the Unicorn See page 94.
Have a Nice Day See page 116.

... and Night designs

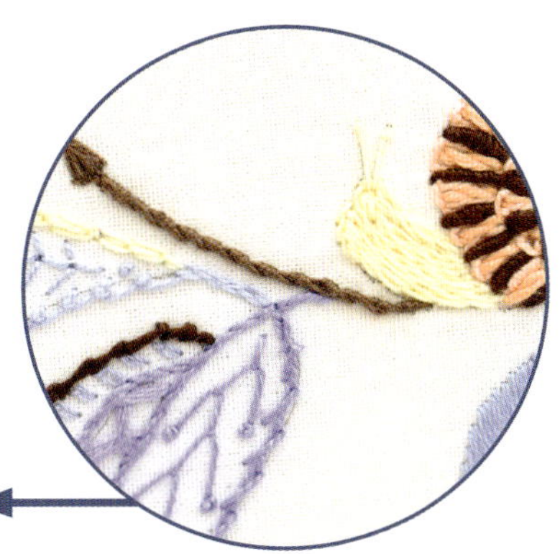

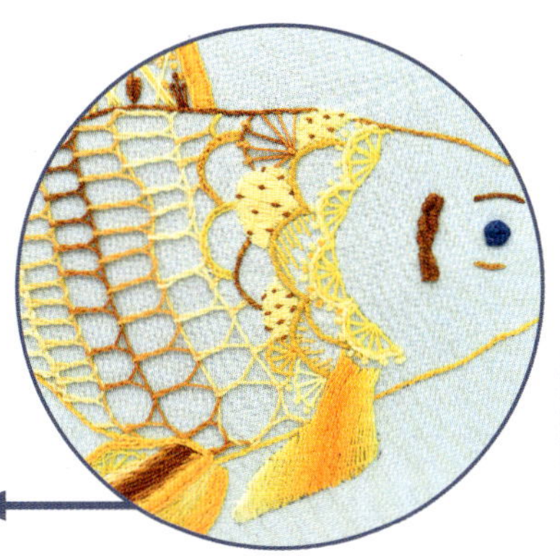

Queen Rose Night See page 62.
Green Brougham See page 82.
Jewels of November See page 104.
Good Night See page 128.

Good news from science

All too often science brings bad news: cakes are no good; sugar and salt are bad for us; we shouldn't stay out in the sun for too long, or go to bed too late; we need to stop what we're doing and start what we don't want to do... And so it is a treat to find out that there are some fields where science approves of what we are inclined to do. Psychologists agree on the therapeutic effects of embroidery: the very routine of hand stitching chronicles our emotions and promotes self-reflection.

Dear psychologists, thank you from all our hearts for some good news! To pay psychology a small tribute in thanks, I will be applying mnemonic rules to some of my stitch instructions. Dear readers, enjoy them.

MATERIALS AND TOOLS

I like work: it fascinates me. I can sit and look at it for hours. No man keeps his work in a better state of preservation than I do.

– Jerome K. Jerome, *Three Men in a Boat*

I have never done crewel. I mean it! I have never worked my embroidery using crewel wool. And since – as we are told – the name 'crewel' derives from those woollen fibres, I confess that I have never done 'proper' crewelwork. I am, however, crazy about crewel patterns and designs. Firstly, they incline me to think I can draw all right. Secondly… well, the above is good enough to make any second reason superfluous!

In this chapter we look at the tools and materials you will need – all of the options available to you; which ones are essential and which are simply nice to have.

Threads

Having confessed that I don't use crewel wool, what do I use for my surface embroidery? I mostly use DMC threads of stranded cotton or pearl cotton in sizes 8 or 12. A list of the threads I have used is given at the start of each project so you can copy it exactly, if you wish.

A TRADITIONAL APPROACH

If you are fond of a more traditional approach to crewel embroidery, use the conversion chart to Appleton wool (see right). If you decide to stitch in Appleton, bear in mind that for some of the areas you might need more or fewer strands than stated. Have a go on a spare piece of fabric first to see whether you are happy with the result.

UNUSUAL THREADS

I occasionally use other types of thread within the designs in this book, and where this is the case, I have included suggestions for substitutions. In addition to the standard stranded cotton or pearl cotton, I use these as well.

DMC Coloris threads These are variegated threads of four colours each. Each of the four component threads is drawn from the DMC range, and therefore each may be substituted by referring to the colour chart to the right. For example, the Coloris thread 4505 'heather' is a combination of greens and purples that correlate to the colours 3051, 3053, 3041 and 3042. In the lists of threads for each project, the component thread colours are given, too.

Silk threads I often use silk threads. I refer to these in the patterns either as 'fine' or 'heavy'. Fine silk threads are as fine as one strand of stranded cotton thread, while heavy silk threads are those around the same size as DMC pearl cotton size 12 thread. To allow for easy replacement, I have used the numbering of the nearest equivalent from the DMC chart, though the thread itself is not by DMC.

Atlas threads These are artificial silk threads produced in Turkey, where they are used to make beautiful Oya lace, used for decorative fringes for ladies' head scarves. The other brand name is Kaplan. I love these threads for their lustre, firmness and more dimensional twists (compared with those of natural silk thread), but be warned that they can be rather tricky to handle.

Metallic threads Also known as Lurex; these embroidery threads have a metallic appearance. They are available from a number of manufacturers, and it does not matter which brand you use for the designs in this book. Metallic threads are used just like other threads, but it is a good idea to work with shorter lengths, bigger needles, and to snip the loose tail often to prevent them from becoming tangled or ragged.

DMC to Appleton conversion chart

DMC	Appleton	DMC	Appleton
B5200	991b	760	143
Ecru	988	761	753
208	894	772	847
211	891	778	711
225	621	794	821
309	227	814	716
311	326	815	305
315	528	816	148
320	644	822	791a
351	124	828	562
352	204	830	336
353	622	841	931
368	402	842	982
369	541	890	835
415	963	902	716
444	312	913	524
501	156	931	323
502	155	938	338
503	643	945	762
517	566	959	463
518	565	987	403
519	462	988	424
522	965	989	402
554	451	3022	965
561	157	3033	971
640	967	3045	343
642	965	3053	154
646	966	3078	872
647	924	3345	256
666	995	3346	426
676	902	3348	401
712	881	3705	502
725	312	3753	561
727	842	3756	991b
733	242	3760	486
738	762	3765	489
739	761	3787	968
741	476	3813	524
742	475	3822	902
743	694	3823	331a
744	842	3842	488
745	851	3865	991b
746	881		

Linen fabric, suitable for both embroidery and backing.

Fabrics

Feel free to use any cotton or high-quality linen, but you must pre-shrink it before transferring the design. To pre-shrink fabric, simply moisten it with water and then iron it with a hot iron (set for cotton or linen, on the highest possible temperature). Another way to pre-shrink fabric is to soak the fabric in cold water for at least a couple of hours, let it dry and then iron it.

For the backing fabric, you can use either a finer cotton/linen/silk fabric, or fusible interfacing (FI), which is a type of unwoven fabric with glue applied on one side. It is better to glue the FI after the design is transferred to embroidery fabric. Put a piece of FI against the embroidery fabric so that the glued side is facing the back of the fabric. Iron the 'sandwich' to melt the glue and join the fabrics together.

If you have never used FI before, practise applying it to a spare piece of fabric first.

Materials for transferring designs

Transferring designs is every embroiderer's least favourite part of the job. These tools will make the job as swift and painless as possible.

Transferring designs to light fabrics I use HB or 2B pencils and fine Sakura Pigma Micron pens. Micron pens produce nice smooth lines and will not smudge once dried. Note that these lines are permanent: no washing will make them come off. Be careful while transferring templates and cover all the lines with your stitching.

Transferring designs to dark fabrics A lightbox is a must, and white fabric markers are very helpful. If you do not have a lightbox, pin the paper with the design to your fabric and hold it up against a window on a sunny day. The design will show through and you can trace it.

TIP

Vilene, manufactured in Germany, is among the highest quality fusible interfacing. Different varieties are available, specialized for sewing, quilting, embroidery and other purposes.

TIP

My way of coping with any lines that remain visible after stitching is to cover them with lines of stem stitch (or similar) worked using thread in the same colour as the embroidery fabric.

Needles

I have a wide selection of needles, but I mostly use chenille needles of sizes 20 to 26. When I'm feeling inspired to be extremely industrious, I also use tapestry needles of similar sizes for needlelace and particular weaving techniques.

Generally, however, I prefer pointed needles to blunt ones. If I need a blunt needle, I simply turn my needle around and lead with the eye end of the needle. It is not the best trick, because I occasionally prick my fingers, but is useful for speed and convenience.

For the finest stitching, like silk shading, I use embroidery needles in size 8 and 10.

HOOPS, FRAMES... OR NEITHER

We can become so focused on the technique while working that we don't notice when stitches start to distort the fabric. At the end, an ugly shrunken surface spoils the appearance of the finished work. Embroidery hoops or frames help us to avoid this, and make managing the fabric easier. They really make our stitching experience more enjoyable.

Choose a hoop or frame that is about 2.5cm (1in) larger than the design you are stitching. A huge variety of hoops and accessories are available: wooden hoops in different sizes; cheaper, more lightweight plastic ones; embroidery stands to help us hold our hoops; small task lamps which can be attached directly to the hoop... what a luxurious variety! However, unless the design is very small, my preference is to use a frame rather than a hoop because I love having the whole design visible to me – it helps when choosing colours, textures and stitches. Of course, if you are following project instructions, seeing the whole design at a time does not matter much, so feel free to use a hoop if you prefer. At present my favourite approach is to use a plain wooden frame with brass push pins to attach the fabric.

I embroider using the stabbing approach (see page 143), where an embroidery hoop or a frame is a must. There are some brave souls who manage to sew without hoops at all, folding embroidery fabric around the index finger of their non-stitching hand. This allows them to use the sewing method (see page 143) to go faster – but I would never run such a risk myself. It is too easy for the fabric to become distorted by overlooking an accidental over-tightening of a stitch or two.

 TIP

You can attach fabric to a frame using a staple gun instead of push pins. Staples hold on the fabric tighter, but are trickier to remove. Sometimes you are forced to carefully cut the embroidered piece out of the fabric and then to remove the staples.

MY WAY OF WORKING

The teacher had been a little bit crazy even for a teacher.

– **Sir Terry Pratchett, *A Hat Full of Sky***

As well as explaining the traditional approach to crewel embroidery, I share my own experience of stitching in this chapter. I hope it satisfies your curiosity about my way of working, and also gives you practical advice for adapting the designs in this book or working out your own original designs. I'll share all my tips and secrets, so you can benefit from the lessons I've learned without making any mistakes of your own!

Where shall we begin? Before I start stitching any project, there are always three choices to be made...

Starting points

1 **Colour choice** Colour is at the heart of all my work. I like to colour the templates of my design using watercolours, coloured pencils or photo-editing software. I make several alternative colourways, to try different ideas and highlight different areas of the design. I explore questions like 'Should the flower centre be darker or paler than its petals?' and 'Which elements should be worked in the same colour?'

Of course, because most stitches involve several threads of contrasting colours and the outcome is patterned, the actual stitching rarely corresponds exactly to these coloured templates. Moreover, as I progress with my stitching, new ideas may emerge, and a lot of changes may be apparent between the initial plan and the finished piece – but this process gives us a good starting point.

2 **Thread choice** I find this part of the process extremely enjoyable. I take my 'thread treasures' (see box to the right) and gather a selection of threads to use in my stitching. These go into a separate bag – ah, what a delight they are! – and with a happy feeling of anticipation, I go to bed. The next morning I have a second look at them, alter a few and start stitching. Gradually I come to find that at least a third of these selected threads need to be substituted – perhaps because I want a shiny thread for outlining, a heavier thread for a key area, or similar practical reasons.

To ensure a design looks harmonious and well-balanced, it is important to use the same thread repeatedly across different areas. To remind myself as I work, I attach lengths of each thread I use to a memo board. As I continue to stitch, I put away the unnecessary leftovers of the initial thread selection and focus only on the threads on the memo board.

3 **Stitch choice** The third part of my preparatory work is making a list of the stitches I want to use – you can create your own list using the magic stitch chart on page 223).

Having worked a particular stitch, I highlight it in my list with a marker. This is to help me remember it, so I can use it again for some other parts of the design I am working on. This helps to ensure that the finished embroidery has a balanced look.

An example of one of my templates that I have begun to colour, in order to explore ideas and options.

Thread treasures – using what you have

I have always felt pity about how unfairly we treat our thread stash – let me explain...

When we buy new threads, we treat them like our treasures. When we stitch with them, they are nice. Having finished, however, we treat them as 'improper' for our next design – but in truth they are still treasures. Therefore, I encourage you to use your thread stash before buying more. Here are some ideas:

- When working the projects, try substituting at least some of the threads I have suggested. You might consider a similar shade or one that contrasts.
- Develop your own colour scheme: it is fun, cheap and good for the environment. It will also save us a lot of time spent shopping.
- You might find it helpful to make a colour chart to help you keep track of your threads. You can use either the official DMC chart, or photographs from the internet as a starting point.

Once I have started

I often find it difficult to pick up my project the next day. If I love how the design is developing, I hesitate over what to do for fear of spoiling it. If I am not happy with what I see, I face a worse question: 'How can I fix it?' Therefore, before I finish each day of working on a piece, I prepare for tomorrow's stitching so I know exactly where I will start and what I will be doing.

Note my plans with pins To assist my colour and thread choice, I place a skein of threads against an unstitched area and, if I am happy with the effect, pin that skein to the area as a reminder for my next day's work. I can remind myself to apply the same thread to other parts of my design by using sewing pins with similarly coloured heads.

Take photographs At the end of my working day I often take a photograph of the current state of my unfinished embroidery. I print the photograph and write names of possible stitches against unstitched parts of my design, to suggest some possibilities to explore during the next session.

Parking threads When you come to finish for the day, make a few stitches along the stitch line, then park the threads outside the stitch area by bringing it to the front, making sure it does not go loose between the anchoring point and the needle. With the correct colour already threaded on the needle, the next day you can pick up your needle straight away and continue stitching.

This practice makes starting afresh much more convenient, so while it takes a little extra work at the end of each session, it is time well spent. Be aware that there is a limit to the number of parked threads you can reasonably fit in an area before you risk the threads getting entangled.

The knotty problem

Securing thread without making a knot has long been a high embroidery standard. Having no knots on the underside keeps embroidery extra tidy and ensures the fabric is soft – crucial for stitching bed linen and underwear, for example.

Historically, the 'No-Knot' idea derived from solid commercial sense. Up until the early 20th century, professional embroiderers made their living by doing bespoke work: custom-made embroidery aimed at decorating clothes. Knots on the underside might ruin months' worth of work, for such stitching was likely to be rejected and not paid for.

Today we mostly embroider for our own benefit: to enjoy the process; to feast our eyes upon colour and texture; to decorate our own homes. Very little of what we make truly requires an underside with no knots, but as many – perhaps most – embroiderers are inclined to be perfectionists, I will share some no-knot tricks with you over the following pages.

Using knots

I confess: I love knots and make them to secure thread for the vast majority of my stitching. I avoid knots only for a few particular techniques such as silk shading – and there simply because stitches in these techniques are so crowded that knots get in the way.

As to the kind of knot I use: I love making quilter's knots, which are technically regular overhand knots, just developed in a special way to guard a knot from nasty loops around it. Since I want to use the space in this book to teach no-knot techniques first and foremost, if you are interested in using knots, I suggest you search for quilter's knots online.

When making a knot, trim off the thread tail very close to the knot. This helps to avoid the tail being caught by the needle and brought through to the right side of the fabric.

No-knot techniques

Whatever method of no-knot securing you choose, start with the same unusual action: bring the needle to the back of the fabric from the front. This is because we want to carefully watch that cunning thread tail until it is well secured. At times it is even worth holding the thread tail with your non-stitching hand to keep it in place.

WASTE KNOT

This is my absolute favourite no-knot technique! There's something very pleasing about trimming off the waste knot and yet doing no harm to the stitching. This technique is also known as an 'away waste knot.'

1. Make a knot at the end of your thread – it does not matter how big or untidy the knot is, as it will be cut away.
2. Starting on the right side of the fabric, bring the needle to the back side 5cm (2in) or so away from the place you want to embroider.
3. Bring the threaded needle up where you want to start your stitching and you are ready to go.
4. Once you finish your work, carefully cut away the knot.

Where possible, I prefer to bring my needle through another area of stitching within the design. For a line stitch or isolated stitches, anchor the waste knot further away from the stitching area – up to 7.5cm (3in). Then, having trimmed off the waste knot, the thread tail will be long enough for you to whip it around the stitches on the back of the fabric.

Waste knot
Shown here is a waste knot placed close to, but outside the design. It is safer to place it inside another stitching area, as the thread of the waste knot may leave fibres on the fabric – and for denser fabrics this can become a nuisance. Where possible, anchor the thread within an area of stitching, as it will be covered with new stitching.

THROUGH THE LOOP

This is a nice and easy way of anchoring, but it only works for double thread.

1 Fold your thread in half and bring the two thread tails through the eye of a needle.
2 Bring the needle to the back of the fabric at the beginning of the stitch line, leaving a small loop on the right side of the fabric.
3 Come up again and go through the loop.
4 Tighten the loop to secure the thread, ready to begin stitching.

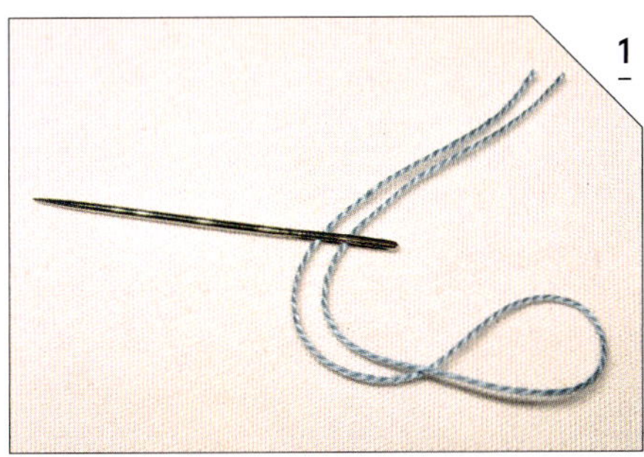

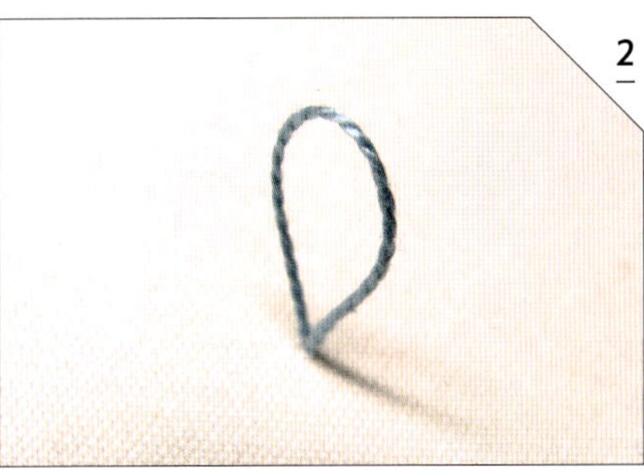

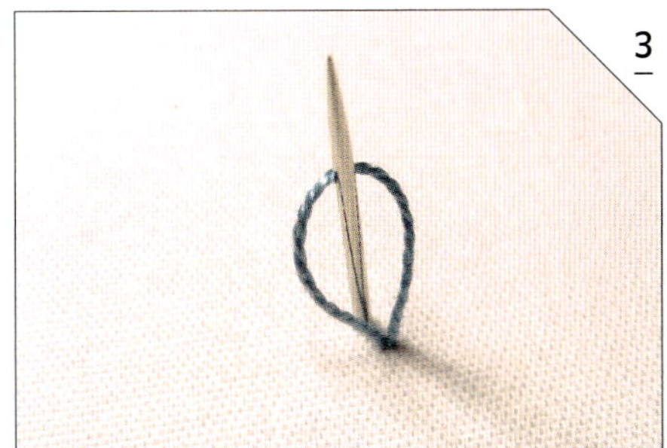

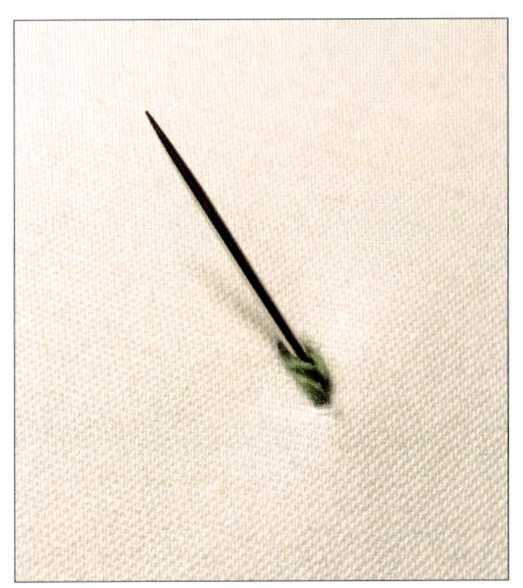

Split stitch

SPLIT STITCH OR SEEDING STITCHES

Split stitch

This is a great way to start your thread that works best for dense filling stitches. When used with line stitches, for example, it makes the tip of the line look bulky.

1 Perform a few split stitches (see page 199).
2 Trim off the thread tail.
3 Cover the stitches with regular stitching.

Seeding stitch

A similar trick can be done with a few seeding stitches (see page 195). This stitch resembles backstitch (see page 144), the only difference is that for the seeding, individual stitches are worked with more space between them.

1 Make two or three seeding stitches, leaving the unknotted thread tail on the right side of the fabric.
2 Make a check: pull on the loose thread tail to make sure it is safely secured. If it is, trim away the excess thread.
3 Proceed with your embroidery, stitching over the anchoring to cover it.

FOUR POINTS

Think of the four points of a square. These are the spots the needle will go through.

1 Bring the needle down, up and down again, as if coming through three of the four points of an imaginary square. Leave the loop loose.

2 Come up through the fourth point of the imaginary square.

3 Bring the loose thread tail through the loop and then tighten the loop.

4 The image of the finished anchoring shows the tightened loop. Together with the thread tail it resembles a tiny cross-stitch.

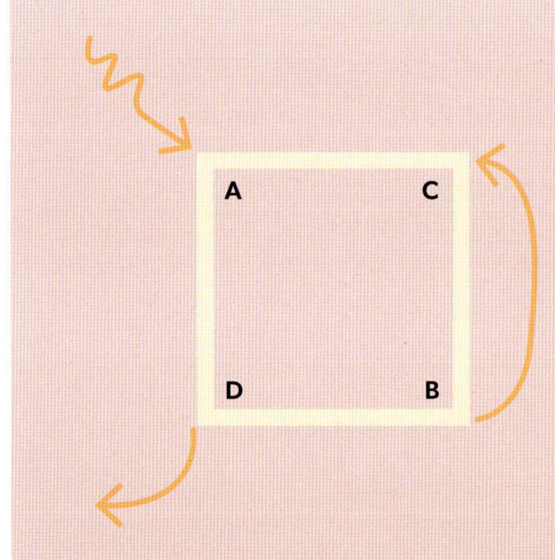

Stitch diagram

This diagram shows the view from the right sight of the fabric. The wavy end of the first arrow represents excess thread to be cut away – but only once it has been taken through the loop between points B and C, and the loop tightened.

It is important to work a tiny cross on the back, as it will secure the threads in a better way. Follow the pattern of the diagram for this; stitching through the points in A–B–C–D order (rather than the more intuitive A–C–B–D.)

 TIPS

- There's no need to draw a square on the fabric – it is only shown in the diagram for clarity.
- Both the photographs and the diagram show the four points of the square more distant from each other than they should be. Reduce the space between the points for a neater result.
- With a smaller square, you can grab the thread tail with the loop while tightening the loop at step 2, instead of step 3.

PIN STITCH

Pin stitch is popular in needlepoint embroidery. The anchoring stitching is almost invisible and so it is great for isolated stitches.

To me this stitch resembles a dance, with steps performed to the right and then to the left of the initial position.

1 Bring the threaded needle to the back and then come up very close to it. Think of it as stepping a few threads to the right of the initial place.
2 Pressing on the thread tail to keep it in place, go down through the same place as in the previous step.
3 Bring the needle up a few threads to the left from where it went down.
4 Draw the thread through.
5 Go down to the back through the same place as in steps 1 and 2.
6 Tighten up the stitch (6A). The result will be two tiny anchoring stitches (6B) formed, one to the right and one to the left of the initial placement. Trim off the excess thread.
7 Cover the place with stitching.

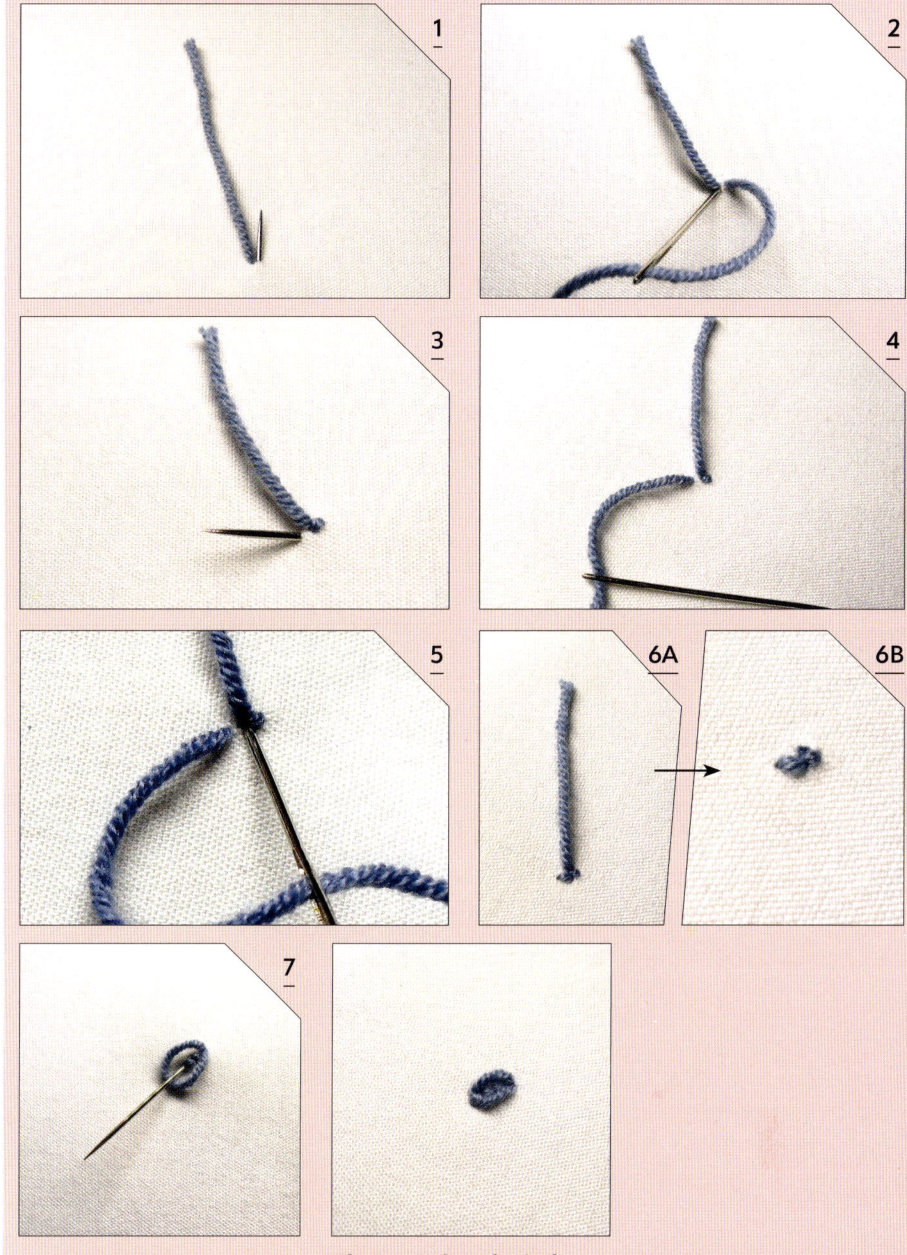

The completed stitch.

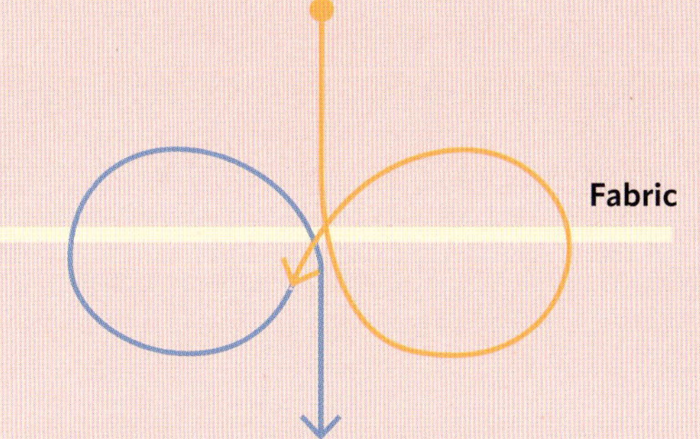

In this diagram, the steps are shown all together, depicting the thread as if seen from the side.

Invisible knot: how I finish a stitch

I call this method the invisible knot, or sliding knot. Having discovered it, I seldom use any other way of securing thread.

I often make knots at the end of my stitching, in order to anchor the thread. There is nothing special about the knot that I use for this: it is a simple overhand knot. The key point is how to ensure it is formed close to the fabric. The method comes from seed beading, and I decided to use it for my embroidery purposes.

TIP

A tightened knot that stands an inch or two above the fabric surface is no good, as it will not make a nice 'anchor' for embroidery thread: pulling on the stitches on the right side of the fabric will produce a nasty loop! Likewise, any free thread tail on the back of the fabric will get in the way of your working.

1. Make a regular overhand knot on the back, but do not tighten it at once.
2. Insert a needle inside the loose loop of the knot, so that it comes half-way through the fabric. A pin or a toothpick can be used instead, but why look for anything else when a needle is at hand?
3. Tighten the knot with the needle inside its loop, by pulling gently on the thread. The needle will guide the knot to slide down to the fabric surface.
4. The result (4A). Trim off the thread tail close to the knot (4B).

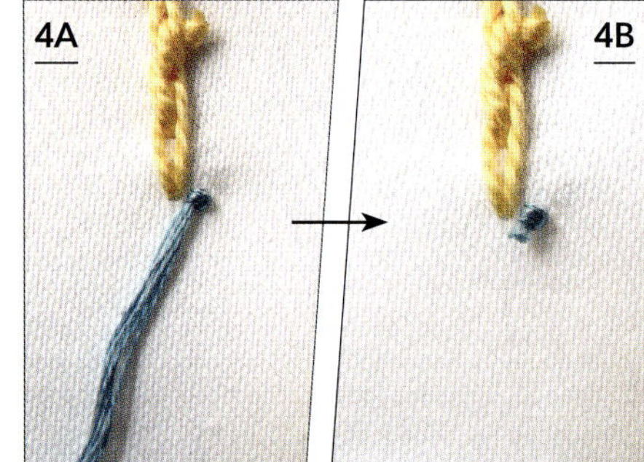

NOTES

Having mastered the invisible knot trick, you can also work it with two or three loops if you want a bigger 'stopper' for your stitching.

My other favourite way of anchoring thread at the end of a stitch is to slide the needle under the stitching on the back of the fabric. I prefer those two methods to whipping the thread tail over the stitches on the back of the fabric, because the whipping produces a rather bulky surface. And the knot I am talking about... ah – it is really tiny!

Unwanted knots and how to avoid them

There is one more kind of knot – one that all of us are all-too-familiar with, though none of us happy about it, I am sure. I am talking about the unwanted knots which form as embroidery thread gets tangled.

The good news is that there are just two most common causes of those knots – and there are also two simple remedies.

LOOSE THREAD TAILS BECOMING UNRAVELLED

Most of our embroidery threads are manufactured by twisting two fibres together. In loose thread tails those fibres often get untwisted as the embroidery thread passes repeatedly through the fabric. That tassel-like thread tail becomes rather over-friendly: it gives hugs to embroidery thread, leading to a nasty entangled knotty mess.

A simple remedy: do not forget to trim off the loose thread tail every now and then. Fresh tails are tightly twisted and will not give you any trouble.

THE THREAD ITSELF GETTING TOO TWISTED

Most embroidery techniques tend to add a slight twist to our needle and thread. Over time, this results in an overtwisted thread which catches on itself, becomes entangled and forms knots.

A simple remedy is to develop the habit of taking short breaks to 'pet' your thread every now and then. Having done some stitching, bring the thread to the right side of the fabric, then push the needle all the way down to the fabric, moving it along the thread. Next, pinch your thread between your forefinger and thumb and gently glide them along the thread, as if straightening a piece of wire. Repeat this action several times then bring the needle to its normal position and resume stitching. You'll find that the happy thread is now in no mood to give you any trouble.

To sum it up: hurray – no more interruptions in our lovely stitching job!

SMART DOODLES

It has long been an axiom of mine that the little things are infinitely the most important.

– Sir Arthur Conan Doyle, *A Case of Identity*

This chapter includes four unusual designs for crewel stitching. Let me let you into a secret – they are stitch samples in disguise! To learn a stitch properly, you have to try your best to get a nice finish, but it is a chore to make such special effort for a sample, which is really just a doodle you make before the 'proper work' begins.

Here then are doodles which are also small, simple designs of their own, each with its own charm. The doodles will allow you to practise the stitches for the larger projects.

Smaller than the designs to which they relate, they include bigger areas for each stitch. The list of stitches for each doodle is the same as the design for which they are a sample. In most cases they use heavier threads than the 'parent' design, which is really helpful when you are practising a stitch for the first time. With only a couple of exceptions, each stitch is used only once, so you can practise things without much repetition, and you will end up with a beautiful piece to show for your efforts.

Below, from left to right:

Doodle 1 – Happy Birthday will teach you the stitches for *Queen Rose Light* on page 52.

Doodle 2 – Tiny the Snail contains all the embroidery techniques you need for *Green Brougham* on page 82.

Doodle 3 – Goldfish will explain the stitches you need for *Jewels of November* on page 104.

Doodle 4 – Columbine will let you practise for *Have a Nice Day* on page 116.

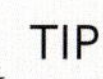

TIP

Have fun: combine your favourite Doodle outlines with stitches used for another Doodle. The magic stitch chart on page 223 will help you in making your own stitch plan for this.

Understanding the embroidery instructions

In our heart of hearts, we remain children – and like children, we likely prefer pictures to text. Therefore, the embroidery instructions in this book are given as pictures with numbers, which are explained in an accompanying coded list. The code explains the stitch to use, along with the type and colour of thread you need, as shown to the right.

Note that the reference numbers do not suggest an order of work, but simply indicate where the stitch should be worked. You can work the stitches in any order you choose.

For easy reference, all of the stitches listed with each project are explained and shown in detail in the stitch menu on pages 140–211.

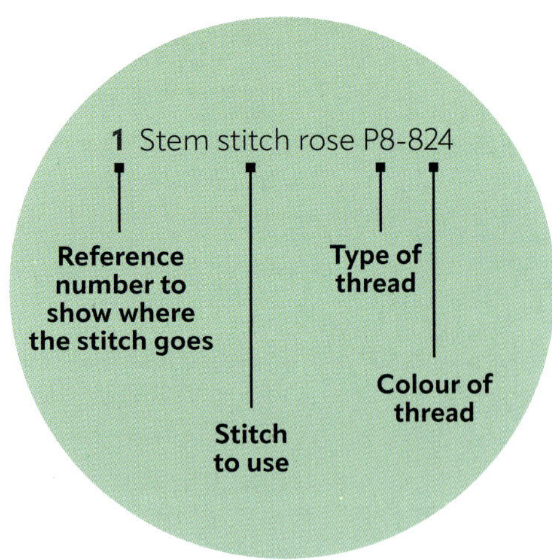

Cracking the code

Let's look at a real example to see this in more depth. The code for this part of the Goldfish reads as follows:

1 Stem stitch rose P8-824
2 Split stitch P8-111
3 Woven bar P8-111
4 Split stitch P8-111
5 Raised stem stitch P8-90
6 Buttonhole scallop + French knot SC-3821(1).

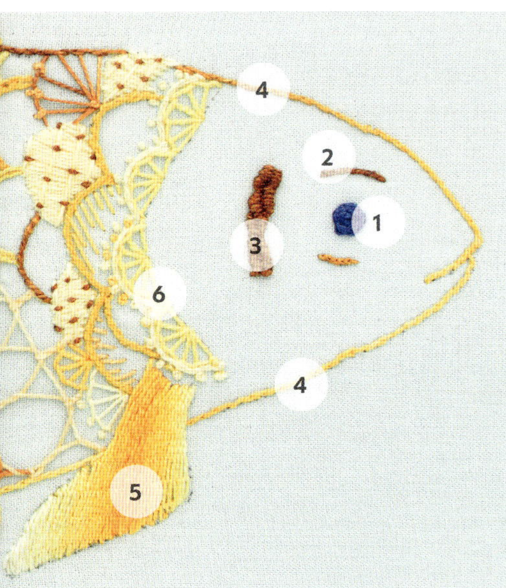

Detail of the Goldfish's head
See page 40 for this doodle project.

1 Stem stitch rose P8-824 – This means you embroider the fish's eye (marked with a '1') like this:

- *'Stem stitch rose'* gives us the name of the stitch we use.
- *'P8'* indicates that we need to use pearl cotton at DMC size 8 ...
- ... and *'824'* tells us the colour of the thread – in this case, 824 Blue – vy dk.

2 Split stitch P8-111; ***3*** *Woven bar P8-111;* ***4*** *Split stitch P8-111* – While the stitch used for these steps varies, we use the same thread for each: DMC pearl cotton size 8 thread in 111 Variegated Orange to Brown dk.

5 Raised stem stitch P8-90 – The fin is worked in raised stem stitch, using DMC pearl cotton size 8 thread in 90 Variegated Yellow to Orange.

6 Buttonhole scallop + French knot SC-3821(1) – This step is a little more complex, but the same rules apply. Here, we use both buttonhole scallop stitch and French knots using stranded cotton thread in 3821 Straw. The figure in brackets – ('1') – is for the number of strands of the thread. In this example, it calls for a single thread.

What sort of thread?

As I have already mentioned, I love cotton threads and use them for my crewel stitching instead of wool. The two types of threads I use most often are pearl cotton and stranded cotton, both produced by DMC.

PEARL COTTON THREAD CODES

Pearl cotton thread takes its name from the French *coton perlé*. It is non-divisible. Unless otherwise stated, always use pearl cotton of any size as a single thread. Size 12 pearl cotton thread is finer and size 8 is heavier. For a few particular stitches I sometimes use size 5 pearl cotton thread, which is heavier still:

P12 DMC size 12 pearl cotton

P8 DMC size 8 pearl cotton

P5 DMC size 5 pearl cotton

EXAMPLES OF PEARL COTTON CODES

- **P8-309** Use DMC size 8 pearl cotton thread, in Dark Rose (309 in the DMC colour chart).
- **P12-3689** Use DMC size 12 pearl cotton thread, in Light Mauve Pink (3689 in the chart).

EXAMPLES OF STRANDED COTTON CODES

- **SC-647(1)** Use a single strand of DMC stranded cotton thread in Medium Beaver Gray (647 in the chart).
- **SC-647(2)** Thread your needle with two strands of DMC stranded cotton thread in Medium Beaver Gray (647 in the chart).

STRANDED COTTON THREAD CODES

Each strand of stranded cotton thread consists of six fine divisible strands, which we can thread onto a needle and use individually, in pairs, or more. The number of strands you need is given in brackets after the colour, so (2) would mean you use a needle threaded with two strands.

Some stitching techniques may call for using stranded cotton threads in different ways, in which case the figures in brackets differ as shown in these examples:

Silk shading SC-640; 642(1) Both colours of threads are used for an area – that is, SC-640 is used for the bottom part of the silk shading, and blended into SC-642 for the top.

Couching SC-647(6;1) All six strands of stranded cotton thread are to be couched with just one strand.

Bayeux stitch SC-647(3;1;2) The figures follow the order of stitching, as the number of threads used for each step of the stitch varies. In this Bayeux stitch example, step 1 (basic satin stitch) is worked using three threads; step 2 (long straight stitches across the area, perpendicular to the direction of satin stitches) are worked in a single thread; and in step 3, long stitches are couched in double thread.

Twisted cord SC-647(1) One thread is used for making a twisted cord, which is then used for the actual twisting. To clarify: when a single thread is twisted and then folded in half to produce a cord, it becomes doubled, and thus effectively two – the number in brackets simply indicates the number of threads used when you start making the cord.

Couching, twisted cord SC-647(1;1) A single thread is used for making the cord, and another single thread is used to attach it to the fabric.

Satin stitch – padded + lattice SC-444 (2;1;1) Use two threads for padding, a single thread for satin stitch, and then another single thread for lattice.

CODES FOR OTHER TYPES OF THREAD

There are only four designs in this book which call for any other types of thread. For each case an option for substitution is suggested. The colour code for these threads is given according to DMC chart to make the substitution as easy as possible.

Silk Silk threads. As explained on page 11, these are noted as either Fine – equivalent to one strand of stranded cotton thread – or Heavy, around the same size as DMC pearl cotton size 12 thread.

At Use Atlas thread (see page 11). Size 12 pearl cotton thread is the best option for substitution. Two or three strands of stranded cotton thread or 100 per cent natural heavy silk thread may also be used instead of Atlas thread.

EXAMPLES OF OTHER THREAD CODES

- **Silk-161** Use grey-blue silk in a colour that corresponds to DMC 161 Gray Blue.
- **At-301** Use Atlas thread in a colour corresponding to DMC 301 Mahogany.

AVOIDING WASTE: HOW MUCH THREAD?

There are a few things I would like to mention before we come to the embroidery instructions.

You would hardly ever use a whole skein of a particular stranded cotton thread for one design, let alone a whole ball of pearl cotton. I always feel a little guilty when my designs include a large number of colour shades and hues – and this is why I often suggest embroiderers cut down the number of threads needed for a particular design.

Happily, this reduction is easily done: select a shade of colour you prefer for the whole 'colourful cluster' – greens, for example – and then make a note for yourself that whenever the other colours of a cluster are featured, you are going to use the chosen one instead of all of them.

Of course, this is only a suggestion. Some of us like using a wide variety of hues in our embroideries, rightly thinking that it enriches the finished stitching.

Whatever your choice is, keep in mind that one skein or one ball of threads is more than sufficient for one design, and that there is no need to purchase more than one of each. If you decide to use your own stash of threads for the projects in this book, partly used skeins will definitely suffice!

Tools, not jewels

This is what my own DMC thread chart looks like – ugh! I am very sorry for its ruined beauty, covered in notes and reference marks, but I do not regret my barbaric actions: the chart is but an instrument. The marks I have made are like the leftover mortar on a bricklayer's trowel – ugly evidence of hard work!

Threading the needle: single vs double

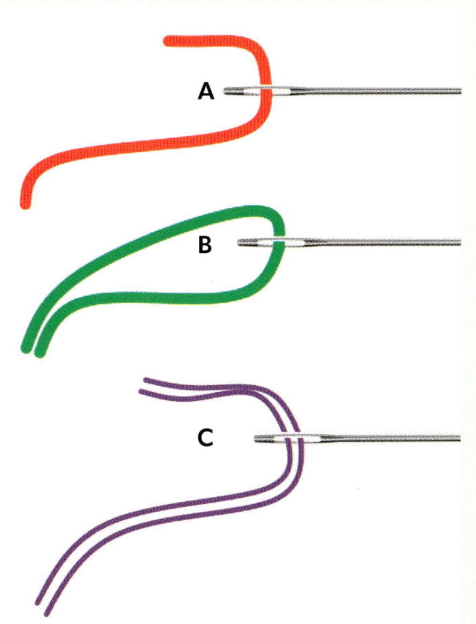

A This shows a single thread, which is how I most often work. Anchoring thread without knotting the thread tail gives a higher quality finish. If you also want to do without a knot, make waste knots or use some other tricks (see pages 17–23 for more on this).

B This shows the double thread used for sewing purposes. While it prevents the needle from slipping off the thread, very few embroidery techniques allow it without sacrifying the quality of a finished stitch, because doubled thread is more likely to get twisted, tangled or simply not give a stitch a smooth finish.

C This shows the double thread most commonly used for embroidery: nothing more than threading the needle with two separate threads. There is nothing to stop the needle from slipping off, but the finish of stitches worked in this way is far more refined and beautiful.

IF DESIGN LINES REMAIN VISIBLE AFTER STITCHING

I confess! I advised you to use permanent pens for transferring designs – and now you have finished your beautiful stitching, some design lines remain, creating untidy outlines where they are unwanted.

Bear in mind this potential problem as you work, and work stitches a little bit outside the design line every time to help hide the design lines. To help avoid this problem happening in the first place, make sure the smallest elements of the design (round berries or very small leaves, for example) are in circles or ovals that are a little bit smaller than you want in the final design.

When using the templates in this book, feel free to use stitching to enlarge the element where necessary, and therefore cover the drawn lines. If, however, some lines are visible in your embroidery after it is completed (it happens to me as well!), here are a few tricks to cope with the problem.

- Hide the stitch line by performing a second line of stem stitch (or similar) along the troublesome part of the design, using thread of the same colour as the one which is already making the outline.
- Using thread in the same colour as the fabric, work either stem or split stitch to cover the line.
- Work twisted cord along the whole element to get a nicely ribbed finish which is not very visible, and yet gives charm to the stitched area.

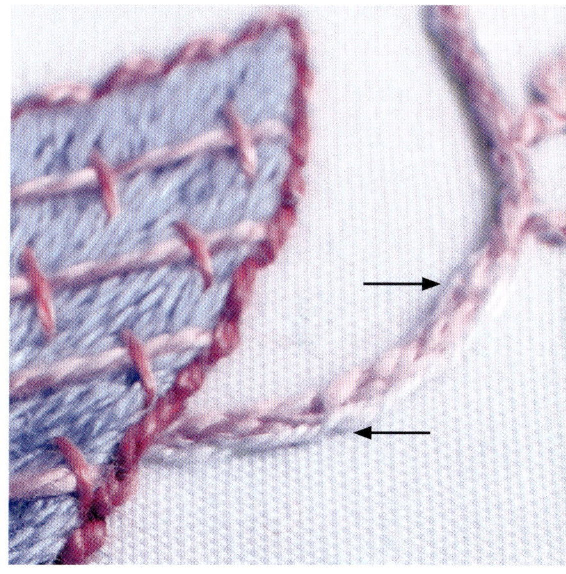

The arrows in the photograph show where extra stitching has been worked to hide visible design lines. Luckily the problem does not happen very often, and fixing it is not too troublesome.

Doodle 1 – *Happy Birthday*

This doodle stitching will help you to practise for the crewel embroidery design on page 52, *Queen Rose Light*. The template is on page 213, and the stitched area of the finished piece measures 19 x 20cm (7½ x 7¾in).

Stitch techniques used in this project

Backstitch see page 144
Backstitch – whipped see page 144
Blanket stitch – whipped see page 146
Bullion knot see page 147
Burden stitch see page 147
Buttonhole stitch see page 148
Buttonhole stitch – padded see page 151
Chain stitch see page 156
Couching (thread) see page 159
Couching (twisted cord) see page 160
Cretan stitch leaf see page 161
Crochet chain see page 161
Double lattice + 4-stitch couching see page 161
Fancy filling – leaf pattern see page 163
Fancy filling – rosebud pattern see pages 164–165
Feather stitch see page 167
Fly stitch – whipped see page 168
French knot see page 171
Heavy chain stitch see page 173
Lattice see page 176
Lattice + woven filling see page 177
Lazy daisy stitch see page 178
Odd flower petal see page 179
Palestrina stitch see page 182
Pistil stitch see page 183
Pistil stitch twigs see page 183
Portuguese knotted stem stitch see page 184
Raised fishbone stitch leaf see page 186
Raised stem stitch see page 187
Rope stitch see page 191
Satin stitch see page 194
Satin stitch – padded see page 194
Silk shading see pages 196–197
Silk shading – padded see page 197
Split stitch see page 199
Stem stitch see page 200
Stem stitch – whipped see page 200

Suggested threads

Rather than being organized by their ID numbers, threads here are arranged according to their actual colour shades: from lighter (or brighter) to darker colours. This is to make thread replacement easier.

DMC STRANDED COTTON THREAD

BURGUNDY
3803 Mauve – dk
3685 Mauve – vy dk
814 Garnet – dk
902 Garnet – vy dk

APRICOT
353 Peach
3824 Apricot – lt
3341 Apricot
352 Coral – lt

SCARLET
349 Coral – dk
347 Salmon – vy dk
815 Garnet – med
221 Shell Pink – vy dk

PINKISH
899 Rose – med
3731 Dusty Rose – vy dk
3804 Cyclamen Pink - dk
777 Raspberry – vy dk

OLD GOLD
739 Tan – ultra vy lt
738 Tan – vy lt
167 Yellow Beige – vy dk
E436 Tan (metallic thread)

SILVERY
3046 Yellow Beige – med
E677 Old Gold – vy lt

DMC PEARL COTTON SIZE 8 THREAD

BURGUNDY
315 Antique Mauve – med dk
902 Garnet – vy dk

APRICOT
224 Shell Pink – vy dk
353 Peach

SCARLET
347 Salmon – vy dk

PINKISH
600 Cranberry – vy dk
602 Cranberry – med
899 Rose – med

SILVERY
644 Beige Grey – med

DMC PEARL COTTON SIZE 12 THREAD

842 Beige Brown – vy lt
712 Cream

Embroidery instructions

See pages 26–28 for how to read the thread code in these instructions.

PART 1

1 Double lattice P8-315 + 4-stitch couching SC-353(2); lazy daisy stitch P8-353; French knot P8-347

2 Buttonhole stitch – padded + pistil stitch. Assorted threads

3 Two rows of rope stitch SC-349(2); P8-347

4 Buttonhole stitch – padded SC-349(6); P8-347

5 Silk shading. Assorted SC(1), shades of burgundy

6 Silk shading. Assorted SC(1 or 2), shades of apricot

7 Silk shading. Assorted SC(1 or 2), pinkish shades

8 Burden stitch P8-224; 353; twisted cord using SC-352(1)

9 Rope stitch SC-902(6)

10 Lattice P8-353; 347

11 Fancy filling – rosebud pattern. Step 1: satin stitch SC-3824(2). Steps 2 and 3: lattice P8-347. Step 4: couching: SC-3341(2). Step 5: dividing SC-3341(2)

12 Rope stitch SC-814(6)

13 Double lattice P8-902 + 4-stitch couching. Assorted SC(2)

14 Raised stem stitch + lattice. Assorted threads

15 Raised stem stitch P8-347

16 Silk shading SC-3731; 3804; 777(1)

17 Fancy filling – rosebud pattern. Step 1: satin stitch SC-352(6). Steps 2 and 3: lattice P8-353. Step 4: couching SC-902(2). Step 5: dividing P8-902

18 Silk shading + lattice. Assorted Burgundy SC(1)

19 Fancy filling – leaf pattern. P8-347; 353; SC-353(2)

20 Heavy chain stitch SC-167(2)

21 Raised fishbone stitch leaf P12-842; stem stitch SC-167(2)

22 Cretan stitch leaf and stem stitch SC-167(2)

23 Whipped fly stitch P8-644; stem stitch SC-167(2)

24 Crochet chain P12-712 + backstitch SC-167(4)

25 Buttonhole stitch and pistil stitch twigs P12-842

26–28 Odd flower petal P8-644; split stitch P8-644; SC-E677 to add an accent

29 Whipped fly stitch, lazy daisy stitch, stem stitch, split stitch. Assorted threads

30 Portuguese knotted stem stitch P12-712

31 Whipped stem stitch SC-3046(2;3)

32 Palestrina stitch SC-167(2)

33 Whipped stem stitch + bullion knot SC-3046(2;3)

34 Couching SC-E436(6) couched with SC-167(2)

35 Cretan stitch leaf SC-167(2); stem stitch SC-167(1)

36 Pistil stitch twig P12-712

37 Raised fishbone stitch leaf P12-842 and stem stitch SC-E436(1)

38 Couching SC-E436(6) couched with SC-167(2)

39 Couching + chain stitch SC-167(2;1)

40 Lattice SC-E677(1); SC-3046(2)

41 Portuguese knotted stem stitch P8-644 around the leaf; stem stitch along one half of the leaf using SC-3046(2)

42 Satin stitch SC-3046(2). Outline: chain stitch SC-E436(2)

43 French knot SC-3046(2); SC-E436(2). Outline: chain stitch SC-167(2)

44 Couching SC-E436(6;1) and French knots along the vein inside the leaf using SC-E436(1)

45 Backstitch for midrib lazy daisy stitch for one half of the leaf and French knots for the other half, all in SC-E436(1)

46 Couching SC-E436(6) couched with SC-167(2)

47 Crochet chain P12-712 attached to the fabric with backstitch SC-167(4)

24
22
26
27
23
21
20
28
25
5
4
6
29
1
30
31
7
2
32
33
3
34
9
10
11
8
14
12
35
13
37
36
15
38
16
39
17
18
19
40
41
42
45
46
43
44
47

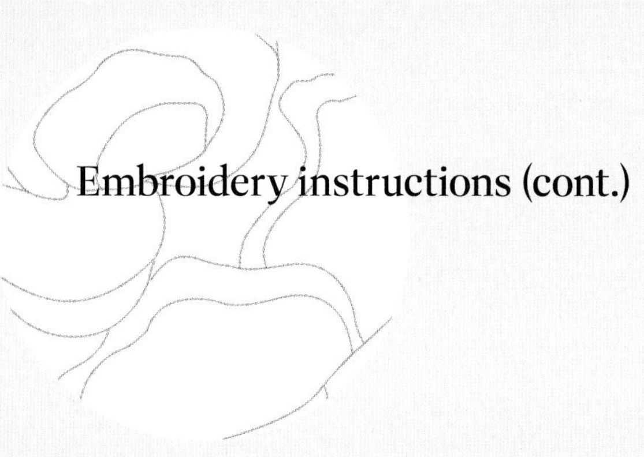

Embroidery instructions (cont.)

PART 2

1 Satin stitch – padded SC-3824(2;1). Atop: lattice P8-353, couched with SC-3341(2)

2 Rope stitch SC-902(6)

3 Fancy filling – leaf pattern. Steps 1 and 2: Lattice P8-602. Skip step 3 (couching to the right and to the left of each intersection). Step 4: long stitches in twisted cord SC-777(1). Step 5: diagonal couching stitches SC-3804(2)

4 Open chain stitch couching P8-602, worked over chain stitch P8-600

5 Burden stitch. Basement stitches P8-600. Burden stitches: alternate P8-600; 602; 899

6 Rope stitch SC-347(6)

7 Double lattice P8-902 + 4-stitch couching. Assorted SC(2)

8 Rope stitch SC-814(6)

9 Silk shading – padded SC-349; 347; 815; 221(1)

10 Lattice + woven filling. Lattice: P8-899, couched with SC-353(2). Weaving: P8-3685

11 Split stitch P8-3685, covered with buttonhole stitch P8-3685

12 Fancy filling – rosebud pattern. Step 1: satin stitch SC-352(6). Steps 2 and 3: lattice P8-353. Step 4: couching P8-902. Step 5. Magic couching SC-902(2)

13 Couching P8-224 with SC-3024(2)

14 Double lattice P8-315 + 4-stitch couching SC-353(2). Each cell is filled with lazy daisy stitch P8-224 with a French knot P8-347 at its tip

15 Rope stitch SC-814(2)

16 Fancy filling – leaf pattern. Steps 1 and 2: lattice P8-347. Do not work step 3 (couching), skip to step 4 instead. Step 4: long stitches in twisted cord SC-353(2). Step 5: diagonal couching stitches P8-353

17 Rope stitch P8-347

18, 19 Whipped fly stitch P8-644; stem stitch SC-167(2)

20 Crochet chain P12-712 + backstitch SC-167(4)

21–23 Palestrina stitch SC-167(2); heavy chain SC-739(2) outlined with stem stitch SC-167(1); couching SCE436(6), couched with SC-167(2); lazy daisy stitch SC-E436(1)

24–26 Blanket stitch and raised stem stitch P8-644; chain stitch SC-738(2); Portuguese knotted stem stitch P8-644

27 Stem stitch P8-644

28–32 Couching around the leaf SC-E677(6), couched with SC-738(2); bullion knot P8-644; French knot SC-738(2); midrib in split stitch SC-3046(2); couching inside the leaf SC-E677(1), couched with SC738(1)

33 Couching SC-E677(6) couched with SC-3046(2)

34–36 Couching, stem stitch, French knot SC-E436(2); 167(2)

37–40 Palestrina stitch SC-167(2); lattice SC-738(2); chain stitch SC-167(2); lazy daisy stitch SC-738(2); stem stitch SC-3046(2)

41–43 Bullion knot SC-3046(6), French knot SC-167(2), stem stitch SC-167; 738(1), heavy chain stitch SC-167(2)

44 Cretan stitch leaf P8-644

45 Couching SC-E677(1) couched with SC-738(2)

46 Raised fishbone stitch leaf P12-842

47 Stem stitch SC-E436(1)

48 Portuguese knotted stem stitch P8-644

49 Cretan stitch leaf SC-167(2)

50 Crochet chain P12-712 attached to the fabric with backstitch SC-167(4)

20
18
19
21
25
24
26
22
23
3
4
2
1
9
27
32
28
29
6
31
30
5
11
33
10
8
36
34
7
13
12
15
35
14
37
39
38
16
40
42
41
17
49
45
43
44
48
46
47
50

Doodle 2 – *Tiny the Snail*

This doodle stitching will help you to practise for the crewel embroidery design on page 82, *Green Brougham*. The template is on page 214, and the stitched area of the finished piece measures 18 x 20.5cm (7 x 8⅛in).

Stitch techniques used in this project

Backstitch see page 144
Blanket stitch see page 146
Bullion knot see page 147
Buttonhole scallops see page 148
Buttonhole stitch see page 148
Buttonhole stitch – padded see page 151
Chain stitch see page 156
Corded single Brussels stitch see page 159
Couching (thread) see page 159
Couching (twisted cord) see page 160
Feather stitch see page 167
Fern stitch see page 167
Fly stitch see page 168
Fly stitch leaf see page 169
French knot see page 171
Heavy chain stitch see page 173
Herringbone stitch see page 174
Hungarian braided chain stitch see page 174
Lattice see page 176
Lattice + woven filling see page 177
Lazy daisy stitch see page 178
Pistil stitch see page 183
Portuguese border stitch see page 184
Portuguese knotted stem stitch see page 184
Raised fishbone stitch leaf see page 186
Rope stitch see page 191
Satin stitch see page 194
Scroll stitch see page 195
Silk shading see pages 196–197
Split stitch see page 199
Stem stitch see page 200
Stem stitch filling see page 201
Straight stitch see page 201
Tuning fork stitch see page 204
Twisted chain stitch see page 204
Twisted cord see page 205
Twisted single Brussels stitch – whipped see page 206
Woven band see page 208
Woven wheel see page 211

Suggested threads

DMC STRANDED COTTON THREAD

951 Tawny - lt
758 Terra Cotta – vy lt
341 Blue Violet – lt
340 Blue Violet – med
3740 Antique Violet – dk
938 Coffee Brown – ultra dk

DMC PEARL COTTON SIZE 8 THREAD

744 Yellow - pale
783 Topaz - med
945 Tawny
353 Peach
341 Blue Violet – lt
340 Blue Violet – med
938 Coffee Brown – ultra dk

DMC PEARL COTTON SIZE 12 THREAD

3823 Yellow – ultra pale

Embroidery instructions

See pages 26–28 for how to read the thread code in these instructions.

PART 1

1 Lattice P8-340 couched in SC-3740(2) + woven filling P8-744

2 Corded single Brussels stitch P8-744

3 Blanket stitch P8-939; the gaps are filled with straight stitch SC-951(6)

4 Heavy chain stitch P8-340

5 Stem stitch filling SC-3740; 340; 341(1) surrounded with pistil stitch P8-341

6 Woven band P8-938; 744

7 Chain stitch, stem or split stitch SC-341(2)

8 Stem stitch using twisted cord SC-951(6)

9 Silk shading SC-3740; 340; 341(1)

10 Rope stitch P8-938; couching P12-3823 anchored with SC-951(1)

11 Filling: fly stitch SC-341(1), outline: rope stitch P8-341

12 Lattice P8-938 couched with SC-951(6), outline: chain stitch P8-783

13 Lazy daisy stitch P12-3823; outline: Hungarian braided chain stitch and backstitch P8-340

14 Woven wheel P8-938

15 Filling: Portuguese border stitch P8-783; outline (bottom part): backstitch and French knots P8-938; outline (top part): two lines of couching P8-353 anchored in SC-758(2)

16 Buttonhole stitch – padded: padding in chain stitch SC-951(6) and buttonhole in P8-783. It is actually the nature of blanket stitch that determine the gaps between individual stitches, but I have kept the name of the technique as-is for simplicity. Fill in each gap with a lazy daisy stitch P12-3823

17 Couching (thread): P8-353 attached with SC-758(2)

18 French knot P8-341 and buttonhole scallop P12-3823

PART 2

1 Filling: twisted single Brussels stitch P8-341; outline: stem stitch P8-340

2 Stem stitch and French knot P8-938

3 Raised fishbone stitch leaf SC-3740(2)

4 Feather stitch P8-938

5 Fly stitch leaf P8-938

6 Corded single Brussels stitch P8-340

7 Twig of the berry: Portuguese knotted stem stitch P8-938. Top part of the main stem: Portuguese knotted stem stitch SC-3740; buttonhole stitch P8-938

8 Stem stitch filling P12-3823; for eyestalks: pistil stitch P12-3823

9 First work bullion knots P8-938, leaving small gaps between them. Fill in each gap with a straight stitch embroidered in twisted cord SC-951(6). Finally, work a lazy daisy stitch around each straight stitch in P8-353

10 Middle: fern stitch P8-341. Top: tuning fork stitch P12-3823. Bottom: scroll stitch P8-341

11 Herringbone stitch SC-340(6), to the right and to the left of it: two lines of stem stitch P8-340

12 Twisted chain stitch P8-938; lazy daisy stitches protruding to the right side P8-341

13 Feather stitch with French knots at the tips P8-340; twisted chain stitch P8-340

14 Two scallops on the tip: satin stitch SC-341(2)

15 Scallop in the middle: buttonhole stitch P8-341. Right-hand scallop: satin stitch SC-341(2)

Doodle 3 – *Goldfish*

This doodle stitching will help you to practise for the crewel embroidery design on page 104, *Jewels of November*. The template is on page 215 and the stitched area of the finished piece measures 25 x 18cm (9⅞ x 7in).

Stitch techniques used in this project

Backstitch see page 144
Bayeux stitch see page 146
Blanket stitch see page 146
Bullion knot see page 147
Burden stitch see page 147
Buttonhole stitch see page 148
Cane weaving – base see pages 153–154
Cane weaving – propeller pattern see page 155
Chain stitch see page 156
Chain stitch – whipped see page 158
Fancy filling – compass pattern see page 162
Fancy filling – cross-whipping pattern see page 162
Fly stitch see page 168
Fly stitch leaf see page 169
French knot see page 171
Granitos see page 173
Heavy chain stitch see page 173
Lattice see page 176
Lattice – lacy pattern see page 176
Lattice + woven filling see page 177
Lazy daisy stitch – open see page 178
Lazy daisy stitch – overlapping see page 178
Loop stitch see page 178
Mountmellick stitch see page 179
Pistil stitch see page 183
Portuguese knotted stem stitch see page 184
Raised chain stitch band see page 185
Raised chain stitch band + woven filling see page 185
Raised fishbone stitch leaf see page 186
Raised stem stitch see page 187
Raised stem stitch – knit pattern see page 188
Raised stem stitch – striped pattern see page 188
Ribbed filling stitch see page 189
Ribbed spider web stitch see page 189
Romanian lace star see page 190
Rope stitch see page 191
Running stitch – double, whipped see page 193
Running stitch – whipped see page 193
Satin stitch see page 194
Silk shading see pages 196–197
Split stitch see page 199
Stem stitch see page 200
Straight stitch see page 201
Trellis cup stitch see pages 202–203
Trellis cup stitch – woven see page 203
Twisted cord see page 205
Woven circle needlelace see page 210
Woven filling – spaced bars see page 211
Woven wheel see page 211

Suggested threads

DMC STRANDED COTTON THREAD

744 Yellow – pale
3820 Straw – dk
3821 Straw
90 Variegated, yellow to orange

DMC PEARL COTTON SIZE 8 THREAD

824 Blue – vy dk
725 Topaz
742 Tangerine – lt
745 Yellow – lt pale
90 Variegated, yellow to orange
105 Variegated, pale yellow to brown
111 Variegated, orange to dk brown

Embroidery instructions

See pages 26–28 for how to read the thread code in these instructions.

PART 1

1 Stem stitch rose P8-824
2 Split stitch P8-111
3 Woven bar P8-111
4 Split stitch P8-111
5 Raised stem stitch P8-90
6 Buttonhole scallop + French knot SC-3821(1). Optional: outline each scallop in chain stitch using any light shade of yellow of SC(1)
7 Bayeux stitch P8-745; 111
8 Buttonhole scallop + French knot. Assorted threads
9 Twisted single Brussels stitch, whipped P8-105
10 Buttonhole stitch – padded P8-742. Along the inner side of it: stem stitch P8-742
11 Lattice P8-745; 725; SC-744(1). Cells of the lattice are filled with a variety of stitches:
- Woven bar P8-105; 111
- Buttonhole scallop + French knot P8-105; 111
- Pistil stitches, radiating from one corner of a cell. May be replaced with straight stitches + French knots P8-105; 111

12 Stem stitch filling P8-90
13 buttonhole scallop + French knot SC-3821(1). Outlined in chain stitch SC-744(6)
14 Stem stitch filling P8-111
15 Silk shading SC-744; 3820; 3821(1)

PART 2

1 Couching (thread) SC-744(6;1) and reverse chain stitch P8-742

2 Bokhara couching and French knots along the top line. Assorted threads

3 Overlapping daisy stitch P8-105; 111

4 Pistil stitch P8-105; 111

5 Lazy fly stitch leaf and raised fishbone stitch leaf. Assorted threads

6 French knot and split stitch. Assorted threads

7 Bayeux stitch P8-745; 111

8 Raised stem stitch P8-111

9 Twisted single Brussels stitch, whipped P8-105. Start with line of backstitch at the tail end of this area

10 Hungarian braided chain stitch P8-111

11 Lattice P8-745; 725; SC-744(1). Cells of the lattice are filled with a variety of stitches:

- Woven bar P8-105; 111
- Buttonhole scallop + French knot P8-105; 111
- Pistil stitches, radiating from one corner of a cell. May be replaced with straight stitches + French knots P8-105; 111

12 Reverse chain stitch P8-111

13 Chain stitch SC-744(6)

14 French knot P8-111

15 Backstitch P8-111

Doodle 4 – *Columbine*

This doodle stitching will help you to practise for the crewel embroidery design on page 116, *Have a Nice Day*. The template is on page 212, and the stitched area of the finished piece measures 21.5 x 17cm (8½ x 6¾in).

Stitch techniques used in this project

Backstitch see page 144
Blanket stitch see page 146
Brick stitch see page 147
Burden stitch see page 147
Buttonhole wheel see page 151
Cane weaving – Japanese mesh pattern see page 155
Chain stitch see page 156
Chain stitch – buttonholed see page 157
Chain stitch – reverse see page 157
Corded single Brussels stitch see page 157
Couching (thread) see page 159
Couching (twisted cord) see page 160
Couching – guided see page 160
Fancy filling – rosebud pattern see pages 164–165
Fancy filling – zebra pattern see pages 166–167
Fly stitch see page 168
Fly stitch leaf see page 169
Fly stitch triangles see page 170
French knot see page 171
German knotted buttonhole stitch see page 172
Lattice see page 176
Lattice – lacy pattern see page 176
Lazy daisy stitch see page 178
Open chain stitch couching see page 180
Satin stitch – padded see page 194
Pekinese stitch see page 182
Pistil stitch see page 183
Portuguese knotted stem stitch see page 184
Raised fishbone stitch leaf see page 186
Raised stem stitch see page 187
Raised stem stitch – knit pattern see page 188
Rope stitch see page 191
Running stitch – double see page 193
Satin stitch see page 194
Satin stitch – padded see page 194
Satin stitch blocks see page 195
Silk shading see pages 196–197
Skeleton leaf – small see page 198
Split stitch see page 199
Stem stitch see page 200
Stem stitch filling see page 201
Straight stitch see page 201
Trellis cup stitch – patterned see page 203
Twisted cord see page 205
Vermicelli stitch see page 207
Woven bar see page 208
Woven filling – spaced bars see page 211

Suggested threads

DMC STRANDED COTTON THREAD

PASTELS
Blanc
3865 Winter White
Ecru
3770 Tawny – vy lt
842 Beige Brown – vy lt
738 Tan – vy lt

LILACs
211 Lavender – lt
155 Blue Violet – med dk
3746 Blue Violet – dk
3835 Grape – med
3834 Grape – dk
3837 Lavender – ultra dk
550 Violet – vy dk

BLUES
794 Cornflower Blue – lt

GREENS
581 Moss Green
469 Avocado Green
935 Black Avocado Green – med

DMC PEARL COTTON SIZE 8 THREAD

PASTELS
Blanc
712 Cream
945 Tawny

LILACS
210 Lavender – med
553 Violet
550 Violet – vy dk
333 Blue Violet – vy dk

YELLOWS
743 Yellow – med
742 Tangerine – lt

GREENS
581 Moss Green
469 Avocado Green
904 Parrot Green – vy dk
937 Avocado Green – med

DMC PEARL COTTON SIZE 12 THREAD

794 Cornflower Blue – lt

Embroidery instructions

See pages 26–28 for how to read the thread code in these instructions.

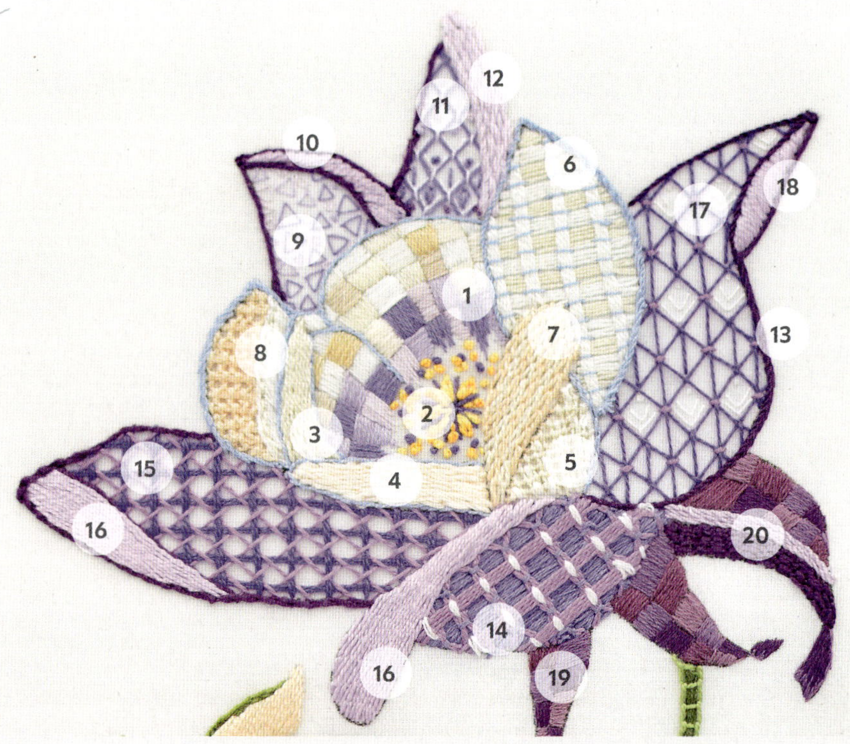

PART 1

1 Satin stitch blocks. Assorted SC(1)

2 Straight stitch, lazy daisy stitch, French knot P8-550; 742

3 Raised stem stitch P8-712; outlined in stem stitch P12-794

4 Woven filling – spaced bars SC-3770(6)

5 Trellis cup stitch – patterned (omit last step) P8-712; SC-Ecru(6)

6 Fancy filling – zebra pattern: Step 1: P8-Blanc, P8-712. Step 2: P8-Blanc. Step 3: P12-794 Outline: couching (guided, twisted cord) P12-794

7 Raised stem stitch – knit pattern P8-945; 712

8 Satin stitch P8-3865; corded single Brussels stitch-2 P8-945

9 Fly stitch triangles SC-211; 3746; 155(1)

10 Rope stitch P8-210; stem stitch P8-550

11 Lattice, options on couching P8-333; SC-211(1)

12 Couching (twisted cord), SC-211(6;1)

13 Couching (twisted cord) P8-210; SC-550(1)

14 Fancy filling – rosebud pattern. Step 1: SC-3746(6). Steps 2–3: P8-553. Step 4: SC-Ecru(2). Step 5: SC-3746(2)

15 Cane weaving – Japanese mesh pattern P8-333; 553

16 Raised stem stitch P8-553 for the upper petal; P8-210 for the lower petal

17 Lattice – lacy pattern P8-333; 553; fly stitch SC-Blanc(1) – two stitches in each cell

18 Satin stitch – padded P8-210, outlined in stem stitch P8-550

19 Satin stitch blocks. Assorted SC(1)

20 Couching (twisted cord) P8-210; SC-210(1); corded single Brussels stitch-2 P8-550

PART 2

1 Open chain stitch couching SC-935(6); P8-581

2 Burden stitch SC-Blanc, 935, 469, 581(6)

3 Trellis cup stitch, patterned. Step 1: Trellis P8-904. Step 2: Weaving SC738(6). Step 3: Seeding stitch P8-Blanc. Outline: couching (thread) SC-937(6;2)

4 Buttonhole wheel P8-581

5 Vermicelli stitch P8-Blanc; SC-Blanc(1). Outline: couching (thread) SC-Blanc(6;1)

6 Woven bar P8-945

7 Satin stitch – padded SC-738(6;1)

8 Skeleton leaf, small. Step 1: Chain stitch P8-Blanc. Step 2: Straight stitches of the basement P8-945. Step 3: Stitching the midrib P8-581

9 Skeleton leaf, small. Assorted threads

10 Fly stitch leaf P8-904

11 Silk shading. Assorted SC(1)

12 Vermicelli stitch P8-Blanc; SC-Blanc(1)

13 Running stitch – double. Assorted threads

14 Blanket stitch P8-937

15 Fly stitch triangles SC-581; 469; 935(1)

16 Brick stitch SC-935; 469; 581(6)

17 French knot P8-581

18 Chain stitch P8-581

19 Satin stitch – padded P8-945. Outline: stem stitch P8-581

20 Chain stitch; reverse chain stitch P8-904. Inside: pistil stitch, individual stitches placed closely together SC-Blanc(1)

21 Chain stitch P8-581

22 Raised fishbone stitch leaf P8-937

23 German knotted buttonhole stitch; pistil stitch P8-581; 945

24 Chain stitch – buttonholed P8-945; 937

25 Stem stitch filling P8-581; SC-581(3). Below: scattered French knots P8-937; Blanc; SC-Blanc(1)

26 Backstitch P8-937; Blanc; running stitch – double P8-904

27 Pekinese stitch P8-904; Blanc

LIGHT & NIGHT

Can you work crewel on colourful fabric?

– A customer

This chapter features four crewel embroidery patterns, each of which has been stitched twice, once on off-white fabric and once on darker fabric – as in the example shown here. Except for *Jewel the Unicorn*, which was made bigger than its 'Night' version, these pairs of designs are of the same size.

Before you begin, read pages 26–28 to familiarize yourself with how to read the code for the embroidery instructions. For easy reference, all of the stitches listed with each project are explained and shown in detail in the stitch menu on pages 140–211.

If you would like to practise the stitches before you begin these larger projects, try out the doodles on pages 30–47, but if you are confident, feel free to dive right in.

1 Queen Rose Light

Size: 22.5 x 20cm (8⅞ x 7⅞in)

You can see the finished pieces at full size on pages 53 and 63.

Template: page 216

Use the same template for both designs.

2 Queen Rose Night

Our highest assurance of the goodness of Providence seems to me to rest in the flowers. All other things, our powers, our desires, our food, are all really necessary for our existence ... But this rose is an extra. Its smell and its colour are an embellishment of life, not a condition of it. It is only goodness which gives extras, and so I say again that we have much to hope from the flowers.

– **Sir Arthur Conan Doyle,** ***The Memoirs of Sherlock Holmes: The Naval Treaty***

Queen Rose Light

Suggested threads

DMC STRANDED COTTON THREAD

10 Tender Green - vy lt
11 Tender Green – lt
15 Apple Green
19 Autumn Gold – med lt
94 Variegated, shades of olive
367 Pistachio Green – dk
368 Pistachio Green – lt
677 Old Gold – vy lt
746 Off White
816 Garnet
834 Golden Olive – vy lt
907 Parrot Green – lt
987 Forest Green – dk
3031 Mocha Brown – vy dk
3052 Green Grey – med
3345 Hunter Green – dk
3346 Hunter Green
3371 Black Brown
3687 Mauve
3688 Mauve – med
3689 Mauve – lt
3782 Mocha Brown – lt
3790 Beige Grey – ultra dk
3803 Mauve – dk
3863 Mocha Beige – med

DMC PEARL COTTON SIZE 8 THREAD

99 Variegated, Burgundy
524 Fern Green – vy lt
640 Beige Grey – vy dk
644 Beige Grey – med
743 Yellow – med
745 Yellow – lt pale

DMC PEARL COTTON SIZE 12 THREAD

356 Terra Cotta – med
712 Cream
758 Terra Cotta – vy lt
814 Garnet – dk

Embroidery instructions

See pages 26–28 for how to read the thread code in these instructions.

The doodle design on page 30, *Happy Birthday,* will help you to practise the stitches you need for this crewel embroidery design.

Stitch techniques used in this project

Backstitch see page 144
Backstitch – whipped see page 144
Blanket stitch – whipped see page 146
Bullion knot see page 147
Burden stitch see page 147
Buttonhole stitch see page 148
Buttonhole stitch – padded see page 151
Chain stitch see page 156
Couching (thread) see page 159
Couching (twisted cord) see page 160
Cretan stitch leaf see page 161
Crochet chain see page 161
Double lattice + 4-stitch couching see page 161
Fancy filling – leaf pattern see page 163
Fancy filling – rosebud pattern see pages 164–165
Feather stitch see page 167
Fly stitch – whipped see page 168
French knot see page 171
Heavy chain stitch see page 173
Lattice see page 176
Lattice + woven filling see page 177
Lazy daisy stitch see page 178
Odd flower petal see page 179
Palestrina stitch see page 182
Pistil stitch see page 183
Pistil stitch twigs see page 183
Portuguese knotted stem stitch see page 184
Raised fishbone stitch leaf see page 186
Raised stem stitch see page 187
Rope stitch see page 191
Satin stitch see page 194
Satin stitch – padded see page 194
Silk shading see page 196–197
Silk shading – padded see page 197
Split stitch see page 199
Stem stitch see page 200
Stem stitch – whipped see page 200

PART 1

1 Backstitch – whipped SC-3345(1)

2 Berries: bullion knot P8-524, 644, 640 with centres in French knot SC-11(1 or 2). Twig: stem stitch SC-3345(1)

3 Cretan stitch leaf SC-3345(1)

4 Backstitch SC-3345(2)

5 French knots SC-907; 3345(2)

6 Cretan stitch leaf SC-10(2), outline: stem stitch SC-3345(2)

7 Cretan stitch leaf SC-3790(2)

8 Buttonhole stitch – padded SC-3031(3;2)

9 Silk shading – padded SC-3790, 19(3;1)

10 Silk shading – padded SC-19, 3345(3;1)

11 Silk shading – padded SC-3345; 10(3;1)

12 Lattice SC-368(2), couched with SC-746(1). Outline: stem stitch SC-834(2)

13 Lattice SC-3790(2) + SC-746(1). Outline: stem stitch SC-367(2)

14 Lattice SC-368(2) + SC-746(1). Outline: stem stitch SC-3371(2)

15 Lattice SC-367(2) + SC-746(1). Outline: stem stitch SC-834(2)

16 Lattice SC-3790(2) + SC-746(1), outline: stem stitch SC-3371(2)

17 Cretan stitch leaf SC-368(2)

18 Silk shading – padded SC-19; 15(3;1)

19 Silk shading – padded SC-3031; 19(3;1)

20 Silk shading – padded SC-3031; 3790(3;1)

21 Buttonhole stitch – padded SC-15(3;2)

22 Silk shading – padded SC-19; 10(3;1)

23 Lattice SC-3031(2) + SC-19(1). Outline: stem stitch SC-834(2)

24 Lattice SC-367(2) + SC-19(1). Outline: stem stitch SC-3371(2)

25 Lattice SC-15(2) + SC-3371(1). Outline: stem stitch SC-367(2)

26 Lattice SC-3031(2) + SC-19(1). Outline: stem stitch SC-834(2)

27–28 Lattice SC-15(2) + SC-3371(1). Outline: SC-3371(2). First work the lattice across both areas (as if they were one petal). Having finished, outline the inner petal in stem stitch using SC-367(2) and the outer petal in stem stitch using SC-337(2)

PART 2

1–4 Fancy filling– rosebud pattern. Thread choice for each petal as follows:

- **Petal 1** Step 1: Background, surface satin SC-816(2). Steps 2–3: Lattice in groups of 4 stitches P12-712. Step 4: Couching lattice SC-816(2). Step 5: Magic stitch SC-3689(2)
- **Petal 2** Step 1: SC-3689(2). Steps 2–3: P12-712. Step 4: SC-816(2). Step 5: SC-3689(2)
- **Petal 3** Step 1: SC-816(2). Steps 2–3: P12-712. Step 4: SC-3689(2). Step 5: SC-816(2)
- **Petal 4** Step 1: SC-3688(2). Steps 2–3: P12-814. Step 4: SC-746(2). Step 5: SC-3688(2)

5 Lattice P12-712 + cross-stitch couching SC-3689(2)

6 Chain stitch SC-677; 746(2)

7 Lattice P12-712 with French knots inside the cells. Assorted SC(1)

8 Heavy chain stitch P8-99

9 Chain stitch, French knots SC-677; 746(2)

10 Four petals at the bottom: rope stitch SC-3687(2) or couching – (twisted cord) SC-3803(2). Optional: split stitch along the couched cord SC-677(2). Two petals at the top: chain stitch, backstitch and French knots P8-99

11 Whipped fly stitch with French knot P12-712 at the tips

12a Portuguese knotted stem stitch P8-99

12b Palestrina stitch P8-99

13 Raised stem stitch P12-356; 758

14 Fishbone stitch leaf assorted SC(2)

TIP

Cover some leaves with feather stitch assorted SC(1).

15 Odd flower petal SC-19(2) and French knot SC-816(2)

16 Options on varying stitches for different leaves: satin stitch, satin stitch – padded, rope stitch or buttonhole stitch assorted SC(1 or 2)

17 Fishbone stitch leaf assorted SC(2)

18 Pistil stitch twig SC-3345(2)

13
13
16
16
16
16
16
16
15
12a
12b
18
11
10
17
7
9
10
8
6
10
9
4
5
1
3
10
2
10
10
14
13

PART 3

1 Fancy filling – leaf pattern P8-640, SC-3782, 3863(1; 2)
2 Stem stitch filling SC-94(2)
3 Satin stitch – padded SC-94(3; 1)
4 Silk shading SC-94(1). Outline: stem stitch SC-94(2)
5 Buttonhole stitch – padded SC-94(2)
6 Chain stitch SC-3345(2)
7 Satin stitch SC-367(2)
8 Raised fishbone stitch leaf SC-907(1)
9 Cretan stitch leaf SC-367(2)
10 French knot SC-10(1 or 2)
11 Buttonhole stitch – padded SC-3346; 94(2;1)
12 Silk shading SC-10; 367; 368; 677(1)
13 Stem stitch filling or silk shading SC-94(1)
14 French knot SC-367; 677(1)
15 Cretan stitch leaf SC-94; 3346(2)
16 Centre: satin stitch – padded SC-19(3;2). Sepals: satin stitch – padded, outlined in stem stitch assorted SC(2;1)
17 Buttonhole stitch – padded SC-368(2;1)
18 Stem stitch SC-3345(1)

11
9
8
10
7
11
4
3
1
2
5
6
17
16
15
18
12
13
14

PART 4

1 Lattice + woven filling (incomplete), both worked in twisted cord SC-11; 907(1)

2 Burden stitch, worked in twisted cord assorted SC(1)

3 Chain stitch SC-816; 3803(2) and P8-99

4 Stem stitch, worked in twisted cord assorted SC(1)

5 Straight stitch, worked in twisted cord SC-3689(1); French knot SC-3687(1)

6 Raised fishbone stitch leaf SC-907(1)

7 Cretan stitch leaf SC-368(2); French knot SC-10(1 or 2). Two sepals: satin stitch SC-3052(1) and buttonhole stitch SC-94(1). Calyx: satin stitch SC-94(1)

8 Stem stitch SC-94(1)

9 Cretan stitch leaf SC-94(2)

10 Centre: satin stitch SC-94(1). Outline: rope stitch SC-3782; 3790; or 3863(2)

11 Stem stitch – whipped SC3345; 94(2)

12 Two or three rows of stem stitch SC-3385(1)

13 Satin stitch SC-3385(2)

14 Centre: French knot SC-94(2). Petals: bullion knot P8-743; 745

15 Centre: French knot SC-94(1). Petals: French knot P8-743; 745, surrounded with lazy daisy stitch SC-10(2)

16 Midrib: stem stitch filling assorted SC(1). Around the midrib (optional): pistil stitch SC-3345(1). Outline: blanket stitch – whipped SC-3345(2)

17 Stem stitch SC-3345(1)

18 Backstitch – whipped SC-15(1)

6
7
8
5
9
2
3
4
1
3
11
3
10
12
16
13
15
17
18
10
11
14

Queen Rose Night

Suggested threads

DMC STRANDED COTTON THREAD

94 Variegated, shades of olive
610 Drab Brown – vy dk
612 Drab Brown – med
640 Beige Grey – vy dk
726 Topaz – lt
727 Topaz – vy lt
834 Golden Olive – vy lt
3031 Mocha Brown – vy dk
3033 Mocha Brown – vy lt
3052 Green Grey – med
3345 Hunter Green – dk
3371 Black Brown
3782 Mocha Brown – lt
4500 Coloris, 'Columbine Gardens' – shades of green grey, khaki green and pink: 3052, 3013, 818, 3354
4505 Coloris, 'Heather' – shades of green grey and violet: 3051, 3053, 3041, 3042

DMC PEARL COTTON SIZE 8 THREAD

469 Avocado Green
471 Avocado Green – vy lt
581 Moss Green
743 Yellow – med
745 Yellow – lt pale
927 Grey Green

DMC PEARL COTTON SIZE 12 THREAD

712 Cream
758 Terra Cotta – vy lt

METALLIC THREAD (OPTIONAL)

Any dark shades. In the original work three metallic threads were used: dk brown, dk blue and dk green

Embroidery instructions

See pages 26–28 for how to read the thread code in these instructions.

You might try cutting down this list and working this embroidery with fewer stitches – or replacing some of the stitches with your own choice. To be creative is half the fun of the embroidery process!

Stitch techniques used in this project

Backstitch see page 144
Battlement couching see page 145
Bayeux stitch see page 146
Buttonhole scallops – padded see page 148
Buttonhole stitch – padded see page 151
Cane weaving – Japanese mesh see page 155
Chain stitch see page 156
Couching (thread) see page 159
Couching (twisted cord) see page 150
Cretan stitch leaf see page 161
Crochet chain see page 161
Double lattice + 4-stitch couching see page 161
French knot see page 171
Granitos see page 173
Lattice see page 176
Lattice – lacy pattern see page 176
Open chain stitch see page 180
Pistil stitch see page 183
Raised chain stitch band see page 185
Raised fishbone stitch leaf see page 186
Raised stem stitch see page 187
Rope stitch see page 191
Satin stitch see page 194
Satin stitch – padded see page 194
Silk shading see pages 196–197
Skeleton leaf – small see page 198
Split stitch see page 199
Stem stitch see page 200
Straight stitch see page 201
Tuning fork stitch see page 204
Twisted cord see page 205
Vermicelli stitch see page 207
Woven bar leaf see page 209

PART 1

1 Satin stitch – padded SC-assorted (3; 1) or buttonhole stitch – padded SC-assorted (3;2)
2 Battlement couching assorted P8
3 Couching, twisted cord SC-3371(1); optional: next to it – couching, thread SC-metallic (1)
4 Battlement couching assorted P8
5 Couching, twisted cord SC-3031(1)
6 Raised fishbone stitch leaf SC-3345(1). Twig: chain stitch SC-3052(1)
7 Buttonhole stitch – padded SC-3371 (3; 2). Twig: chain stitch SC-3052(1); tip: French knots SC-3052(1)

PART 2

1 Centre: French knot assorted SC(2); petals: granitos SC-4505(2)
2 Raised stem stitch SC-94(2)
3 Buttonhole stitch – padded SC-94(3;1)
4 Rope stitch SC-3345(2)
5 Satin stitch – padded SC-3033; 3345(3;1)
6 Raised stem stitch SC-3052(2)
7 Raised fishbone stitch leaf SC-3345(1)
8 Leaf: buttonhole stitch – padded SC-94(3;2). Twig underneath the leaf: split stitch SC-3345(2)
9 Woven bar leaf SC-610; 612(2)
10 Raised stem stitch SC-3033; 3052(2)
11 Vermicelli stitch: two threads couched with on SC-610; 3033; 3371(1;2). Outline: stem stitch SC-3345(1)
12 Couching, twisted cord SC-3052(1)
13 Pistil stitch SC-94(1); French knot SC-726; 727; 834(1 or 2); P8-743
14 Satin stitch – padded SC-3033(3;2) or buttonhole stitch – padded SC-3033(3); P12-712. Optional: the finished stitch is covered with lattice SC-3033(1)
15 Silk shading SC-726; 727; 3033(1)
16 Raised chain stitch band P8-745
17 Double lattice + 4-stitch couching SC-834(1)
18 Woven bar leaf SC-610; 3371(2)
19 Raised stem stitch SC-3033; 3052(2); base of the stem is outlined in stem stitch P12-712
20 Stem stitch SC-612(1)

1
2
3
4
5
6
7
8
9
10
11
12
12
13
14
15
16
17
18
19
20

PART 3

1 Petals: French knot SC-4505(1 or 2). Between the petals: satin stitch and stem stitch SC-94(1)

2 Satin stitch SC-94(1)

3 Rope stitch SC-94(2)

4 Stem stitch, broad variation SC-94(1)

5 Raised fishbone stitch leaf SC-94(2)

6 Satin stitch SC-94(2)

7 Buttonhole stitch – padded SC-94(1;2)

8 Stem stitch filling SC-94(1)

9 Chain stitch SC-3345(1)

10 Lattice metallic thread (2), couched with SC-4505(2)

11 Chain stitch P8-745; P12-758

12 French knot SC-4505(1). Outline: rope stitch SC-3031(2)

13 French knot SC-4505(1), Outline: metallic thread (2), couched with SC-3031(1)

14 Straight stitch metallic thread (1) with French knots at tips SC-3031(1)

15 Vermicelli stitch metallic thread (1), couched with SC-4505(1)

16 Straight stitch metallic thread (1). Outline: rope stitch SC-3031(2) with French knot SC-94(1)

17 Satin stitch – padded or straight stitches, assorted threads

18 Tuning fork stitch SC-4500(2)

19 Padded buttonhole scallops assorted SC(2;1)

20 Granitos SC-610; 3782(2)

21 Skeleton leaf SC-3052(2); SC-94(1). Outline: backstitch SC-94(1)

22 Bayeux stitch SC-3345(2;1). Outline: backstitch SC-94(1); midrib: chain stitch SC-94(1)

23 Raised chain stitch band SC-3345(2). Outline: backstitch SC-94(1). Midrib: chain stitch SC-94(1)

24 Skeleton leaf SC-94(2). Outline: stem stitch SC-3345(2)

25 Chain stitch SC-3345(2)

PART 4

1 Vermicelli stitch, two threads couched with one SC-4505(2;1)

2 Satin stitch, outlined with stem stitch SC-612(1)

3 Rope stitch SC-3371(2). Optional: next to the rope stitch work couching of metallic thread with SC-3371(1)

4 Rope stitch assorted SC(2)

5 French knot assorted SC(1)

6 Stem stitch SC-3052(1)

7 Raised fishbone stitch leaf SC-3052(1)

8 Sepals: satin stitch – padded SC-3052(2;2). Outline: stem stitch SC-4500(1). Bud: rope stitch SC-4500(2); French knot SC-4500(1 or 2)

9 Raised fishbone stitch leaf SC-4500(1)

10 Tuning fork stitch P12-758

11 Cane weaving, Japanese mesh P12-712; P8-471

12 Cane weaving, Japanese mesh P12-712; P8-469

13 Bayeux stitch P12-758

14 Rope stitch SC-94(2)

15 Split stitch SC-3345(2)

16 Tip of petal: satin stitch assorted SC(1). Bud and sepals: satin stitch – padded SC-4505(2;1)

17 Raised fishbone stitch leaf SC-3052(2)

18 Stem stitch SC-4500(1)

3 Captured by Flora

Size: 29 x 18.5cm (11½ x 7¼in)

You can see the finished pieces at full size on pages 72–73 and 82–83.

Template: page 217

Use the same template for both designs.

4 Green Brougham

Good night little ones: bear cubs, hedgehogs, mice and small froggies. Tomorrow, very early in the morning you will be woken up by the sound of horseshoes. And when you look out of your windows you will see Spring's Brougham standing there out in your yards.

– **Ovsey Driz, *The Green Brougham***

Captured by Flora

Flora was the goddess of flowers in Greek mythology. This design is about the irresistible power of nature and its beauty, which overwhelms man-made technology. It is also about going green, the urgent necessity for mankind to keep ecology in mind. Besides, it makes a nice play of colour and shapes: focus on floral elements and you will find the car seemingly disappearing among them.

A funny fact: some people failed to spot the car within the stitched design when it was displayed at craft shows – so fixated were they on leaves and flowers.

Embroidery instructions

See pages 26–28 for how to read the thread code in these instructions.

Suggested threads

DMC STRANDED COTTON THREAD

10 New colour, Tender Green - vy lt
164 Forest Green – lt
347 Salmon – vy dk
647 Beaver Gray – med
677 Old Gold – vy lt
830 Golden Olive – vy dk
833 Golden Olive – lt
986 Forest Green – vy dk
988 Forest Green – med
989 Forest Green
3328 Salmon – dk
3371 Black Brown
3687 Mauve
3689 Mauve – lt
3856 Mahogany – ultra vy lt
4180 Variegated, Rose Petals vy pale to med pink: 603, 604, 605

DMC PEARL COTTON SIZE 8 THREAD

471 Avocado Green – vy lt
640 Beige Grey – vy dk
741 Tangerine – med
840 Beige Brown – med
53 Variegated, Steel Gray
67 Variegated, Baby Blue
69 Variegated, Terra Cotta
90 Variegated, Yellow
92 Variegated, Avocado
94 Variegated, Khaki Green
99 Variegated, Mauve

Stitch techniques used in this project

Backstitch see page 144
Basket stitch see page 145
Blanket stitch see page 146
Bokhara couching see page 146
Bullion knot see page 147
Buttonhole stitch see page 148
Buttonhole stitch – closed see page 149
Buttonhole wheel see page 151
Cable chain stitch see page 152
Chain stitch see page 156
Corded single Brussels stitch see page 159
Couching (thread) see page 159
Cretan stitch leaf see page 161
Fancy filling – strawberry pattern see page 165
Feather stitch see page 167
Fly stitch see page 168
Fly stitch triangles see page 170
French knot see page 171
German knotted buttonhole stitch see page 172
Gordian knot stitch see pages 172–173
Herringbone stitch see page 174
Interlaced band stitch see page 174
Lattice – mitre pattern see page 177
Lattice + woven filling see page 177
Lazy daisy stitch see page 178
Loop stitch see page 178
Open chain stitch see page 180
Open chain stitch – whipped see page 181
Portuguese knotted stem stitch see page 184
Raised chain stitch band see page 185
Raised fishbone stitch leaf see page 186
Raised stem stitch see page 187
Ribbed filling stitch see page 189
Rope stitch see page 191
Rose leaf stitch – Brazilian embroidery see page 192
Running stitch see page 193
Satin stitch see page 194
Scroll stitch see page 195
Seeding stitch see page 195
Silk shading see pages 196–197
Split stitch see page 199
Stem stitch see page 200
Stem stitch filling see page 201
Straight stitch see page 201
Tuning fork stitch – lazy variation see page 204
Twisted cord see page 205
Wheel spike technique see page 207
Woven filling – solid 2 × 2 see page 211
Woven filling – spaced bars see page 211

PART 1

1 Silk shading SC-4180; 164; 988; 989(1)
2 Woven filling (spaced bars) SC-830; 833(2); stem stitch SC-986(1)
3 Fly stitch leaf with straight stitches added, both in P8-94
4 Chain stitch and straight stitches P8-69 and French knots SC-4180(1). Outline: couched thread P8-840; SC-3371(1)
5 Lattice SC-3687(2;1). Outline: stem stitch SC=986(1)
6 Raised fishbone stitch leaf SC-986(1)
7 Seeding stitch SC-986; 164(1). Outline: stem stitch SC-164(1)
8 Stem stitch filling SC-986(1)
9 Split stitch P8-92 or P8-840 and French knot SC-986(1 or 2)
10 Silk shading SC-4180(1)
11 Satin stitch SC-3328(1)
12 Fly stitch triangles SC-3371(1). Midrib: split stitch P8-840
13 Buttonhole stitch P8-741; SC-833(2), two lines facing each other
14 Open chain stitch – whipped and backstitch, both in P8-69
15 Raised fishbone stitch leaf SC-164; 988; 989(1). Twig: stem stitch P8-840
16 Portuguese knotted stem stitch P8-840
17 Lazy daisy stitch SC-4180(2). Twigs: stem stitch SC-4180(1)
18 Silk shading SC-164; 988; 989(1)
19 Fancy filling, 'Strawberry' SC-347; 3328(1)
20 Stem stitch filling SC-830; 833(2), covered with herringbone stitch P8-90
21 Backstitch and blanket stitch SC-3371(1)
22 Midrib: split stitch SC-4180(2). Left-hand side: blanket stitch P8-99 and outlined in stem stitch SC-3328(1). Right-hand side: buttonhole stitch – closed SC-3328(1) and outlined in stem stitch P8-99. Leaf tip: silk shading SC-4180(1), outlined in backstitch SC-3328(1)
23 Feather stitch SC-3371(1). Outline: backstitch SC-3371(1)
24 Interlaced band stitch SC-988; 986(1)
25 Wheel spike technique P8-67
26 Raised stem stitch P8-53
27 Buttonhole stitch and split stitch P8-67; bullion knot P8-94
28 Backstitch P8-840; cable chain stitch P8-471
29 Rope stitch P8-640; outlined from the bottom in blanket stitch P8-840
30 Stem stitch filling SC-164; 988; 989(1)
31 Silk shading SC-4180(1). Outline: straight stitch SC-3328(1)

1
2
3
4
5
6
7
8
9
10
11
12
13
14
15
16
17
18
19
20
21
22
23
24
25
26
27
28
29
30
31

PART 2

1 Bokhara couching P8-94 couched with SC-164(1)
2 Lazy daisy stitch SC-4180 (2); stem stitch SC-4180 (1)
3 Gordian knot P8-92. Outline: split stitch P8-92
4 German knotted buttonhole stitch P8-92
5 Portuguese knotted stem stitch P8-840
6 Scroll stitch SC-830; 833(2)
7 Blanket stitch, outlined in stem stitch P8-90
8 Woven filling, solid P8-69. Outline: rope stitch SC-3687(2)
9 Raised fishbone stitch leaf SC-169; 989(1). Twig: stem stitch P8-92 or P8-840; French knot (on the tips of twigs) SC-986(1)
10 Silk shading SC-4180(1), covered with lattice SC-3328(1 and 2) – one side of lattice is done in double thread and the other side in single thread. The left-hand side is outlined in stem stitch SC-4180(2)

 TIP

Try couching just one thread of the double thread to add interest to the pattern, SC-4180(1).

11 Two lines of Portuguese knotted stem stitch with French knots evenly spaced between them P8-69
12 Silk shading SC-164; 989; 988(1)
13 Bullion knot P8-69. Twig: stem stitch SC-986(2)
14 Buttonhole stitch P8-741; SC-833(2)
15 Stem stitch P8-640, couched thread P8-640; SC-647(1) and bullion knot (for the car door handle) P8-640
16 Raised chain stitch band P8-99
17 Rose leaf of Brazilian embroidery P8-94
18 French knot P8-94
19 Split stitch P8-94
20 Tuning fork stitch – lazy variation P8-94
21 Backstitch P8-840 and herringbone stitch P8-94
22 Cable chain stitch P8-471
23 Blanket stitch P8-94
24 Rope stitch P8-640; outlined from the bottom in blanket stitch P8-840
25 Raised fishbone stitch leaf SC-986(1) with stem stitch filling background SC-647(1)
26 Stem stitch filling SC-164; 988; 989(1)
28 Blanket stitch P8-741
29 Centre: French knot SC-164(1). Petals: buttonhole stitch SC-164(1 or 2)
30 Buttonhole stitch P8-741; SC-3856(2)
31 Lazy daisy stitch SC-647(2)
32 Ribbed filling stitch SC-647(2)
33 Silk shading SC-164; 989; 988(1)
34 Portuguese knotted stem stitch P8-92
35 Herringbone stitch with feather stitch around it. Outline: stem stitch, all SC-3689(1)
36 Loop stitch SC-3687(1). Outline: stem stitch SC-3689(1), with some French knots along the inside part SC-3689(1)
37 Backstitch SC-3328(1) and satin stitch SC-3687(1)
38 Couched twisted cord with French knots along it SC-3328(1)
39 Lattice SC-986(2), couched with SC-833(2). Filling in the cells: satin stitch SC-989(2) and French knot SC-988(1)
40 Stem stitch filling SC-164; 988; 989(1). Outline: split stitch SC-3328(2)
41 Loop stitch P8-840
42 Split stitch SC-988(2)
43 Silk shading SC-4180(1). The circular part: satin stitch SC-833(1)
44 Silk shading SC-4180(1). Outline: straight stitch SC-3328(1)
45 Midrib: split stitch P8-69. Filling, every other leaf: French knot SC-830(1)
46 Outline: three rows of rope stitch SC-830; 833(2)
47 Running stitch SC-3371(1). Outline: scroll stitch SC-3371(1)

1
5
9
2
6
7
9
2
8
11
3
6
4
10
14
12
16
13
21
15
17
22
19
17
23
20
17
18
24
42
44
25
41
43
26
39
47
28
45
40
29
27
38
46
32
33
35
34
36
44
31
30
32
37
31

PART 3

1 Split stitch P8-92 or P8-840 and French knot SC-986(1 or 2)

2 Leaves, left to right: buttonhole stitch – closed. Outline: stem stitch. Lattice: Cretan stitch leaf – all in SC-986(1)

3 Buttonhole wheel P8-741

4 Silk shading SC-4180(1). Outline: straight stitches SC-3328(1)

5 Lattice – mitre pattern SC-3371(1)

6 Raised fishbone stitch leaf SC-164; 988; 989(1). Twig: stem stitch P8-92. Background: fly stitch triangles SC-830; 833(1)

7 Rope stitch SC-833(2)

8 Blanket stitch P8-741

9 Silk shading SC-164; 989; 988(1)

10 Lazy daisy stitch SC-647(2)

11 Ribbed filling stitch SC-647(2)

12 Split stitch P8-92 and French knot SC-986(1 or 2)

13 Outline: split stitch. Filling in: straight stitch. Calyx: French knot – all P8-69

14 Chain stitch P8-53. French knots SC830(1)

15 Leaves: rose leaf of Brazilian embroidery P8-94. Outline: split stitch P8-67

16 Basket stitch P8-640

17 Middle part: herringbone stitch P8-90. Outer parts: chain stitch and French knot P8-69, couched thread P8-69, SC-3689(1)

18 Two leaves: silk shading SC-164; 988; 989(1). Three leaves: raised fishbone stitch leaf P8-94. Two half-leaves in the background: buttonhole stitch SC-986(1)

19 Lattice P8-741 couched with SC-3856(1). Filling, every other cell: cross-stitch SC-3856(2)

20 Chain stitch P8-69

21 Chain stitch SC-830, 833(2). Fine line inside petals: couched twisted cord SC-3856(1)

22 Rope stitch SC-3371(2)

23 Vine: couched twisted cord SC-986(1). Leaves: raised fishbone stitch leaf SC-164, 988, 989(1)

24 Satin stitch SC-3328(1)

25 Lazy daisy stitch, stem stitch SC-4180(2)

26 Wheel spike technique P8-67

27 Raised stem stitch P8-53

1
1
2
4
3
7
10
9
1
6
17
5
8
11
12
15
13
1
14
26
27
16
18
20
25
19
6
22
21
23
6
24

Green Brougham

A lyric lullaby called *The Green Brougham* (or *The Green Carriage*) is one of my favourite pieces of guitar music. Its original text was written in Yiddish by Jewish poet Ovsey Driz. The poem was later translated into many languages and made into a song with the music by the bard singer Alexandre Sukhanov.

The song is about Spring hurrying to our parts on a green brougham in the dead of night, while all the children and little creatures are fast asleep. When they all wake up and look out of their windows, Spring has arrived in the midst of their gardens!

Embroidery instructions

See pages 26–28 for how to read the thread code in these instructions.

The doodle design on page 36, *Tiny the Snail,* will help you to practise the stitches you need for this crewel embroidery design.

Suggested threads

DMC STRANDED COTTON THREAD

As well as being organized by their ID numbers, threads here are arranged in colour shades to make thread replacement easier.

PINKS

225 Shell Pink – vy lt
3689 Mauve - lt
3608 Plum - lt
3805 Cyclamen Pink

GREENS

3817 Celadon Green - lt
368 Pistachio Green – lt

VARIEGATED AND MULTICOLOURED

4060 Variegated, shades of yellow, pale green and lt blue, equivalent to 964, 164, 772, 165
4505 Coloris 'Heather' – shades of green, grey and violet: 3051, 3053, 3041, 3042
4513 Coloris 'London'– shades of grey, off-white and garnet: B5200, 413, 814, 318

DMC PEARL COTTON SIZE 8 THREAD

600 Cranberry – vy dk
744 Yellow - pale
48 Variegated, shades of red to pink

DMC PEARL COTTON SIZE 12 THREAD

223 Shell Pink - lt
640 Beige Grey – vy dk
642 Beige Grey – dk
676 Old Gold - lt
927 Grey Green – lt

SILK THREAD

HEAVY

3046 Yellow Beige – med
3345 Hunter Green – dk

FINE

Blanc Off-white
3803 Mauve – dk

Stitch techniques used in this project

Backstitch see page 144
Blanket stitch see page 146
Bullion knot see page 147
Buttonhole scallops see page 148
Buttonhole stitch see page 148
Buttonhole stitch – padded see page 151
Chain stitch see page 156
Corded single Brussels stitch see page 159
Couching (thread) see page 159
Couching (twisted cord) see page 160
Feather stitch see page 167
Fern stitch see page 167
Fly stitch see page 168
Fly stitch leaf see page 169
French knot see page 171
French knot – loose see page 171
Heavy chain stitch see page 173
Herringbone stitch see page 174
Hungarian braided chain stitch see page 174
Lattice see page 176
Lattice + woven filling see page 177
Lazy daisy stitch see page 178
Pistil stitch see page 183
Portuguese border stitch see page 184
Portuguese knotted stem stitch see page 184
Raised fishbone stitch leaf see page 186
Rope stitch see page 191
Satin stitch see page 194
Scroll stitch see page 195
Silk shading see pages 196–197
Split stitch see page 199
Stem stitch see page 200
Stem stitch filling see page 201
Straight stitch see page 201
Tuning fork stitch see page 204
Twisted chain stitch see page 204
Twisted cord see page 205
Twisted single Brussels stitch – whipped see page 206
Woven band see page 208
Woven wheel see page 211

PART 1

1 Silk shading SC-225; 3689; 3805(1). Left side outline: blanket stitch SC-225(2)
2 Corded single Brussels stitch SC-4505(2). Outline: stem stitch Silk-Blanc
3 Fly stitch leaf SC-4505(2)
4 Fly stitch leaf SC-368(2). Outline: split stitch SC-4505(2)
5 Lattice Silk-3045, couched with SC-225(1)
6 Raised fishbone stitch leaf Silk-Blanc
7 French knot SC-4505(1). Outline: stem stitch Silk-3803
8 Woven band P12-927. Outline: couching (twisted cord) SC-368(1)
9 French knot P8-48
10 Filling: fern stitch Silk-3803 and French knot SC-4060(1). Outline: split stitch SC-368(2)
11 Buttonhole stitch SC-4513(2). Filling: French knot P8-48
12 Stem stitch Silk-3046; rope stitch SC-4505(2); split stitch SC-368(2)
13 Straight stitch, lazy daisy stitch and stem stitch Silk-Blanc
14 Rope stitch Silk-3803
15 Stem stitch Silk-Blanc; lazy daisy stitch P8-600
16 Split stitch SC-3817(2); straight stitch SC-368(2)
17 Lattice Silk-3803 couched with SC-4513(2). Outline: stem stitch SC-368(2)
18 Outline: stem stitch Silk-Blanc. Filling: chain stitch P8-48
19 Woven band P8-744
20 Filling: woven wheel and French knot SC-4513(2). Outline: split stitch P8-744
21 Blanket stitch Silk-3345
22 Centre: French knot Silk-Blanc; eight straight stitches starting from the centre and eight shorter ones in each of the gaps; Portuguese border stitch P12-640. Outline: tuning fork stitch P12-223
23 Pink side: buttonhole stitch – padded P8-48. Green side: buttonhole stitch Silk-3345
24 Buttonhole stitch – padded P8-48
25 Split stitch SC-4060(2)
26 Chain stitch Silk-3803; herringbone stitch Silk-3345
27 Split stitch and French knot P8-48

1
2
3
4
5
6
7
7
8
9
10
11
12
12
13
13
13
13
13
14
15
16
17
18
19
20
21
22
23
24
25
26
27

PART 2

1 Silk shading SC-3689; 3608; 3805(1)
2 Backstitch; chain stitch; lazy daisy stitch Silk-Blanc
3 Chain stitch P8-48; French knot SC-3608(1)
4 Tuning fork stitch SC-4060(2); backstitch SC-4505(2)
5 Buttonhole scallops P12-676; Silk-3803
6 Corded single Brussels stitch P12-927; French knot SC-4505(1)
7 Stem stitch Silk-Blanc; lazy daisy stitch P8-48
8 Split stitch Silk-Blanc; lazy daisy stitch P8-48
9 Twisted single Brussels stitch Silk-3345. Outline: Portuguese knotted stem stitch SC-4513(2); stem stitch Silk-Blanc
10 Buttonhole stitch SC-4513(2); French knot P8-48; split stitch Silk-3803(2)
11 Stem stitch filling SC-4060(1)
12 Backstitch Silk-3345; French knot (loose) Silk-3803
13 Blanket stitch P12-676; French knot Silk-3345; stem stitch P8-48
14 Woven band P12-642; 927
15 Corded single Brussels stitch P12-223
16 Chain stitch; straight stitch Silk-Blanc
17 Raised fishbone stitch leaf; French knot; backstitch Silk-Blanc
18 Tuning fork stitch; backstitch P12-223
19 Buttonhole stitch – padded P8-48
20 Split stitch, straight stitch SC-4060(2)
21 Raised fishbone stitch leaf SC-4060(1); French knot SC-368(1); stem stitch SC-368(2)
22 Backstitch Silk-3803; French knot Silk-3345; chain stitch P12-927; herringbone stitch Silk-3345; stem stitch P12-927
23 French knot SC-4505(1). Twigs: split stitch P8-600 and French knot Silk-Blanc
24 Silk shading SC-3689; 3608; 3805(1)
25 Buttonhole stitch SC-4513(2); French knot Silk-3046
26 Buttonhole stitch SC-4513(2); buttonhole scallops P8-600; pistil stitch SC-4505(1)
27 Stem stitch P8-600; couching (thread) SC-4505(6;1); couching (twisted cord) P12-223 SC-3805(1); lazy daisy stitch Silk-3345
28 Lattice SC-3817(2). Woven filling SC-368(1)
29 Silk shading SC-3689; 3608; 3805(1)
30 Woven wheel SC-4513(2); pistil stitch Silk-Blanc
31 Straight stitch SC-4060(1); Silk-3345
32 Buttonhole stitch – padded P12-676
33 Satin stitch SC-4060(1). Outline: fly stitch Silk-Blanc
34 Feather stitch SC-4505(2). Outline: couching (twisted cord) SC-368(1)
35 Heavy chain stitch SC-368(2). Tendrils: chain stitch and French knot SC-3689(2)
36 Hungarian braided chain stitch Silk-Blanc; French knot and split stitch P8-48
37 Bullion knot P12-676; French knot Silk-Blanc
38 Satin stitch SC-4060(1). Outline: fly stitch Silk-Blanc

PART 3

1 French knot P8-48; SC-4513(1); split stitch P8-48
2 Raised fishbone stitch leaf Silk-Blanc; SC-4513(2)
3 Woven wheel SC-4513(2); buttonhole scallops Silk-3345
4 Straight stitch; stem stitch; lazy daisy stitch; raised fishbone stitch leaf Silk-Blanc
5 Buttonhole scallops P12-676; Silk-3803
6 Stem stitch SC-Blank; SC-3345; French knot Silk-3345
7 Buttonhole stitch SC-4513(2)
8 Lattice Silk-3803
9 Raised fishbone stitch leaf SC-368; 3817(1); stem stitch SC-3817(2); French knot SC-4505(1). Base: backstitch Silk-3345
10 Twisted single Brussels stitch Silk-3345
11 Woven band P12-642; 927
12 Corded single Brussels stitch P12-223
13 Chain stitch Silk-Blanc, split stitch and French knot P8-48
14 Bullion knot P12-676
15 Satin stitch SC-4060(1). Outline: fly stitch Silk-Blanc
16 Split stitch, chain stitch, French knot, raised fishbone stitch leaf Silk-Blanc
17 Portuguese border stitch P8-48; French knot SC-4060(1)
18 Centre: French knot Silk-Blanc; eight straight stitches starting from the centre and eight shorter ones in each of the gaps; Portuguese border stitch P12-640. Outline: tuning fork stitch P12-223
19 Split stitch SC-4060(2); twisted chain stitch Silk-3345
20 Raised fishbone stitch leaf SC-4505(1). Inside the five leaves: French knot SC-3608(2)
21 Lazy daisy stitch SC-4513(2). Outline: split stitch SC-3817(2)
22 Filling: chain stitch, French knot P8-48. Inner side outline: scroll stitch Silk-Blanc, French knot SC-4505(1). Outer side outline: stem stitch Silk-3803
23 Straight stitch SC-4060(1), Silk-3345
24 Buttonhole stitch – padded P12-676
25 Twig: stem stitch Silk-Blanc. Leaves: lazy daisy stitch P8-48. Berries: cluster of French knots P8-48

1
5
2
4
3
6
13
7
8
9
10
14
15
11
16
12
17
21
18
19
20
25
4
22
24
23
4
25

5

Jewel the Unicorn

It was the Unicorn who summed up what everyone was feeling.
He stamped his right fore-hoof on the ground and neighed and then cried:

"I have come home at last! This is my real country! I belong here. This is the land
I have been looking for all my life, though I never knew it till now."

– C. S. Lewis, *The Chronicles of Narnia: The Last Battle*

Size: 33 x 33cm (13 x 13in)

You can see the finished piece at a larger size on pages 95.

Template: page 218

6 Jewels of November

Size: 23 x 23cm (9 x 9in)

You can see the finished piece at full size on page 105.

Template: page 218

Omit the central unicorn for *Jewels of November*.

5
Jewel the Unicorn

Suggested threads

DMC STRANDED COTTON THREAD

315 Antique Mauve med dk
316 Antique Mauve med
321 Christmas Red
355 Terra Cotta dk
356 Terra Cotta med
778 Antique Mauve vy lt
817 Coral Red vy dk
3345 Hunter Green dk
3346 Hunter Green
3726 Antique Mauve dk
3727 Antique Mauve lt
3778 Terra Cotta lt
3802 Antique Mauve vy dk
3830 Terra Cotta
3834 Grape dk
3835 Grape med
3836 Grape lt
92 Variegated, shades of olive – bright
4500 Coloris, 'Columbine Gardens' – shades of green grey, khaki green and pink: 3052, 3013, 818, 3354
4504 Coloris, 'Hydrangea' – shades of mocha brown and mauve: 3781, 3032, 3803, 316
4508 Coloris, 'Frosted Countryside' – shades of olive green, yellow, brown grey and terra cotta: 734, 3078, 3024, 3771

DMC PEARL COTTON SIZE 8 THREAD

223 Shell Pink lt
224 Shell Pink vy lt
352 Coral lt
471 Avocado Green vy lt
580 Moss Green dk
581 Moss Green
640 Beige Grey vy dk
937 Avocado Green med
92 Variegated, shades of olive – bright

DMC PEARL COTTON SIZE 12 THREAD

316 Antique Mauve med
524 Fern Green vy lt
712 Cream
758 Terra Cotta vy lt
818 Baby Pink

SILK THREAD

FINE
154 Purple vy dk
Blanc Off-white
HEAVY
3362 Green dk

Shown at two-thirds of actual size.

Embroidery instructions

This design is meant to be a stitched framing for... anything! It could surround a warm greeting, a favourite saying, a photograph or even a Unicorn. The Unicorn's name, Jewel, is from the *Narnia* series by C. S. Lewis.

See pages 26–28 for how to read the thread code in these instructions.

Stitch techniques used in this project

PART 1

1 Berries: woven wheel. Stems: split stitch or stem stitch. All in SC-4500; 4504(2) – choose sections of these multi-coloured threads to make berries and stems of the appropriate colours.

 TIP

It is important not to bend these threads in two to get a double thread. Instead, take two threads out of a strand, so that sections of the same colour shades go together.

2 Double lattice + 4-stitch couching (Silk-Dark green + Silk-Blanc for couching). Outline: split stitch P8-92

3 Twigs: backstitch P12-524. Florets: pistil stitch P12-524; French knots SC-4508; 3345(1 or 2); Silk-Dark green

4 Stem stitch P8-92. Pink part: raised stem stitch P8-224, outlined in stem stitch P12-818. Green part: stem stitch P8-92

 TIP

Start working the raised stem along the centre of the creeper and then fill in the spaces to the right and to the left of it.

5 Raised chain stitch band (optional: with woven filling) SC-92; 4508(3); P8-580 and 640

6 For solid leaves: fly stitch leaf P8-92. For openwork leaves: skeleton leaf – small technique. Steps 1–3: blanket stitch; chain stitch P12-542. Step 4: lazy daisy stitch Silk-Blanc

7 Jacobean star – pattern 1: Step 1 SC-4504(2). Step 2 SC-3345(2). Step 3: Silk-Blanc. Step 4 P8-92. Step 5: Silk-3362. Jacobean star – pattern 2: Step 1 SC-4504(2). Step 2 Silk-3362; Silk-Blanc; SC-3346(2); Silk-3362. Steps 3 and 4 Silk-Blanc.

8 Stem stitch, split stitch P8-92

9 Central leaf: start with chain stitch along the midrib; then work straight stitches on the right and on the left of it – each of those is surrounded with a lazy daisy stitch. Add straight stitches to fill gaps. Outline in stem stitch. Assorted threads. Top side leaves: silk shading, SC-3835; 3836(1). Middle side leaves: work fly stitch leaf SC-316(2) and then work blanket stitch SC-3835(2) to fill in the gaps. Bottom side leaves: work woven filling, spaced bars SC-4504(6) and cover it in blanket stitch Silk-Blanc

10 Blanket stitch P8-92

11 Petals: granitos SC-4500(3). Centre: French knot SC-3346(2)

PART 2

1 Bud: French knots, outlined in chain stitch all in SC-4504(2). Upright sepals: Bayeux stitch Silk-Blanc, outlined in heavy chain stitch P12-524. Bottom sepals: rows of chain stitch in Silk-Blanc alternating with rows of stem stitch SC-3346(2), outlined in Mountmellick stitch SC-3345(2). Optional: work French knots in Silk-Blanc to fill in the gaps of Mountmellick stitch

2 Raised stem stitch P8-224, outlined in stem stitch P12-818

3 Granitos SC-321; 817(3); French knot P12-712; Silk-Blanc and Silk-154

4 Bottom part of the leaf: lattice in Silk-3362, couched with SC-3345(1) + woven filling in Silk-Blanc(1 or 2). Outline: heavy chain stitch P12-524. Top part of the leaf: raised chain stitch band P8-640 + woven filling P8-937

5 Twigs: backstitch P12-524; umbels: pistil stitch P12-524; French knots SC-4508; 3345(1 or 2); Silk-3362

6 Raised chain stitch band SC-92; 4508(6). Outline: stem stitch in Silk-3362

7 Berries: woven wheel. For stem: stem or split stitch, same thread. Leaf: fly stitch leaf. All in SC-4500; 4504(2) – choose sections of these multi-coloured threads to make berries, leaves and stems in appropriate colours

8 Centre: lazy daisy stitch, pistil stitch, French knot P8-224; Silk-Blanc and Silk-154. Receptacle (i.e. where the parts of the flower are attached): ribbed filling stitch P8-640. Petals as follows:

- **Openwork petals** Lattice – lacy pattern SC-3830(2)
- **White petal** Bayeux stitch or satin stitch in Silk-Blanc, chain stitch for midrib in SC-355(2); stem stitch – also decorated with French knots and Pistil stitch – in SC-355(2)
- **Pastel-coloured petal** (pointing to the top) Raised stem stitch – striped pattern – two rows in SC-3778(2) alternating with one row in P12-758
- **Terra Cotta petal** (pointing to the right) Satin stitch SC-356(2), covered with lattice SC-3830(1 or 2)
- **Two-coloured petal** Lazy daisy stitch, couched with pistil stitch SC-355(2); chain stitch SC-355; 3830(2). White part: lazy daisy stitch in Silk-Blanc; French knot P12-758

9 Tendrils and stems: running stitch – double, whipped. Spikelet: bullion knots. Use the lightest shade of olive for grains on the tips. P8-471, 580, 581

10 Woven circle needlelace P8-92; raised stem stitch SC-92(2); loop stitch SC-3345(1); raised chain stitch band SC-3346(2); French knot SC-3345(1). Middle part: satin stitch in Silk-Blanc. Outline: backstitch, stem stitch or split stitch SC-3345(1); P8-92 and P8-640

11 Double lattice + 4-stitch couching (Silk-3362 + Silk-Blanc for couching). Outline: split stitch P8-92

12 Romanian lace star SC-3346; 4508(2)

13 Split stitch SC-3345(2)

14 Fancy filling – compass pattern in Silk-3362 and Silk-Blanc. Outline: stem stitch SC-3345(2)

1
2
3
4
7
6
5
8
9
13
10
14
11
9
12
7

PART 3

1 Berries: woven wheel. Stem: stem or split stitch, same thread. Both in SC-4500; 4504(2) – choose appropriate sections of these multi-coloured threads to get fitting colours. Leaf: Bayeux stitch in Silk-Blanc, outlined in stem stitch P12-524

2 Centre: lattice in Silk-154; French knots in Silk-Blanc inside some of the cells; outline with woven filling, spaced bars SC-4504(6), covered with blanket stitch in Silk-Blanc and Silk-154. Petals: Burden stitch in twisted cord. Grape set of threads: SC-3726; 3802; 315(1). Mauve: SC-778; 3727; 316(1). Lilac: SC-3836; 3835; 3834(1). Apply these to different petals. Receptacle: raised stem stitch P12-524

3 Twigs and tendrils: heavy chain stitch P8-92. Leaves: fly stitch leaf P8-92 and skeleton leaf – small P12-524; Silk-blanc

4 Raised chain stitch band + woven filling SC-4508(3); P8-580; 640. Outline: stem stitch, assorted thread

5 Lattice, French knot, stem stitch, chain stitch SC-3345, 3346(1 or 2); Silk-3362 and Silk-Blanc

 TIP

Use SC-3345(1) for one layer of lattice stitches and Silk-Blanc for the other.

Outline: two rows of chain stitch in Silk-Blanc. Work a line of French knots along the outer line of chain stitch SC-3345(1). Finish by outlining the whole area with either stem stitch or chain stitch SC-3346(2)

6 Twigs: backstitch P12-524. Floret: pistil stitch P12-524; French knots SC-4508; 3345(1 or 2); Silk-3362

7 Petals: granitos SC-4500(3); centre: French knot SC-3346(2); twigs, stem stitch P8-92

8 Creeper: raised stem stitch P8-224, outlined in stem stitch P12-818.

 TIP

Start working the raised stem along the centre of the creeper and then fill in the spaces to the right and to the left of it.

9 Flower centre: lazy daisy stitch P8-224; Silk-Blanc and Silk-154. Options for the petals:

- **Option 1** Cane weaving – Japanese mesh pattern P8-223; SC-355(2)
- **Option 2** Raised stem stitch – knit pattern SC-3830(2)
- **Option 3** Trellis cup stitch – woven P12-312; P8-223
- **Option 4** Fancy filling – compass pattern SC-316(2); SC-778(1)

Outline: rope stitch SC-3778(2); chain stitch SC-355(2). Receptacle: satin stitch SC-92(2)

10 Bayeux stitch Silk-Blanc. Outline: heavy chain stitch P12-524

11 Berries: Granitos SC-321; 817(3); French knot P12-712; Silk-Blanc and Silk-154. Stem: split stitch P8-92. Leaf: skeleton leaf – small. Steps 1–3: blanket stitch; chain stitch P12-542. Step 4: lazy daisy stitch in Silk-Blanc

1
2
3
4
5
6
7
8
9
10
11

PART 4

1. Berries: granitos SC-321; 817(3); French knot P12-712; Silk-Blanc and Silk-154. Stem: split stitch P8-92. Leaf: Cretan stitch leaf SC-3345
2. Flower centre: French knot, pistil stitch, lazy daisy stitch P8-224; P12-524; Silk-154 and Silk-Blanc. Options for petals:
   - **Option 1** Fancy filling – compass pattern P8-352; SC-3830(1).
   - **Option 2** Lazy daisy stitch – overlapping variation, starting from outer edge SC-3778; 3830; 355(2) or P12-758; P8-352; P12-758 or in the reverse order
   - **Option 3** Trellis cup stitch P8-352

   Outline: rope stitch or split stitch SC-355(2). Receptacle: raised stem stitch – knit pattern P12-524
3. Tendrils and stems: running stitch – double, whipped. Spikelets: bullion knots. Use the lightest shade of olive for grains on the tips. P8-471, 580, 581
4. Midrib: raised stem stitch P8-224, outlined in stem stitch P12-818. Top part: chain stitch Silk-Blanc; French knot SC-3345(1); outlined in Mountmellick stitch with stem stitch along the tip of the leaf SC-3346(1). Bottom part: Cane weaving – Japanese mesh pattern (partly worked) Silk-3362 and Silk-Blanc. Outline: stem stitch SC-3346(2)
5. Solid leaves: fly stitch leaf P8-92. Openwork leaves: skeleton leaf – small. Steps 1–3: blanket stitch, chain stitch P12-542. Step 4: lazy daisy stitch Silk-Blanc
6. Creeper: raised stem stitch P8-224, outlined in stem stitch P12-818

 TIP

Start working the raised stem along the centre of the creeper and then fill in the spaces to the right and to the left of it.

Stems and tendrils: chain stitch or stem stitch P8-92 or P12-524

7. Fancy filling, cross-whipping pattern Silk-3362 and Silk-Blanc. Outline: stem stitch SC-3346(2)
8. Petals: granitos SC-4500(3). Centre: French knot SC-3346(2)
9. Leaves: raised chain stitch band + woven filling P8-580; 640 or SC-4508(3). Outline: split stitch P12-524 or stem stitch SC-3346(2)

PART 5

1. Petals: silk shading assorted SC(1). Flower centres: French knot assorted green SC(1)
2. Leaves: raised fishbone stitch leaf, satin stitch, buttonhole stitch Assorted green SC(1)
3. Woven circle needlelace Silk-Blanc. Along the curved lines: backstitch, worked atop of needlelace Silk-154
4. Forelock: lazy daisy stitch – overlapping variation Silk-Blanc. Outline: backstitch Silk-154
5. Running stitch – double (optional: also whipped) Silk-154
6. One row of blanket stitch, alternating longer and shorter stitches Silk-Blanc
7. Buttonhole stitch Silk-154
8. Horn: twisted cord SC-4508(3). After twisting and folding up, the cord will be made of six threads. Knot the end of the cord as usual, but do not tighten it. Take an awl and make a hole at the bottom of the horn, right above the forelock. Using a large needle, bring the twisted cord to the right side of the fabric, coming through the hole. The knotted tail of the cord is on the back of the fabric. Attach the cord, using SC-4508(1) (see tip below). Outline: two straight stitches along both sides of the twisted cord Silk-154

TIP

We want the base of the cord to be wider than its tip, so that it resembles the shape of a horn. Keep that in mind while working couching stitches along both parts of the cord. Having finished, bring the rest of the twisted cord down to the back of the fabric before outlining.

Suggested threads

DMC STRANDED COTTON THREAD

As well as being organized by their ID numbers, threads here are arranged in colour shades to make thread replacement easier.

STRAW-YELLOWS

677 Old Gold vy lt
3046 Yellow Beige med
834 Golden Olive vy lt
832 Golden Olive
831 Golden Olive med

PINKISH-REDS

3731 Dusty Rose vy dk
3687 Mauve

GREENS

772 Yellow Green vy lt
368 Pistachio Green lt
522 Fern Green
523 Fern Green lt
501 Blue Green dk
936 Avocado Green vy dk

DARK BLUES

3808 Turquoise ultra vy dk

VARIEGATED AND MULTICOLOURED

4240 Variegated, shades of dark blue
4500 Coloris, 'Columbine Gardens' – shades of green grey, khaki green and pink: 3052, 3013, 818, 3354
4504 Coloris, 'Hydrangea' – shades of mocha brown and mauve: 3781, 3032, 3803, 316

DMC PEARL COTTON SIZE 8 THREAD

69 Variegated, shades of burgundy

SILK AND SILKLIKE THREAD

Manufactured from viscose filaments, rayon threads have a silk-like appearance and soft sheen in the light. DMC rayon comes in skeins of six divisible threads, but for this design, always use all strands of this thread and do not divide them.

FINE

3325 Sky blue lt

DMC RAYON FLOSS

712 Sand yellow, vy lt

Embroidery instructions

In this dark version, which can be used as a frame for whatever you like, the colours resemble fading autumnal leaves upon the darkening background – just as they appear in November in Kiev. It is a kind of tribute to my homeland, which I may be destined never to see any more.

See pages 26–28 for how to read the thread code in these instructions.

The doodle design on page 40, *Goldfish,* will help you to practise the stitches you need for this crewel embroidery design.

Stitch techniques used in this project

Backstitch see page 144
Backstitch – whipped page 144
Bayeux stitch page 146
Bokhara couching page 146
Buttonhole stitch page 148
Buttonhole stitch – padded page 151
Buttonhole scallops – padded page 148
Chain stitch page 156
Chain stitch – reverse page 157
Chain stitch – whipped see page 158
Couching (thread) page 159
Couching (twisted cord) page 160
Fly stitch leaf – lazy variation page 169
French knot page 171
Hungarian braided chain stitch page 174
Lattice page 176
Lazy daisy stitch page 178
Lazy daisy stitch – overlapping page 178
Pistil stitch page 183
Raised fishbone stitch leaf page 186
Raised stem stitch page 187
Satin stitch page 194
Satin stitch – padded page 194
Silk shading pages 196–197
Split stitch page 199
Stem stitch page 200
Stem stitch filling page 201
Stem stitch rose page 201
Straight stitch page 201
Twisted cord page 205
Twisted single Brussels stitch – whipped page 206
Woven bar page 208

PART 1

1 Berries: stem stitch rose P8-69. Twig: chain stitch SC-831(1)

2 Leaf: Bayeux stitch, different threads for each step. Step 1: satin stitch SC-834(2). Step 2: straight stitches in twisted cord SC-832(1). Step 3: couching SC-3808(2). Bottom sections of the leaf: stem stitch SC-834(1). Outline: stem stitch SC-677; 832(1)

3 Umbels: French knots SC-4240(1); straight stitches SC-831(1). Stem: straight stitch in twisted cord SC-831(1)

4 Raised stem stitch Rayon thread

5 Leaf: satin stitch – padded SC-4504(1). Outline: chain stitch SC-4504; 4540(1)

6 Raised fishbone stitch leaf SC-368; 772(1 or 2). Optional: outline in stem stitch SC-936(2). Alternative technique: first work backstitch – whipped SC-368(1); then, using the backstitch as a base, work fly stitch leaf – lazy variation SC-4500(2)

7 Petals: woven bar SC-4240(2)

8 Hungarian braided chain stitch SC-831; 832(1); chain stitch SC-522(1)

9 Five upright leaves. Step 1: lattice SC-3046(1). Step 2: midrib in chain stitch Silk-3325. Step 3: outline in chain stitch SC-3808(1). Two dark blue sepals: buttonhole scallops – padded SC-3808(3;1), outline in chain stitch or twisted cord, assorted SC(1;2). Receptacle: pistil stitch SC-772(1).

10 Bayeux stitch SC-3731; 4504(1). Outline: stem stitch SC-4540(1)

11 Woven bar SC-368; 772(2)

PART 2

1 Bud: satin stitch Rayon thread. Two upright sepals: lazy daisy stitch – overlapping SC-4500(2). Larger downward sepal: raised fishbone stitch leaf SC-936(2). Smaller downward sepal: French knots SC-3808(1), outlined in chain stitch SC-936(1)

2 Creeper: raised stem stitch Rayon thread. Fine tendril: twisted cord SC-936(2), attached in SC-936(1)

3 Berries: three rows of chain stitch SC-3687(2) with three pistil stitches on tips SC-4504(2). Stem: chain stitch SC-4500(1). Leaf: raised fishbone stitch leaf SC-772(2)

4 Bottom part of the leaf: twisted single Brussels stitch – whipped SC-843(2); outline: backstitch – whipped SC-832(2;1). Top part of the leaf: raised stem stitch SC-368(2)

5 Umbels: French knot SC-4240(1); straight stitch SC-831(1); twigs: chain stitch SC-831(1)

6 Satin stitch – padded Rayon thread

7 Petals: woven bar SC-368; 522(2); twigs: chain stitch SC-831(1); leaf: satin stitch SC-722(2)

8 Flower centre: lazy daisy stitch SC-831; 3046(1). Options for petals:
- **Option 1** Bayeux stitch SC-3731; 3687(2;1)
- **Option 2** Lazy daisy stitch – overlapping SC-4500(2)

Anther: French knot SC-4240(1). Receptacle: satin stitch – padded SC-936(2;1)

9 Leaves: woven bar, assorted SC(2). Tendrils: stem stitch SC-3687(1)

10 Silk shading, assorted SC(1).

 TIP

Work chain stitch along the outlines of the leaf and whip just the outer side of the chain SC-523(1). Next, start working silk shading, so that the first row of stitches come inside the chain, over the part of the chain stitch which is not whipped. The whipped part will make a nice rib placed along the leaf outlines.

10 (*cont.*) Leaf stalk: several rows of stem stitch, SC-523(1)

11 Leaf: Bayeux stitch, different threads for each step. Step 1: satin stitch SC-834(2). Step 2: straight stitches in twisted cord SC-832(1). Step 3: couching SC-3808(2). Bottom parts of the leaf: stem stitch SC-834(1). Outline: stem stitch SC-677; 832(1)

12 Petals: woven bar SC-4240(2)

13 Chain stitch SC-831(1)

14 Silk shading, assorted SC(1).

 TIP

Use the technique described in step 10 for the leaf.

15 Berries: stem stitch rose P8-69. Twig: chain stitch SC-831(1)

1
2
3
4
5
6
7
8
9
10
13
11
14
9
12
15

PART 3

1 Berries: stem stitch rose P8-69. Twig: chain stitch SC-831(1). Leaf: Bayeux stitch, different threads for each step. Step 1: satin stitch SC-772(2). Step 2: straight stitches in twisted cord SC-523(1). Step 3: couching SC-936(2).

2 Flower centre: lattice SC-3046; 831(1); decorate every other cell with a French knot SC-3808(1). Outline: buttonhole stitch – padded SC-3808(6;2) and stem stitch SC-772(1). Petals: chain stitch SC-834; 3046(1) and French knot SC-772; 831(1). Receptacle: stem stitch filling SC-936(2)

3 Stem: chain stitch SC-936(1). Tendrils: chain stitch SC-4500(1). Options for leaves:
- **Option 1** Raised fishbone stitch leaf SC-368(2)
- **Option 2** Lazy daisy stitch – overlapping SC-4500(2)

4 The leaf on the tip: Bayeux stitch SC-4504(2;1). Outline: backstitch SC-4500(1). Two leaves on the sides: lazy daisy stitch – overlapping SC-4500(2). Stem: chain stitch SC-831(1)

5 Leaf: padded satin stitch SC-936(3;2). Tendrils: twisted cord SC-936(2)

6 Umbels: French knot SC-4240(1); straight stitch SC-831(1); twigs: chain stitch SC-831(1)

7 Petals: woven bar SC-501; 522(2); twigs: chain stitch SC-522(1)

8 Creeper: raised stem stitch Rayon thread. Fine tendril: chain stitch SC-831(1)

9 Flower centre: lazy daisy stitch SC-522; 936(1). Options for petals:
- **Option 1** Satin stitch – padded SC-3046(2;1)
- **Option 2** Twisted single Brussels stitch – whipped SC-3046(2). Outline: chain stitch or stem stitch SC-831; 3809(1). Receptacle: satin stitch SC-936(1)

10 Satin stitch – padded SC-3731(2;1)

11 Berries: satin stitch SC-772(1) and pistil stitch SC-4500(2). Stem: split stitch SC-936(2). Leaf: lazy daisy stitch – overlapping SC-522(1)

1
2
3
4
5
6
7
8
9
10
11

PART 4

1 Berries: three rows of chain stitch SC-3687(2); pistil stitch SC-4500(2). Stem: chain stitch SC-3687(2). Leaf: raised fishbone stitch leaf SC-368(2)

2 Flower centre: satin stitch and lazy daisy stitch SC-4240; 831(1). Options for petals

- **Option 1** Silk shading, assorted SC(1 or 2)
- **Option 2** Lazy daisy stitch – overlapping, assorted SC(1 or 2)

Optional: outline some petals in chain stitch, assorted SC(1)

3 Leaves: woven bar, assorted SC(2). Tendrils: stem stitch SC-3046(1)

4 Midrib: Bokhara couching SC-4240(2) couched with SC-4504(2). Leaf: satin stitch P8-223. Outline: twisted cord SC-772(2)

5 Leaves: lazy daisy stitch – overlapping SC-501; 936(2). Twig: chain stitch SC-501(1)

6 Creeper: raised stem stitch Rayon thread. Fine tendril: twisted cord SC-936(2), couched with SC-936(1)

7 Silk shading, assorted SC(1)

8 Petals: woven bar SC-4240(2). Stem: chain stitch SC-3687(2)

9 The leaf on the tip: Bayeux stitch SC-4504(2;1). Outline: backstitch SC-4500(1). Two leaves on the sides: lazy daisy stitch – overlapping SC-4500(2). Stem: chain stitch SC-831(1) or twisted cord SC-831(2;1)

1
2
3
4
5
6
7
8
9

7
Have a Nice Day

Size: 37 x 22cm (14⅝ x 8⅝in)

You can see the finished pieces at full size on pages 116–117 and 128–129.

Template: pages 219

Use the same template for both designs.

8 Good Night

To makes things clear for embroiderers all around the world, I decided to give these pieces English names – both suggested by the plot of the design: the bird in the bush in broad daylight and then in darkness. The original name for *Have a Nice Day*, however, was *Miłego Dnia*, which is the Polish version of this greeting – I enjoy a personal connection with the Polish language, as some of my grandparents were Polish. It was so sweet to hear my Polish friends saying '*Miłego Dnia!*' when we met at the Golden Hands craft show in Kiev, Ukraine.

Have a Nice Day

The charm of lattice work can hardly be overestimated, and this design shows dozens of variations of this technique. Besides this, there are a few intricate combinations of traditional crewel stitches, as well as some tips regarding well-known stitches such as stem stitch filling or fly stitch triangles.

I hope that this design will bring you some fresh ideas, too. Have you ever tried working vermicelli stitch over a surface covered with padded satin stitch, for example? Pay special attention to the skeleton leaf technique here, for you will certainly find it desirable for your other embroideries. Finally, I bet that you have never tried the patterned trellis cup stitch, so have a go!

Embroidery instructions

See pages 26–28 for how to read the thread code in these instructions. The doodle design on page 44, *Columbine,* will help you to practise the stitches you need for this crewel embroidery design.

Suggested threads

DMC STRANDED COTTON THREAD

As well as being organized by their ID numbers, threads here are arranged in colour shades to make thread replacement easier.

VERY PALE PASTELS
3865 Winter white
3823 Yellow – ultra pale
3856 Mahogany – ultra vy lt

GREENS
772 Yellow Green – vy lt
369 Pistachio Green – vy lt
165 Moss Green – vy lt
472 Avocado Green – ultra lt
3819 Moss Green – lt
166 Moss Green – med lt
906 Parrot Green – med
905 Parrot Green – dk
904 Parrot Green – vy dk
986 Forest Green – vy dk
890 Pistachio Green – ultra dk

EARTH TONES
3774 Desert Sand – vy lt
842 Beige Brown – vy lt
407 Desert Sand – dk
3772 Desert Sand – vy dk
3778 Terra Cotta – lt
356 Terra Cotta – med

ORANGES
970 Pumpkin – bright
947 Burnt Orange

REDS
351 Coral
90 Burnt Orange – dk
321 Christmas Red
817 Coral Red – vy dk
815 Garnet

VARIEGATED
51 Variegated, shades of orange
92 Variegated, shades of olive

DMC PEARL COTTON SIZE 8 THREAD

315 Antique Mauve – med dk
353 Peach
640 Beige Grey – vy dk
760 Salmon
94 Variegated, shades of Olive

DMC PEARL COTTON SIZE 12 THREAD

223 Shell Pink – lt
642 Beige Grey – dk
666 Christmas Red – bright
758 Terra Cotta – vy lt
3865 Winter White

SILK THREAD

FINE
Blanc Off-white. May be replaced with DMC 3865 Winter White stranded cotton thread
Dark blue violet may be replaced with DMC 3746 Blue Violet – dk stranded cotton thread

Stitch techniques used in this project

Backstitch see page 144
Blanket stitch see page 146
Brick stitch see page 147
Burden stitch see page 147
Buttonhole wheel see page 151
Cane weaving – Japanese mesh pattern see page 155
Chain stitch see page 156
Chain stitch – buttonholed see page 157
Chain stitch – reverse see page 157
Corded single brussels stitch see page 159
Couching (thread) see page 159
Couching (twisted cord) see page 160
Couching – guided see page 160
Fancy filling – rosebud pattern see pages 164–165
Fancy filling – zebra pattern see pages 166–167
Fly stitch see page 168
Fly stitch leaf see page 169
Fly stitch triangles see page 170
French knot see page 171
German knotted buttonhole stitch see page 172
Lattice see page 176
Lattice – lacy pattern see page 176
Lazy daisy stitch see page 178
Open chain stitch couching see page 180
Pekinese stitch see page 182
Pistil stitch see page 183
Portuguese knotted stem stitch see page 184
Raised fishbone stitch leaf see page 186
Raised stem stitch see page 187
Raised stem stitch – knit pattern see page 188
Rope stitch see page 191
Running stitch – double see page 193
Satin stitch see page 194
Satin stitch – padded see page 194
Satin stitch blocks see page 195
Silk shading see pages 196–197
Skeleton leaf – small see page 198
Split stitch see page 199
Stem stitch see page 200
Stem stitch filling see page 201
Straight stitch see page 201
Trellis cup stitch – patterned see page 203
Twisted cord see page 205
Vermicelli stitch see page 207
Woven bar see page 208
Woven filling – spaced bars see page 211

PART 1

1 Upper part of the head: brick stitch, worked in twisted cord SC-772(1). Lower part of the head: burden stitch, worked in twisted cord SC-369(1). Eye: buttonhole wheel P12-3865; pupil: French knot P8-640; Eyelash: French knot P12-3865; 223

2 Crown: three lines of rope stitch P8-315; 760; 353

3 Beak: woven bar P12-3865. Outline: backstitch P8-353

4 Breast: fancy filling – zebra pattern. Step 1: P8-315; 353. Step 2: P8-760. Step 3: P12-223

5 Top part of the wing: lazy daisy stitch and straight stitch, assorted P8

6 Middle part of the wing: a group of five straight stitches 760, covered with German knotted buttonhole stitch P8-315. Bottom part: a group of five straight stitches P12-758, covered with German knotted buttonhole stitch P8-223. The space between those parts may be filled in stem stitch P12-3865

7 Tail: open chain stitch couching SC-369(6), couched with P12-223; 315

8 Thighs: satin stitch – padded SC-369(2). Legs and feet: backstitch P12-223

9 Middle leaf: woven filling SC-3819(2). Outline: stem stitch SC-92(2)

10 Two side leaves: raised fishbone stitch leaf SC-986; 890(2)

11 Woven filling, covered with pistil stitches P12-3865. Inside outline: chain stitch P12-666. Outer outline: chain stitch – buttonholed P8-335; P12-666

12 Midrib: open chain stitch couching SC-92(6;2). Leaf: French knot SC-92(1). Outline: stem stitch SC-92(1)

13 Woven filling, covered with pistil stitches P12-3865. Inside outline: chain stitch P12-758. Outer outline: chain stitch – buttonholed P8-3865; P12-758

14 Middle leaf: woven filling P8-353. Two side leaves: raised fishbone stitch leaf P8-94

15 Petals: split stitch P12-666. Flower centre: French knot P12-666

16 Stem: Pekinese stitch P8-94, SC-906(6)

17 Three leaves: satin stitch P8-94; 758. Flower top: woven filling partly filling in the space. Inside outline: woven filling P12-223. Outer outline: chain stitch – buttonholed P12-758; 223

18 Twig: stem stitch P12-223 and SC-986(3). Two smaller leaves: raised fishbone stitch leaf SC-986; 890(2). Options for the two larger leaves:

- **Option 1** Fly stitch triangles SC-986(1), stem stitch SC-890(1), outlined in stem stitch SC-986; 92(1)
- **Option 2** Background: French knot SC-986; 890(1). Twig and outline: SC-890(1). Raised fishbone stitch leaf SC-986(1)

19 Berries: French knot SC-817; 321; 815(1). Sepals and twig: stem stitch and straight stitch SC-986(1)

2
3
1
5
6
4
8
12
7
19
15
16
10
9
14
13
18
11
17

PART 2

1 Petals: cane weaving – Japanese mesh pattern SC-3746(2); twisted cord SC-3823(1). Outline: stem stitch SC-51(2)

2 Flower centre: French knot, assorted SC(1)

3 Silk shading SC-3746; 51(1)

4 Fly stitch triangles SC-3746(1)

5 Flower centre: French knot, assorted SC(1)

6 Fine stem: stem stitch SC-986(1). Heavy stem: chain stitch SC-890(2). Small leaves: lazy daisy stitch SC-890(2)

7 Stem stitch filling SC-91(1)

8 Corded single Brussels stitch, using double thread for cording P8-94

9 Skeleton leaf – small P8-640; P12-3865

10 Satin stitch P8-94 or SC-166(2)

11 Stem stitch SC-890(1)

12 Raised fishbone stitch leaf SC-92(2)

13 Backstitch or stem stitch SC-890(1)

14 Flower petals: silk shading, assorted SC(1). Flower basement: straight stitch, assorted SC(1), two lazy daisy stitches to the right and to the left SC-890(1)

15 Flower centre: French knot, straight stitch SC-842(1)

16 Buds: lazy daisy stitch SC-356; 3778(2). Stem: stem stitch SC-890(1). Small leaves: lazy daisy stitch SC-890(1)

17 Stem stitch filling SC-92(1)

18 Raised fishbone stitch leaf and stem stitch SC-890(1); French knot, assorted SC(1). Outline: stem stitch P8-94

PART 3

1 Lattice – lacy pattern SC-3774; 3823(2;1).

2 Raised stem stitch – Knit P8-640

3 Combination of chain, stem and blanket stitch SC-890; 906(1;2)

4 Open chain stitch couching SC-165(6;1)

5 Chain stitch – buttonholed P8-94

6 Flower centre: French knots SC-51(1)

7 Flower petals: options. Lattice Silk-Blanc, couched with Silk-Dark blue violet, or cells filled in with French knots/ triple straight stitches worked in that thread. Outline: stem stitch Silk-Dark blue violet

8 Stem stitch filling SC-51; 986(2)

9 Satin stitch blocks, assorted SC(1)

10 Raised stem stitch – knit pattern P8-640

11 Woven filling P12-3865. Outline: stem stitch and backstitch P8-640; SC-890(1)

12 Skeleton leaf – small. Chain stitch P12-642, straight stitches P12-3852; midrib in chain stitch SC-890(1). Outline: backstitch SC-890(1)

13 Chain stitch P8-640; backstitch SC-890(1)

14 Stem stitch SC-986(2)

15 Petals: cane weaving – Japanese mesh pattern, incomplete. SC-51(2); 3746(1). Outline: stem stitch SC-51(1)

16 Flower centre: French knot SC-51(1)

17 Petals: lattice – lacy pattern SC-3746(2). Outline: stem stitch SC-51(1)

18 Flower centre: French knot SC-51(1)

19 Satin stitch blocks SC-92(1) – choose sections of thread of contrasting colour shades for neighbouring blocks. Outline: same thread, darker shade

20 Satin stitch darker shade of SC-92(1). Outline: stem stitch in same thread, lighter shade

21 Stem stitch SC-92(1)

22 Trellis cup stitch – patterned P12-642; P8-94; SC-772(6)

23 Corded single Brussels stitch – double thread used for cording P8-94

24 Pekinese stitch P8-94, SC-906(6). Split stitch P12-666

25 Satin stitch P8-94

PART 4

1 Petals: silk shading, assorted SC(1). Base: straight stitch Assorted SC(1), two lazy daisy stitches SC-890(1). Flower centre: French knot, straight stitch SC-842(1)
2 Lazy daisy stitch, assorted SC(2). Stem or split stitch SC-92(2) or 906(2)
3 Fly stitch leaf with satin stitch around it SC-92(1)
4 Silk shading, assorted SC(10
5 Top: fly stitch leaf SC-890(1). Bottom: split stitch SC-905(2) or SC-92(2)
6 Raised stem stitch SC-92(1)
7 Satin stitch SC-772(2); fly stitch leaf P8-640. Outline: backstitch SC-92(1)
8 Stem stitch SC-890; 986(2); Portuguese knotted stem stitch P8-640
9 Raised fishbone stitch leaf SC-890(2)
10 Buttonholed chain stitch P8-94
11 Blanket stitch – arranged in scallops SC-3778; 356(1)
12 Leaf: blanket stitch P12-666. Stem: split stitch P12-666
13 Couching SC356(6;1)
14 Satin stitch SC-166(2); P8-94
15 Skeleton leaf – small P12-642; 3865
16 Raised fishbone stitch leaf and stem stitch SC-890(1); French knot, assorted SC(1). Outline: stem stitch P8-94
17 Blanket stitch P12-223 and stem stitch SC-986(2)
18 Every other petal: pistil stitch P12-3865. Outline: rope stitch SC-3746(2). Flower centre: French knot SC-51(1)
19 Leaf: stem stitch filling, Assorted SC(1)
20 Petals: silk shading in one colour SC-3746(1). Optional: leave some petals as they are and work lattice over the others Silk-Blanc. Outline: rope stitch SC-51(2)
21 Flower centre: French knot SC-51(1)
22 Fly stitch leaf P8-94
23 Optional: first cover the area in chain stitch – or work satin stitch instead SC-842(2). Next, work lattice on top P12-223. Fill in the cells in fly stitch SC-815(2). Outline: stem stitch P12-223
24 Chain or satin stitch for background SC-3778(2). On top, vermicelli stitch P8-353, couched with SC-3774(1). Outline: stem stitch P8-315
25 First work groups of five long straight stitches SC-900(6). Now work a line of German knotted buttonhole stitch over each group P8-353. Outline: split stitch P8-353
26 Flower centre: buttonhole stitch, arranged in a circle
27 Satin stitch SC-351(2), covered with lattice P12-758; cells filled in with French knots, assorted SC(1)
28 Fancy filling – rosebud pattern. Step 1: satin stitch SC-900(2). Step 2: lattice in groups of four stitches P8-353. Step 3: couching SC-321(2). Step 4: couching SC-3865(2). Outline: split stitch P12-223
29 Satin stitch SC-3772(2), covered with lattice P12-758 couched with SC-321(2)

2
3
2
4
5
1
6
7
12
8
10
9
3
13
22
14
11
5
15
16
17
22
15
10
18
19
20
24
23
21
26
25
27
28
29

PART 5

1 Lattice; fill in every other cell with three straight stitches in Silk-Blanc. On top, work lines of chain stitch in assorted SC(2)

2 Lattice Silk-Blanc, couched with SC-51(2). On top, work lines of reverse chain stitch SC-3778(2). Outline: reverse chain stitch SC-900(2) and double running stitch SC-817(1)

3 Fly stitch triangles SC-947; 970(1). Outline: chain stitch SC-947(2)

4 Raised fishbone stitch leaf or raised fishbone stitch leaf SC-92(1)

5 Stem stitch, stem stitch filling SC-92(1)

6 Chain stitch SC-900(2); French knot SC-817(1)

7 Lattice worked in twisted cord SC-3823(1) and couched with Silk-Blanc. Add straight stitches in Silk-Blanc into every other cell

8 Pink sepal: corded single Brussels stitch – double thread used for cording P8-353. Red sepal: satin stitch SC-817(2)

9 Satin stitch – padded with split stitch outline, assorted SC(2)

10 Berries: French knot SC-815; 817(1). Twigs: running stitch – double, straight stitch SC-986(1)

11 Blanket stitch SC-3772(1). Stems: running stitch – double SC-3772; SC-986(1)

12 White half-circle: woven filling P12-3865. Outline: chain stitch – buttonholed P8-353; P12-223

13 Central leaf: raised fishbone stitch leaf P8-640. Two side leaves: satin stitch P8-94. Twig: stem stitch P8-640

14 Stem stitch filling, assorted SC(1)

15 Raised fishbone stitch leaf and stem stitch for twigs SC-986(1); French knot, assorted SC(1). Outline: stem stitch SC-905(1). Two lines of the leaf stalk: running stitch – double SC-905(1)

16 Skeleton stitch leaf P12-642; 3865

17 Corded single Brussels stitch, using double thread for cording P8-94

18 Blanket stitch P12-666. Twigs: stem stitch and Portuguese knotted stem stitch P12-666

19 Chain stitch – buttonholed P8-94

20 Satin stitch blocks, assorted SC(1)

21 Lattice Silk-Blanc, cells filled in with fly stitch SC-970(2). Outline: rope stitch SC-51(2) and chain stitch SC-906(2)

22 Lattice Silk-Blanc, couched with SC-51(2). Outline: Portuguese knotted stem stitch P12-666

23 Fly stitch triangles and French knots SC-92(1). Outline: split stitch SC-92(2)

24 Rope stitch with French knots SC-51(2); stem stitch Silk-Blanc; SC-51(1). Outline: Running stitch – double SC-906(1); rope stitch SC-51(2)

25 Satin stitch – padded SC-472(3;2), covered with Vermicelli stitch in P8-94 couched with SC-472(1)

26 Lattice Silk-Blanc, cells filled in French knots SC-51(1). On top: lines of rope stitch SC-321; 900(2). Outline: stem stitch SC-92(2) and Portuguese knotted stem stitch P12-666

27 Satin and satin stitch – padded, assorted SC(2;1). Outline: split stitch SC-51(2)

28 Satin stitch – padded SC-165(2;2). Outline: chain stitch SC-3778(2). Smaller leaf: raised fishbone stitch leaf SC-356(1). Twig: stem stitch SC-3778(2)

1
2
3
4
5
6
7
8
9
10
11
12
13
14
15
16
15
17
18
17
19
20
21
22
23
24
25
11
23
28
27
26

Good Night

I love experimenting with fabrics, and I often try new fabric for embroidery – though such an approach has its drawbacks at times! So it was with this design. I picked up a piece of dark blue linen fabric and left home on another long-term business trip.

When I started stitching, I found the fabric to be excellent for some stitches but simply awful for others. Thus a lot of imperfections are shown in close-up images; I believe this may prove instructional – or, at the very least, reinforce the importance of testing your fabric thoroughly before you begin a final piece.

Embroidery instructions

See pages 26–28 for how to read the thread code in these instructions.

Suggested threads

DMC STRANDED COTTON THREAD

3866 Mocha Brown – ultra vy lt
932 Antique Blue – lt
168 Pewter – vy lt
318 Steel Grey – lt
524 Fern Green – vy lt
3811 Turquoise – vy lt
927 Grey Green – lt
926 Grey Green – med
3042 Antique Violet – lt
3041 Antique Violet – med
3740 Antique Violet – dk
310 Black
53 Variegated, greyish to black

DMC PEARL COTTON SIZE 8 THREAD

644 Beige Grey – med
53 Variegated, greyish to black

DMC PEARL COTTON SIZE 12 THREAD

712 Cream
842 Beige Brown – vy lt
3743 Antique Violet – vy lt
3042 Antique Violet – lt
927 Grey Green – lt
3813 Blue Green – lt

Stitch techniques used in this project

Backstitch see page 144
Backstitch – buttonholed see page 144
Backstitch – double-threaded see page 144
Battlement couching see page 145
Bayeux stitch see page 146
Brick stitch see page 147
Bullion knot see page 147
Buttonhole scallops see page 148
Buttonhole stitch see page 148
Buttonhole stitch – closed see page 149
Buttonhole stitch – overlapping see page 150
Buttonhole wheel see page 151
Cable chain stitch see page 152
Chain stitch see page 156
Chain stitch – whipped see page 158
Couching (thread) see page 159
Couching (twisted cord) see page 160
Cretan stitch leaf see page 161
Cretan stitch leaf – openwork variation see page 161
Fern stitch see page 167
Fly stitch leaf see page 169
Fly stitch leaf – lazy variation see page 169
French knot see page 171
French knot – loose see page 171
Gordian knot stitch see pages 172–173
Granitos see page 173
Heavy chain stitch see page 173
Herringbone stitch see page 174
Interlaced band stitch see page 174
Lattice see page 176
Lattice + woven filling see page 177
Lazy daisy stitch see page 178
Mountmellick stitch see page 179
Open chain stitch couching see page 180
Open fishbone stitch see page 181
Pekinese stitch see page 182
Pistil stitch see page 183
Portuguese border stitch see page 184
Raised chain stitch band see page 185
Raised chain stitch band – striped see page 185
Raised fishbone stitch leaf see page 186
Raised stem stitch see page 187
Ribbed filling stitch see page 189
Ribbed filling stitch – false lattice variation see page 189
Rope stitch see page 191
Satin stitch see page 194
Satin stitch – padded see page 194
Satin stitch – surface see page 194
Seeding stitch see page 195
Split stitch see page 199
Stem stitch see page 200
Stem stitch – whipped see page 200
Stem stitch filling see page 201
Stem stitch rose see page 201
Straight stitch see page 201
Trellis cup stitch see pages 202–203
Tuning fork stitch see page 204
Twisted cord see page 205
Vermicelli stitch see page 207
Woven band see page 208
Woven circle needlelace see page 210
Woven wheel see page 211

PART 1

1 Head: no stitching. Eye: French knot P12-712

2 Crown: twisted cord P12-712

3 Beak: straight stitch P12-712

4 Breast: battlement couching SC-932; 3866; 168(2), the latter is couched with SC-3042(2)

5 Wing: trellis cup stitch P12-3042

6 Base: satin stitch P8-53. Covering: herringbone stitch P12-927. Outline: backstitch P8-53

7 Tail: chain stitch SC-3866; 3042(2)

8 Left thigh: satin stitch SC-927(2). Right thigh: satin stitch SC-926(2). Legs and feet: backstitch P12-712

9 Three leaves: Cretan stitch leaf P8-53

10 Pistil stitch P8-53

11 Three flowers: woven wheel P8-53; SC-3042; 3041; 3740(2)

12 Whipped stem stitch SC-3866(2;1)

13 Two leaves: Cretan stitch leaf P12-3042. Remaining area: brick stitch SC-53(6), with buttonhole scallops SC-3866(1) worked over its lower part

14 The leaf pointing upwards: split stitch SC-3866(2). The leaf pointing downwards: fern stitch P12-927, outlined with backstitch P8-53

15 Lazy daisy stitch P12-712; SC-3041(2)

16 Open chain stitch couching SC-926(6), couched with P12-927

17 Two leaves: Cretan stitch leaf P12-3743. The rest of the area: brick stitch SC-53(6), with buttonhole scallops SC-310(1) worked over its lower part

18 Bayeux stitch SC-310(2;1), outlined in backstitch P12-3813

19 French knot, lazy daisy stitch P8-53

20 Tuning fork stitch P12-3042

PART 2

1 French knot P12-712

2 Raised fishbone stitch leaf SC-932(2)

3 Raised chain stitch band SC-932(2)

4 Ribbed filling stitch SC-932(2). Outline: stem stitch P12-712

5 Upper part of the stem: couching SC-926(2;1). Small leaves: lazy daisy stitch SC-926(2). Lower part of the stem: chain stitch – whipped SC-926(2)

6 Fern stitch P12-842 or 3813, outlined in backstitch P8-53

7 Fly stitch leaf – lazy variation. Midrib: backstitch SC-3866(2). Leaf: straight stitches SC-310(2), each passing under the midrib. Outline: stem stitch SC-3866(1)

8 Cretan stitch leaf P12-712 or 927 or 3813

9 Stem stitch P12-712

10 Petals: surface satin stitch SC-927 or 3811(6), radiating from flower centres. Optional: work lattice SC-3811(1) over some of the petals. Outline: stem stitch SC-3811(1)

11 Buds: lazy daisy stitch SC-927 or 926(2). Sepals: lazy daisy stitch P12-712. Stem: stem stitch P12-712

12 Leaves: satin stitch or fly stitch leaf P8-53

PART 3

1 Woven circle needlelace P12-3813
2 Stem stitch filling SC-3740(1)
3 Midrib: stem stitch filling SC-3740(2). Leaf: stem stitch filling (rows worked apart from each other, leaving some space between them) P12-3813
4 Two lines of backstitch P12-3813; SC-310(2)
5 Bullion knot P8-53
6 No stitching. Optional: French knot SC-310(2)
7 Brick stitch SC-932(6)
8 Lattice SC-932(1); with French knot in each cell P8-53
9 Ribbed filling stitch – false lattice variation SC-932(2)
10 Raised chain stitch band SC-932(2). Outline: two rows of stem stitch SC-932 and 310(1)
11 Bottom part of each leaf: straight stitches in P8-53. Top part of each leaf: P12-712
12 Cable chain stitch P12-712
13 Raised chain stitch band P8-53
14 French knot P12-712
15 Portuguese border stitch P12-3813. One side is outlined in backstitch – buttonholed P12-712. The other side is outlined in backstitch P12-712
16 Split stitch P8-53
17 Satin stitch – padded P8-53. Outline: backstitch and stem stitch SC-927(1)
18 Couching P12-712; SC-3866(1)
19 Midrib: French knots arranged in flower patterns, centres SC-3740(2), petals P8-53. Outline: chain stitch SC-3740(2)
20 Central scallop: buttonhole scallops SC-926(1). Side scallops outline: chain stitch SC-3042(2)
21 Brick stitch SC-524(6). Optional: cover one or two of the leaf scallops in buttonhole scallops SC-926(1)
22 Mountmellick stitch P8-53
23 Open chain stitch couching SC-3042(6); P12-3042
24 Satin stitch – padded P8-53. Outline: stem stitch SC-932(1)
25 Bayeux stitch SC-932(2;1;1)
26 Raised chain stitch band P8-53
27 Lattice P8-53 + woven filling (incomplete), using twisted cord SC-932(1)
28 Vermicelli stitch P8-53 couched in SC-932(2). Outline: chain stitch SC-932(1)
29 French knot SC-932(2)
30 Lattice SC-932(2)
31 Satin stitch SC-932(2)

18
17
16
15
8
19
7
7
5
4
6
9
1
20
10
2
3
21
22
23
11
13
12
29
24
28
25
12
30
29
26
14
31
27

PART 4

1 Surface satin stitch SC-927 or 3811(6): alternate colour for different petals of the same flower

2 Buds: lazy daisy stitch SC-927 or 926(2). Sepals: lazy daisy stitch P12-712. Stem: stem stitch P12-712

3 Cretan stitch leaf – openwork variation P12-3813

4 Satin stitch SC-318(2)

5 Satin stitch P8-53. Outline: stem stitch P12-712. Decoration: three groups of buttonhole stitch – closed SC-310(2)

6 Open fishbone stitch P12-3813. Outline: backstitch P8-53

7 Heavier stem: rope stitch P8-644. Finer twig: cable chain stitch P12-712

8 Raised stem stitch P12-3813

9 Raised chain stitch band P12-3813. Outline: backstitch P8-53

10 Woven band P8-53; P12-842. Outline: backstitch P12-712

11 Petals: lazy daisy stitch in SC-3041; 3740 or 3844(6), couched with another thread P12-3743. Flower centre: French knot P12-3743. Flower stems: P12-3743 couched with SC-310(1). Twigs: split stitch P12-3743

12 Raised fishbone stitch leaf P12-3813

13 Stem stitch SC-3866(1)

14 Fern stitch P12-842 or 3813, outlined in backstitch P8-53

15 Satin stitch P8-53

16 Blanket stitch filling P8-53. Outline: backstitch P8-53

17 Bullion knot P8-53

18 Lazy daisy stitch SC-3042(1)

19 Pistil stitch SC-3740(2)

20 Raised chain stitch band SC-3041(2)

21 Midrib: stem stitch filling P12-3042. Leaf: stem stitch filling (rows worked apart from each other) P12-927

22 Lattice SC-3740(1), couched with SC-3866(1). Inside each cell: French knot P8-53

23 Satin stitch P12-712

24 Raised chain stitch band SC-3041(2). Outline: stem stitch SC-932(2)

25 Lattice P8-53. Outline: stem stitch SC-932(2)

26 Brick stitch SC-310(6). Outline: stem stitch SC-932(2)

27 Vermicelli stitch SC-310(6;1). Outline: stem stitch SC-932(2)

28 Buttonhole wheel P12-3042

29 Centre: Gordian knot stitch SC-3740(6). Sides: seeding stitch SC-3740(2). Outline: open chain stitch couching SC-3740(6) couched with P12-712. Outside the outline: French knots SC-3740(2)

30 Centre: Gordian knot stitch SC-3041(6). Optional: work two lines of backstitch P8-53 along the two edges of Gordian knot stitch. Filling in the petal: French knot P8-53. Outline: chain stitch SC-3042(2)

31 Raised chain stitch band – striped variation: alternate rows in P8-53 and in SC-53(6). Outline: Pekinese stitch, P8-644 for backstitch and SC-3740(6) for whipping

32 Centre: interlaced band stitch. First work two lines of couching: SC-3740(6) couched with P8-644, then use P8-53 to perform the interlaced band stitch between the two lines (the stitch is barely visible in the photograph). Work French knots P8-644 at equal intervals around the stitching. Outline: chain stitch SC-3042(2). Outside the petal: French knots SC-3746(2)

33 Woven circle needlelace P8-53. Outline: Pekinese stitch, P8-644 for backstitch and SC-3042(6) for whipping

34 Buttonhole stitch – closed P8-58. Outline: chain stitch SC-3042(2). Outside the petal: French knots SC-3746(2)

2
2
3
4
1
5
6
9
7
12
11
10
8
15
13
14
16
17
18
19
22
20
21
24
34
33
23
25
27
28
26
32
29
30
31

PART 5

1 Buttonhole stitch – closed P8-53. Twisted cord SC-3740(1), attached using single thread of the same colour. Outline: open chain stitch couching SC-3740(6;1)

2 Raised chain stitch band P12-712. Outline: chain stitch P12-3740

3 Vermicelli stitch, worked in twisted cord SC-3041(1) and attached in one strand of the same thread. Twig: stem stitch and lazy daisy stitch P12-712. Outline, inner row: couching P12-927 couched with SC-310(1). Outline, outer row: backstitch P8-53

4 Lazy daisy stitch P12-927; stem stitch P12-3813

5 Raised stem stitch P8-53

6 Outline, inner row: couching P12-927 couched with SC-310(1). Outline, outer row: backstitch P8-53

7 Centre: interlaced band stitch. First work two lines of couching: P12-3042 couched with SC-53(1). Now interlace the two lines in P8-53. Finally work French knots along the outer sides of the lines P12-712, as shown. Outline: heavy chain stitch P12-3813

8 The bigger sepal: ribbed filling stitch P12-3813; smaller sepals: French knots along the outline P8-53; raised stem stitch P12-3813

9 Centre: satin stitch SC-310(2), outlined in backstitch P8-53. Outline: couched thread P12-927, couched using SC-310(1)

10 Berries: French knot – loose variation SC-3041(3). Twigs: stem stitch and backstitch P8-53

11 Petals: lazy daisy stitch SC-3041; 3042 and 3740(3) – each loop couched in contrasting thread P12-712

12 Cretan stitch leaf P12-3813

13 Three flowers: Buttonhole wheel P8-53 with straight stitches inside the gaps SC-3740(2). Inside: French knot SC-3740(2). Outside: French knot P8-53

14 Woven band P8-53; P12-842. Outline in twisted cord SC-3041(1;1)

15 Blanket stitch as filling P8-53. Outline: stem stitch P12-712

16 Open fishbone stitch leaf P12-3813. Outline: backstitch P8-53

17 Satin stitch SC-3042; 926(2). Outline in stem stitch SC-310 or 53(2) and couching P8-53 attached with SC-524(1)

18 Buttonhole scallop P12-3743; lazy daisy stitches to the sides of the scallop P12-712. Twigs: couching P12-3743 attached with SC-3041(1)

19 Leaf: raised chain stitch band P8-53. Leaf stalk: tuning fork stitch P8-53

20 Bullion knot P8-53

21 Chain stitch SC-168(1)

22 Bigger leaf: chain stitch, with three straight stitches inside the leaf shape SC-168(1). Smaller leaf: raised fishbone stitch leaf SC-53(1)

23 Petals: granitos SC-53; 3811(2). Centres: French knot SC-53; 3811(1)

24 Heavier line inside the petal: backstitch – double-threaded P12-3913. Finer line inside the petal: couching P12-842 with SC-310(1). Outline: chain stitch SC-3740(2) and backstitch – double-threaded SC-3740(2); 53(1)

25 French knot P8-53 and Pekinese stitch P12-3813; SC-3740(2)

26 Portuguese border stitch P12-842. Outline: backstitch – buttonholed P12-712

27 Battlement couching SC-3042; 3041; 3740(2) – couched with SC-3042(1). Outline: twisted cord SC-3740(1;1)

28 Lattice P12-712 + woven filling SC-3866; 3041(2). Outline: twisted cord SC-3041(1;1)

29 Satin stitch SC-53; 3740; 3866(2)

1
2
3
4
5
6
7
8
9
10
11
12
13
14
15
16
17
18
19
20
21
22
23
24
25
26
27
28
29

THE STITCH MENU

Knowing things is magical, if other people don't know them.

– Sir Terry Pratchett, *A Hat Full of Sky*

This chapter show you how to work all of the stitches used for the designs. Some are very simple, and you can just follow the step-by-step photographs; while I have given extra written guidance for more complex stitches.

Offering a wide range of stitches from the fundamental to the purely ornamental, you can pick and choose from this stitch menu, and use it in a number of different ways:

- Refer to it while following the instructions for a particular design. You will find a list of the required stitches at the beginning of each doodle and project, with the page numbers included for easy reference.
- If you spot a reference to an embroidery stitch or technique which is unfamiliar to you – either in this book or elsewhere – you can have a close look at it here in the stitch menu.
- You can simply browse the pages of this chapter to explore the world of embroidery. I have tried my best to fill it with a number of things to catch your eye.
- You can choose a selection of stitches from this menu to make your own magic stitch chart – see page 223 for more details on this.
- And finally, you can use it to substitute one stitch for another. This stitch menu will help you to pick an alternative technique you will enjoy.

Stitch naming

I always try my best to make learning new stitches as easy as possible. This is not always simple, because historical, geographical and even economic reasons mean that the same stitch can be called something very different depending on where you are in the world – which can be very confusing!

The confusion inherent in stitch naming has been particularly clear to me, as I was born in Ukraine, and like most Ukrainians, I speak both Russian and Ukrainian fluently (indeed, they share the same root language). In these languages almost every embroidery stitch comes under several different names. I had hoped that the English names would be more consistent, but it turns out that the same issue applies here, too.

Needless to say, this can cause some confusion or uncertainty when it comes to writing stitching instructions, and for this stitch guide I have tried to make things as simple and consistent as possible. For this book, when choosing a name for a stitch from the variety of options, I determined that the name should be distinct to prevent (as far as possible) mixing up the stitch with others. I also give one or two alternative names as well, if those versions are also popular.

Stitch order in this book

Rather than listing things strictly alphabetically, all the related variations of a stitch are grouped together – whipped backstitch, for example, appears alongside backstitch as '*backstitch – whipped*', rather than being at the very end of the stitch menu.

To see the whole 'stitch family' at one glance like this helps understanding and learning.

If you are struggling to find a particular stitch, refer to the stitch index on pages 220–222, or try looking for another combination of the words.

Diagrams and photographs

You will find a few special symbols in the diagrams and in some of the photographs. They are there to help make things clear, so do bear them in mind.

Rainbow colours

As everybody knows, a rainbow shows a spectrum of colours in the following order: red, orange, yellow, green, blue, indigo and violet. The sequence of work for some stitches in this chapter is shown in the colours of the rainbow. It means that a stitch marked in red should be performed first, then the one in orange, followed by the one in yellow, and so on. See the example for basket stitch to the right.

Black dots

A black dot symbol on a stitch indicates its starting point – the place where you come up with your needle, as shown here.

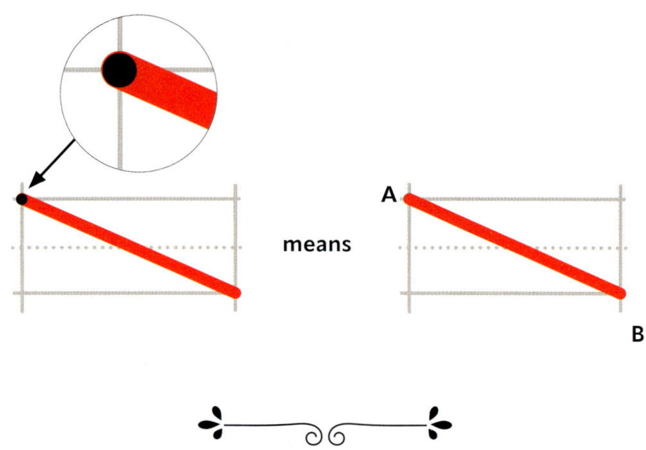

Black arrows

A black arrow next to the needle in some of the photographs indicates the direction of needle movement.

SEQUENCE OF WORK FOR BASKET STITCH

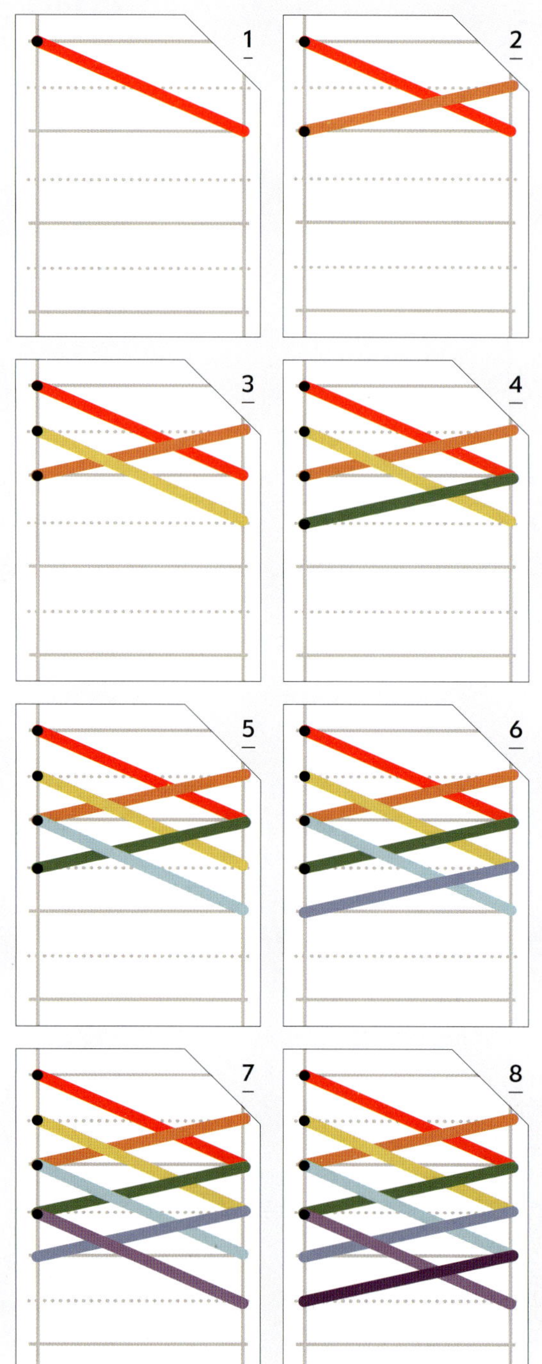

Thread colour and texture

Now and then the photographs show a stitch worked in thread of two or three contrasting colours. This is just for clarity in the demonstrations: you should work using just one colour of thread.

The heavier the thread, the easier it is to see and understand the demonstration, so for clarity, I have often used the whole strand of stranded cotton thread for the examples in this chapter. In some pictures, you will see fluffy-looking thread because tapestry wool has been used to help make the pictures as clear as possible.

RIGHT- OR LEFT-HANDED?

All the stitches in this chapter were performed by right-handed embroiderers. If you are a left-handed stitcher, work them in mirror image. Note that sometimes it can be really helpful to use an actual mirror for this!

Sewing vs stabbing

There are two ways of stitching: the first is the sewing method, where you take the needle up and down through the fabric in one movement. This is a quick way of embroidering, but it is not as precise as the stabbing method, which involves bringing your needle up with one movement and taking it down in a separate movement.

If you are using a small embroidery hoop and feel confident with the stitches, the sewing method is better as it speeds up your work. The sewing method often appears in the pictures in the stitch menu because it provides a better needle position for photographs, and helps to reduce the number of pictures needed to demonstrate a stitch. However, when it comes to practice, I always encourage you to use the stabbing method!

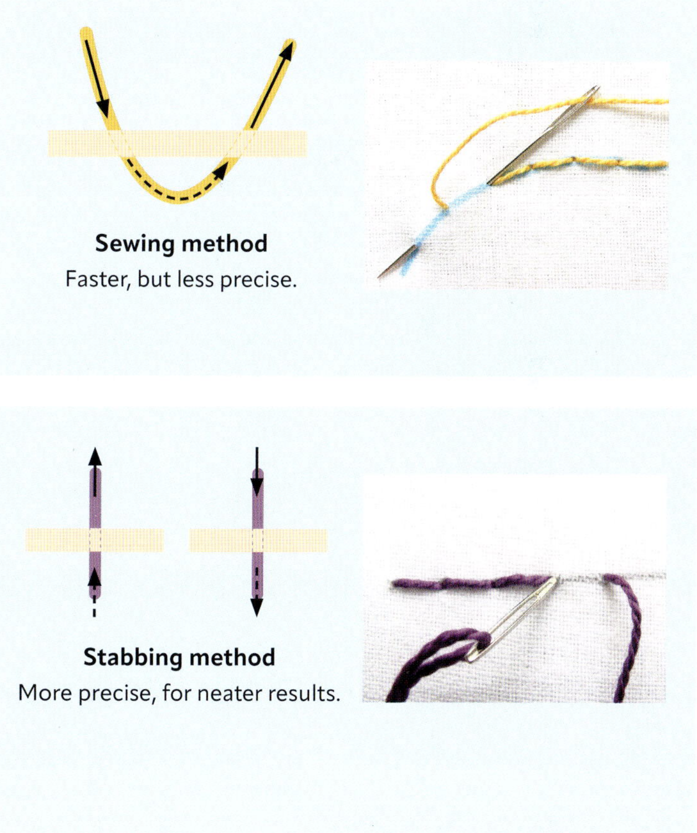

Sewing method
Faster, but less precise.

Stabbing method
More precise, for neater results.

BACKSTITCH

1

2

Stabbing method
More precise, for neater results.

Sewing method
Faster, but less precise.

BACKSTITCH – BUTTONHOLED

1

2

3

4

BACKSTITCH – DOUBLE-THREADED

1

2

3

4

BACKSTITCH – WHIPPED

1

2

3

BASKET STITCH

The stitches in the photographs are spaced out for clarity. Work them closer together.

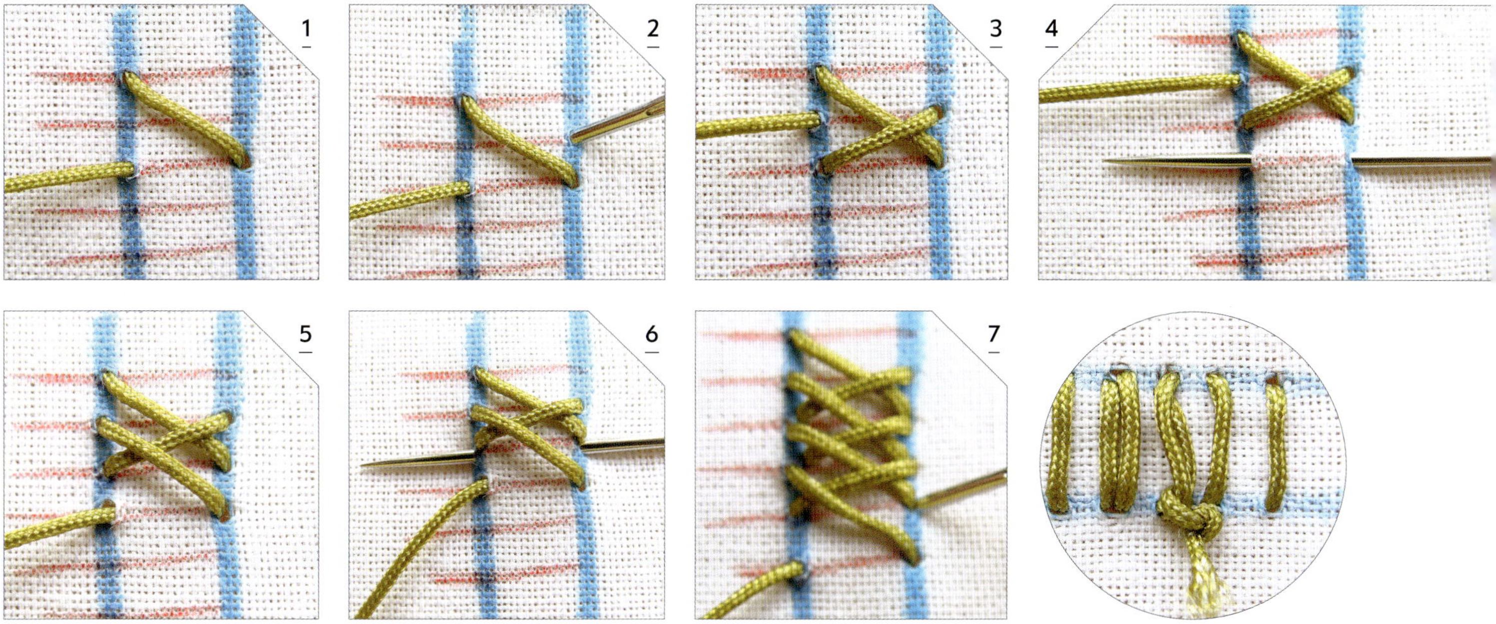

The back

BATTLEMENT COUCHING

Work three to five layers of lattice, placing them on top of each other with a small shift. Couch the top layer only.

BAYEUX STITCH

The single-colour stitch variation (the stitches shown in blue at the top of the shape in step 4) is traditional.

The back

BLANKET STITCH

When closely worked, this is known as buttonhole stitch.

BLANKET STITCH – WHIPPED

Also known as buttonhole stitch – whipped.

BOKHARA COUCHING

There are various options for the placing of couching stitches, as shown.

Vertical couching stitches

Diagonal couching stitches

Staggered couching stitches

BRICK STITCH

Brick stitch is made up of rows of backstitch worked side by side, with each row staggered with a half-stitch-length shift – like the pattern in a brick wall. Keep your stitch size consistent for a more uniform look to the finished stitch.

BULLION KNOT

1 Bring the needle up at A, where you want the knot, down through B, then up at C. Note the position of the needle!
2 Work as many wraps around the needle tip as needed so that the length of the wrapped part is equal to the length of the space marked B–C. Gently pull the needle through the wraps.
3 Couch down the finished bullion knot.

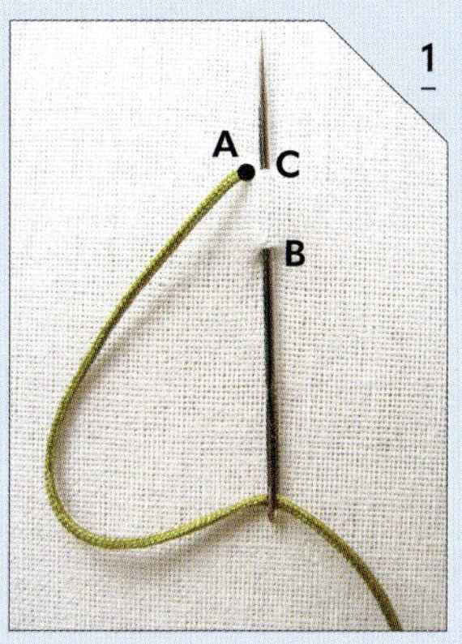

BURDEN STITCH

BURDEN STITCH 2

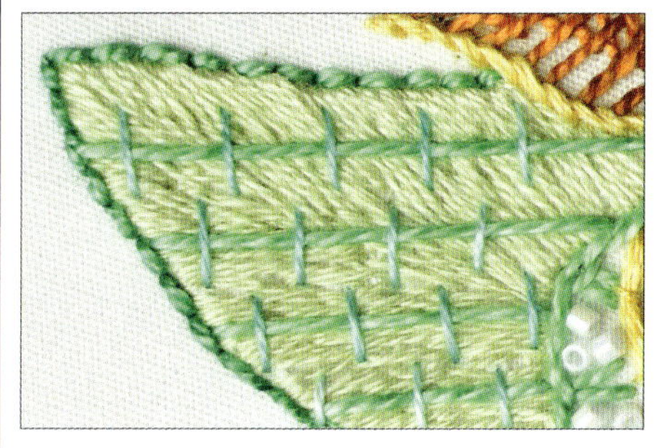

Option 1

Couching stitches are more spaced out than in burden stitch (see left) and go over just one couched stitch.

Option 2

Couching stitches (blue) go over two couched stitches (green).

BUTTONHOLE SCALLOPS

You may find it easier to work a straight stitch (see page 201) first – shown here in yellow thread.

BUTTONHOLE SCALLOPS – PADDED

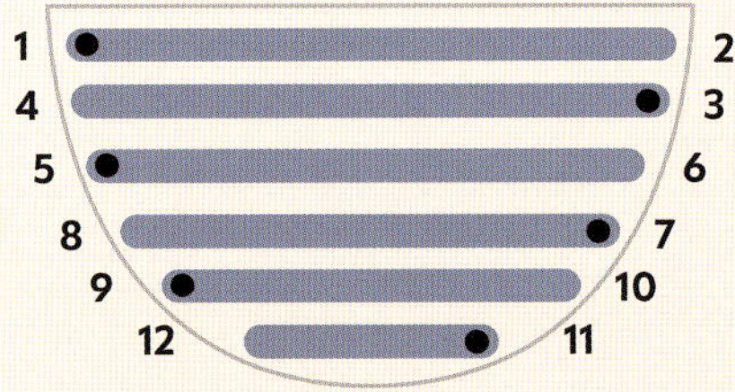

1 Pad a scallop in satin stitch (see page 194), using three to six strands of stranded cotton thread.

2 Using just one or two strands of the same thread you used for padding, work buttonhole stitch (see below) over the padded area, so that the stitches fan out from the centre of the area (see the dot in the diagram).

BUTTONHOLE STITCH

BUTTONHOLE STITCH – CLOSED

This is simply a row of buttonhole with neighbouring individual stitches tilted towards each other.

Simpler option

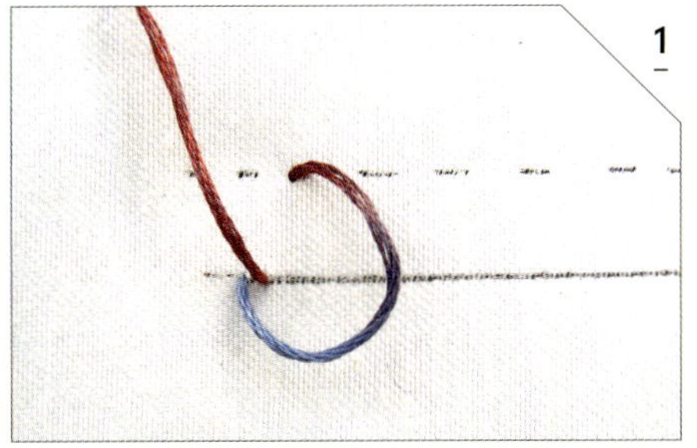

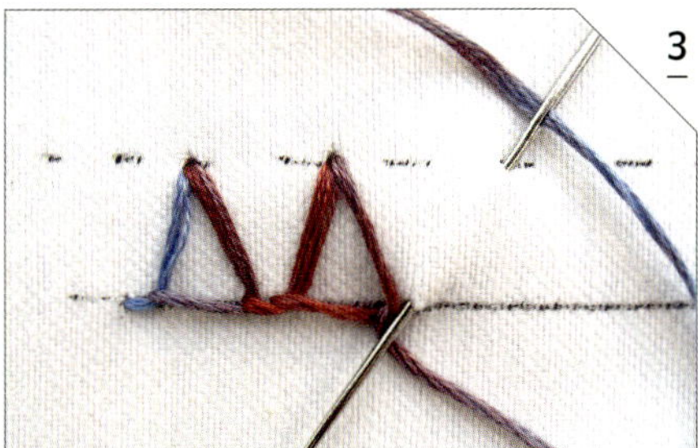

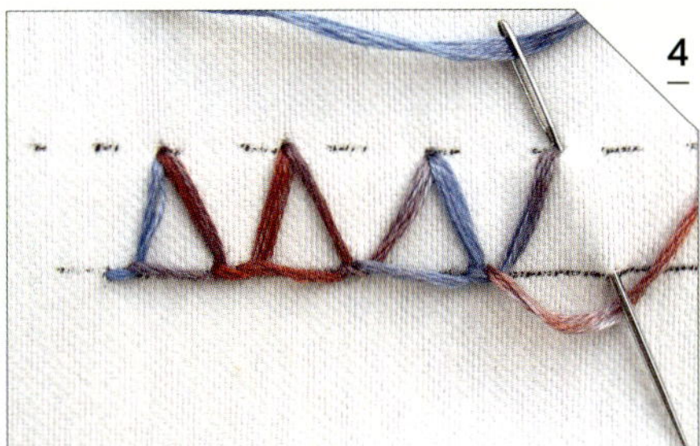

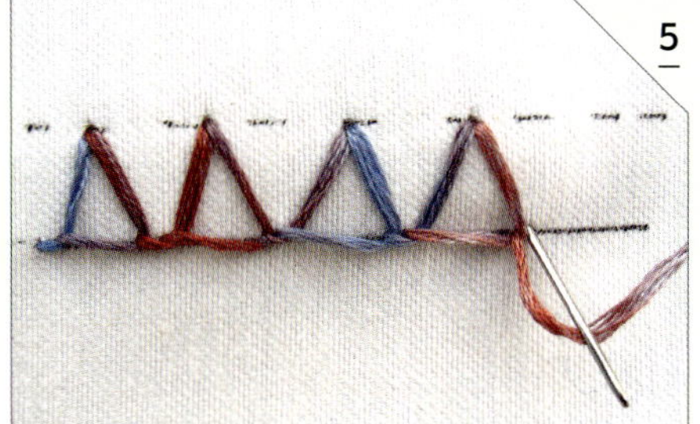

More complex option

This option gives an alternative to using water-soluble fabric marker – useful if we do not have a marker at hand, or when working on types of fabric that do not work well with marker.

Make guiding stitches (shown in yellow thread here) and remove them as you progress.

TIP

When guiding stitches are removed, stray fibres can remain trapped at the spots where the thread passed through the fabric – so never use a colourful thread for guiding stitches.

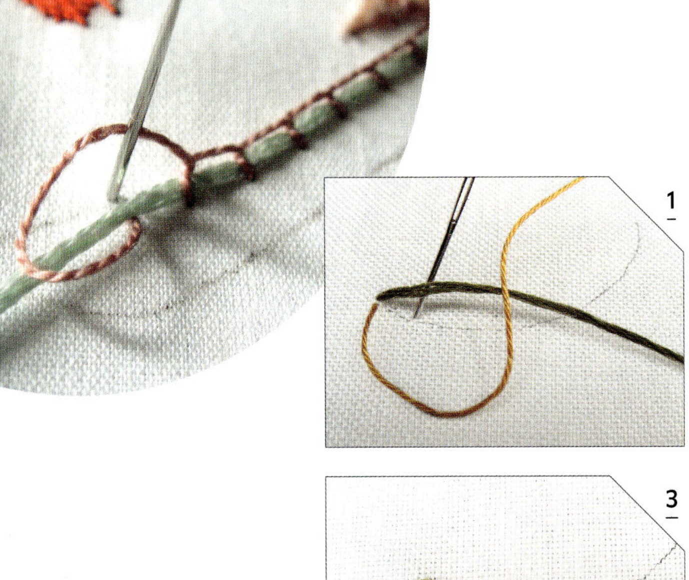

BUTTONHOLE STITCH – COUCHING

When couching (see pages 159–160), you can use buttonhole stitches instead of small straight stitches to couch the working thread across the design line.

Thread two needles, one with a couching thread and the other with a working thread. The couching thread is usually finer.

The interval between the couching stitches may vary.

BUTTONHOLE STITCH – OVERLAPPING

Also known as blanket stitch filling.

1 For the first row, work a line of buttonhole stitches (see page 148), half their normal length. Leave a small gap between each stitch, just large enough to fit one stitch.
2 For the second row, work full-size stitches, placing them in the gaps in the previous row so they overlap.
3 For the third row: repeat the first row, but this time make the stitches full-size.

Correct sequence of stitching.

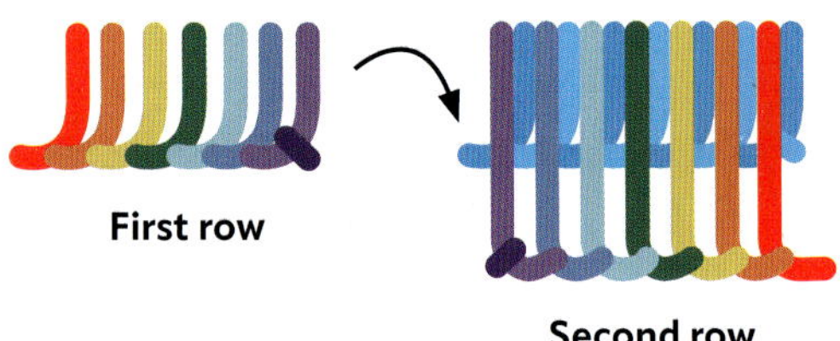

BUTTONHOLE STITCH – PADDED

1 Make guiding stitches (see page 149).
2 Using the same thread as for stitching, take the needle under as shown to create padding.
3 Stitch buttonhole stitches (see page 148) over the padding. Remove a guiding stitch when you approach it with your stitching (see inset).
4 Work stab stitches to finish. If gaps appear, fill them with straight stitch (see page 201), as shown in the inset.

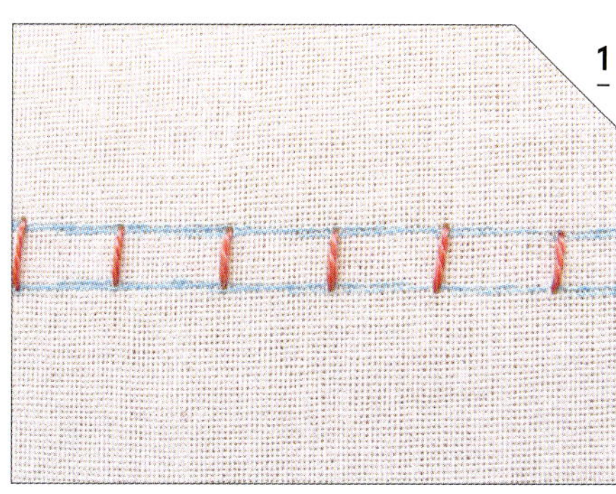

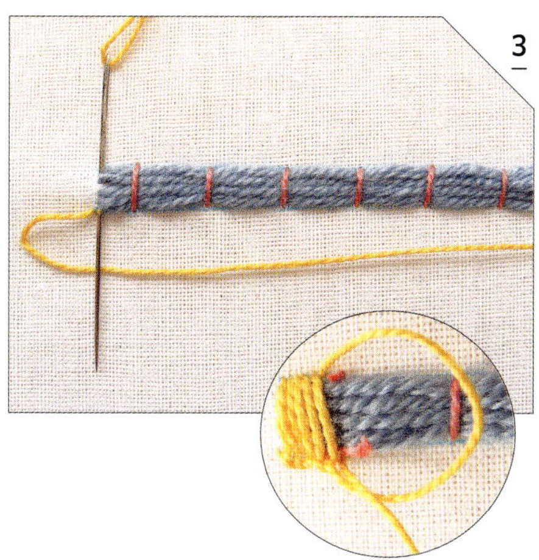

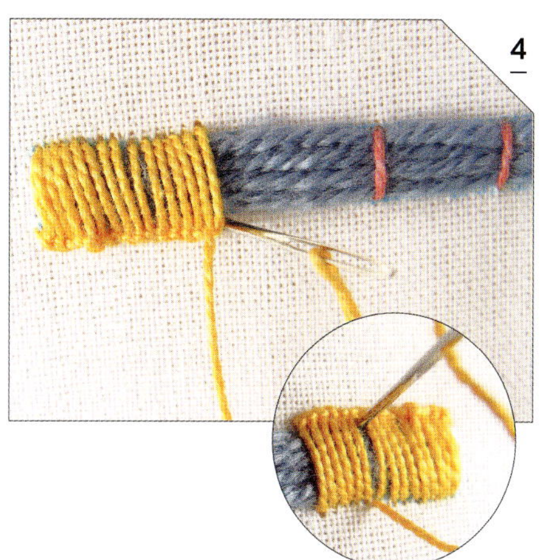

BUTTONHOLE WHEEL

CABLE CHAIN STITCH

Unusually for embroidery, the sewing method of stitching (see page 143), in which the needle comes up through and goes down into the fabric in a single pass, is used for this stitch.

1 To make the first loop, wrap the thread around the needle tip.

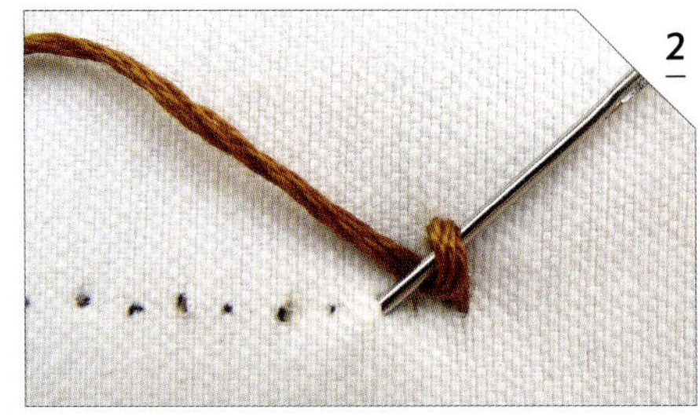

2 Bring the needle halfway down through the fabric…

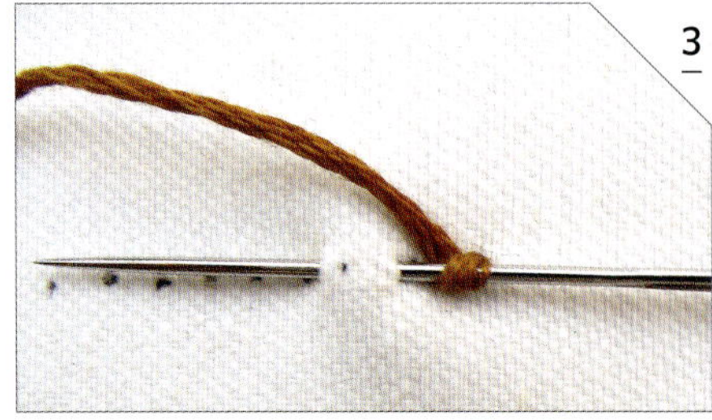

3 …then immediately bring it up, as if you were parking the needle.

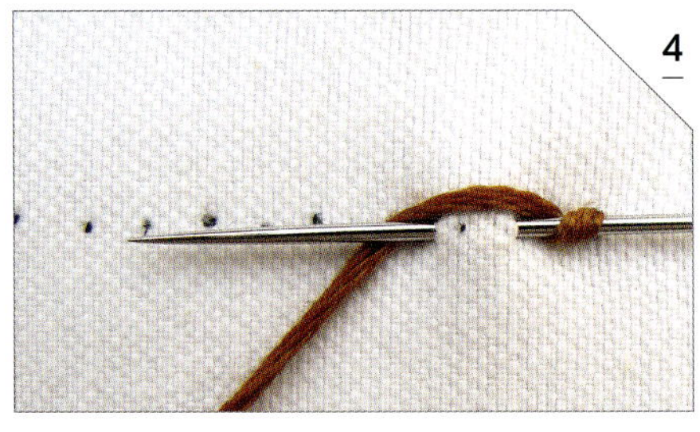

4 Bring the thread under the tip of the needle.

5 Bring the needle through the fabric, tightening the loop.

6 All the rest is just a repeat. To finish off, work a small couching stitch.

CANE WEAVING – BASE

There are a number of patterns for cane weaving. It is particularly popular in the Far East, where the patterns are used for making decorative cane furniture.

I have called this pattern 'Cane weaving – base', or basic cane weaving, as it is the foundation for the other cane weaving patterns explained on the following pages. It has its own beauty, and can be used as a completed stitch in its own right – indeed, you will see it used in some of the designs in this book.

It is important not to make a mistake following the pattern for weaving, so to help you remember, think of the lattice as joyfully-coloured multi-storey buildings standing side by side. The vertical stitches of the mesh are impassable walls – we never, ever, go under vertical stitches with our needle.

Imagine our needle is paying a visit to each house in turn. We bring the needle up at the ground floor, then visit a friend who lives on the first floor of the first house (that is, go under the thread marked '1'). Next we 'skip over the wall' by taking the needle over them to get into the second house, where a friend awaits you on the second floor; and then on to the third house on the third floor, and so on. Continue to the end of the first diagonal line.

Why such an intricate explanation for such a simple action? This will become clear when you come to stitching the other cane weaving patterns.

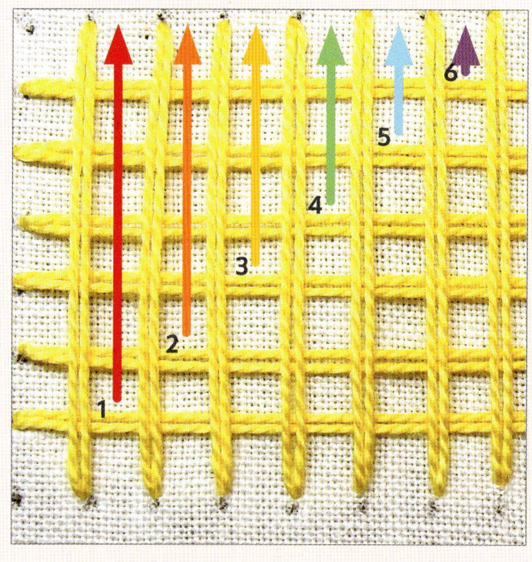

Visiting houses

The rainbow colours show the sequence of work: we visit the red 'house' first, then the orange, and so on.

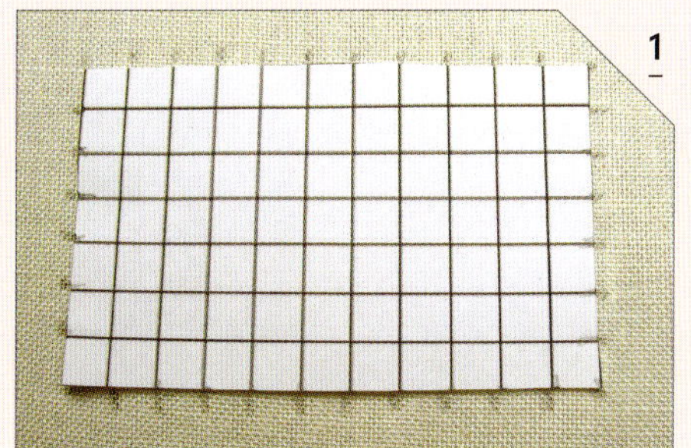

1 Cut a piece of squared paper to the size and shape of the area you want to stitch. Use this to help you mark a grid by placing it on your fabric and making dotted marks on the fabric around the edges, to make the shape of a rectangle.

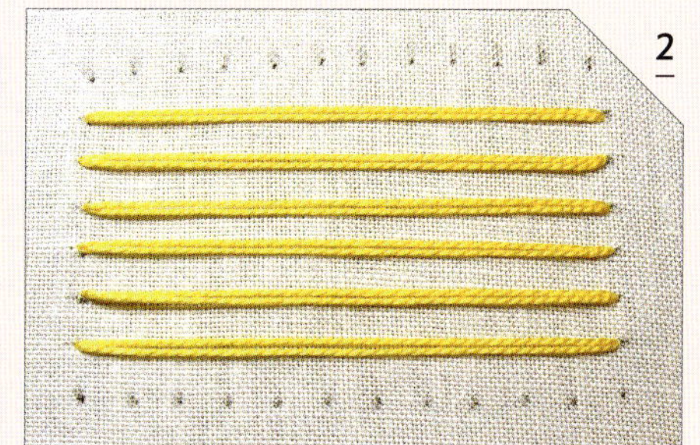

2 Prepare a long piece of double thread and knot the tail. Work the longer lines first (here, the horizontal lines) using the method for satin stitch – surface, on page 194.

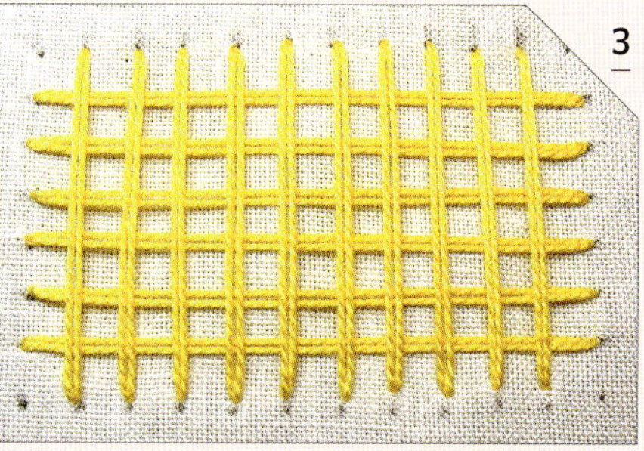

3 Stitch the vertical lines, but do not couch the intersections yet. Once complete, prepare a single thread. You can use the same colour as the mesh, but a contrasting thread is helpful when learning.

Continued overleaf.

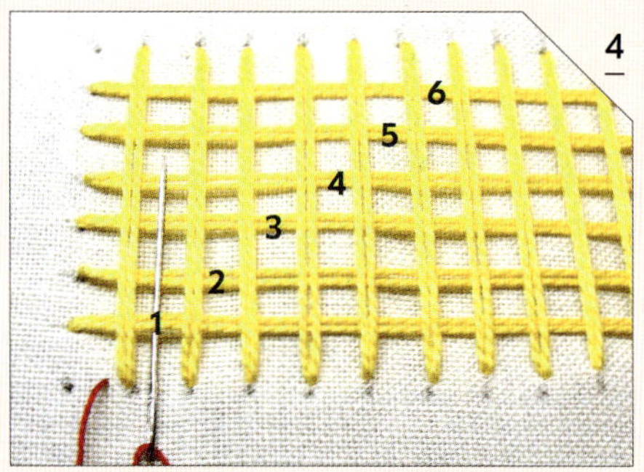

4 Bring the needle up to the left of the first vertical line (1).

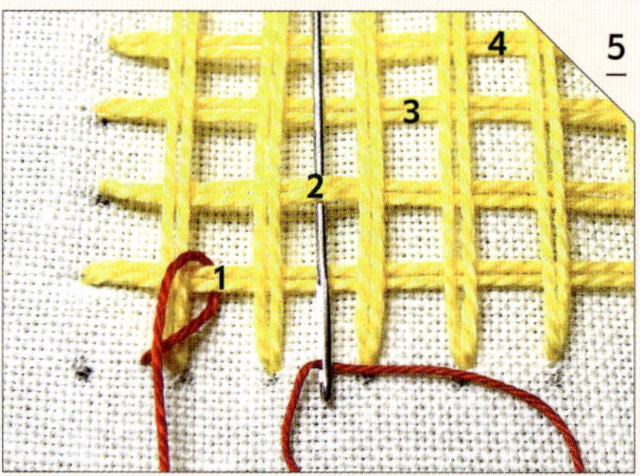

5 Take the thread up, over and back under the second vertical line (2), as shown.

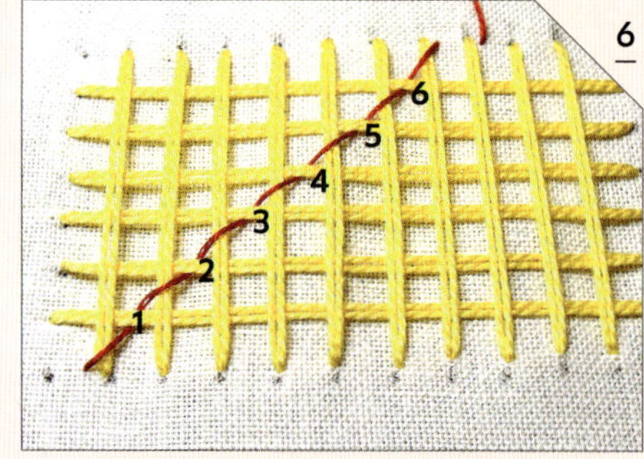

6 Follow the pattern to weave the first diagonal line. Bring the needle down at the end of the line and come up for the second diagonal line.

 TIP

Why start here, when this stitching divides the area in half diagonally? We start at the bottom left because it is good to weave a long line first while practising. Having stitched one half, we will anchor the thread and return to the other side.

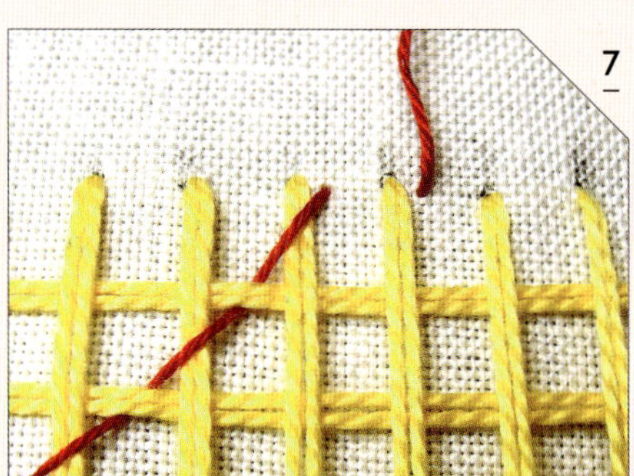

7 Bring the needle down at the end of the line and come up for the second diagonal line.

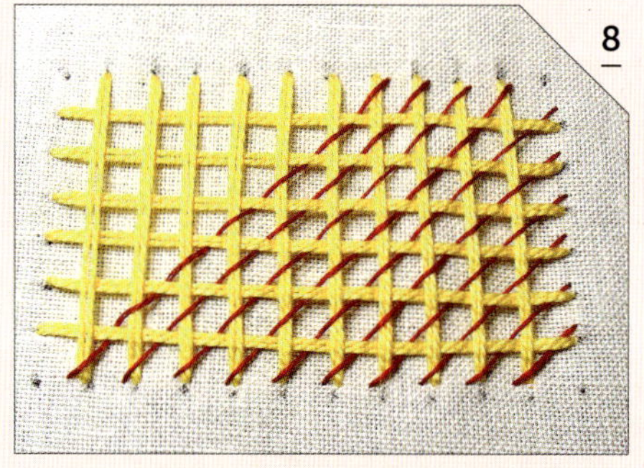

8 Work back down, then continue until one half of the area is woven.

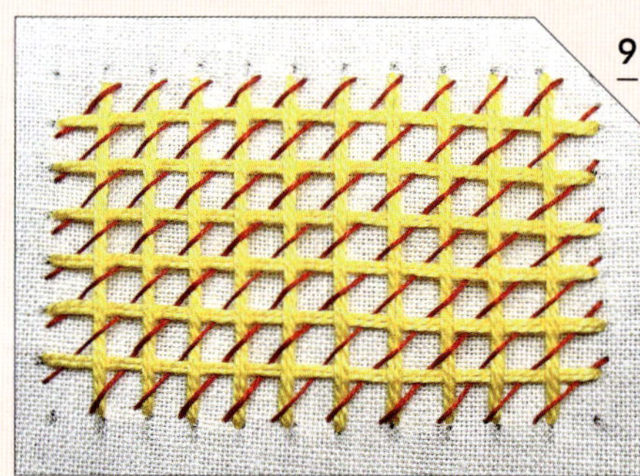

9 Work the other half in a similar way.

CANE WEAVING – JAPANESE MESH PATTERN

This variation takes its name from a very skilful embroiderer friend, who gave me the idea of using cane weaving patterns for embroidery.

While designing a flower bouquet, she searched for a technique to stitch a basket for the bouquet. Looking into her Granny's stock of embroidery books, she found a Japanese magazine, with instructions for a cane weaving pattern. Because of her Japanese origin, she told me, she was able to read the pattern – so happily used it for her design.

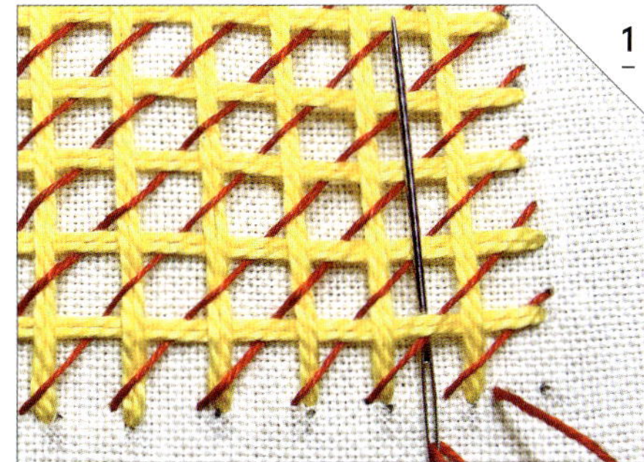

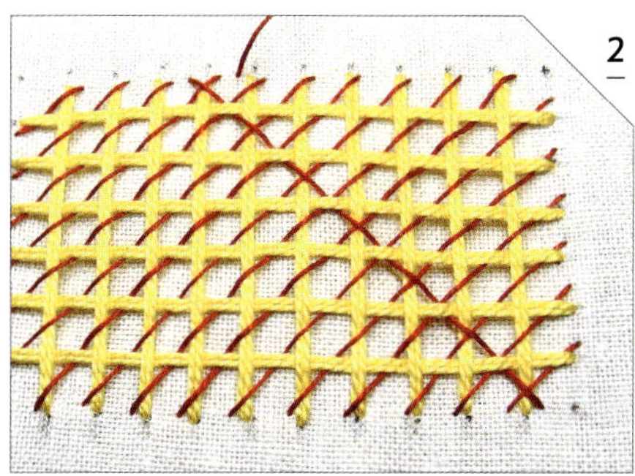

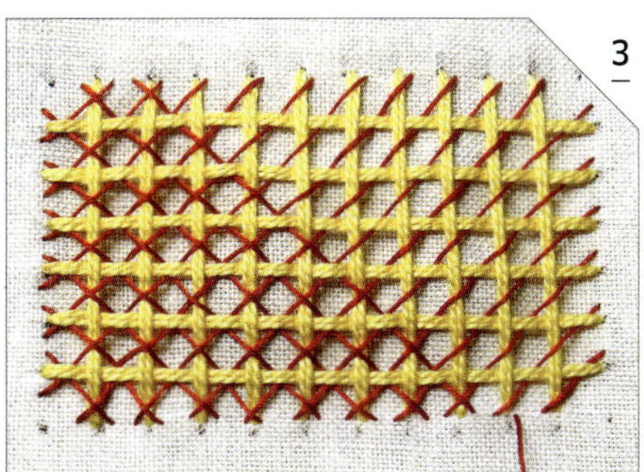

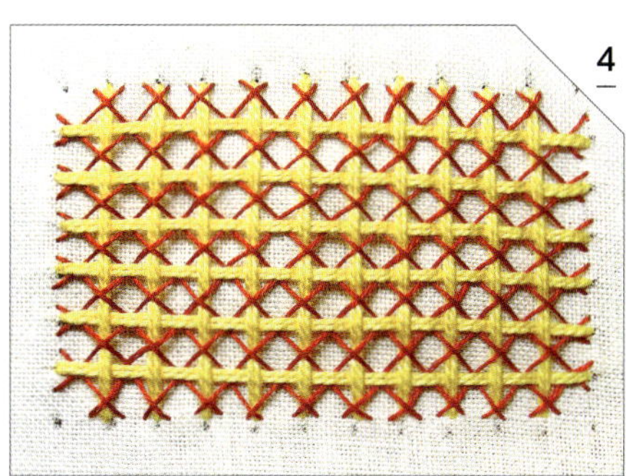

1 Work cane weaving – base (see pages 153–154). Weave another set of diagonal stitches into the pattern in a similar way – but placed as a mirror image of the earlier stitches.

2 Ignore the first set of diagonal stitches as you work; focus on the mesh itself. It is helpful to break the space into two parts and weave one first, starting from the longest diagonal stitch.

3 Having finished weaving one part of the mesh, anchor your thread and start a fresh one at the other part.

4 Finally, you will get a pattern with small 'crosses' placed over vertical lines. Make sure that you pass the needle underneath all the horizontal lines of your weaving.

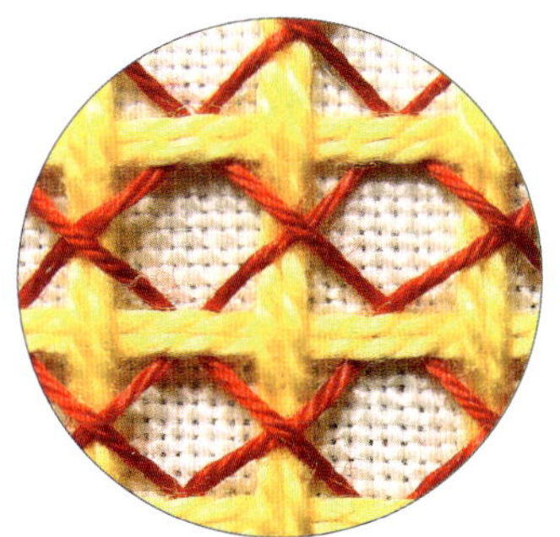

Detail of the crosses worked over the vertical lines.

TIP

To avoid making mistakes like this (A), always come *over* vertical stitches and *under* horizontal ones.

CANE WEAVING – PROPELLER PATTERN

The name comes from the finished stitch's resemblance to a paper toy windmill, as the pattern of weaving forms a kind of tiny propeller around each of the intersections of the mesh.

First, work cane weaving – base (see pages 153–154) and then work diagonal weaving, placing it the other way to that of the Japanese mesh. Having finished this stage, turn your embroidery 90 degrees clockwise (shown in step 1) and repeat.

We follow the story of visiting houses (see page 153) for this variation, too – though of course, as you turn the work, the lines which were impassable walls become floors – as shown in the steps below.

TIP

Try working the mesh in black thread and then use a heavier red or purple thread to make a weaving – the result will be a pattern resembling a field of poppies.

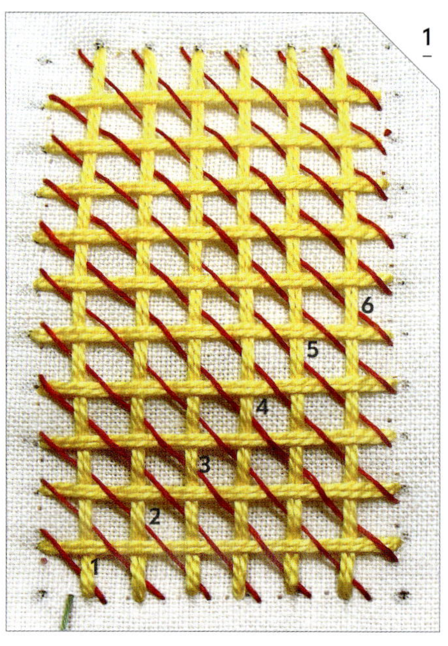

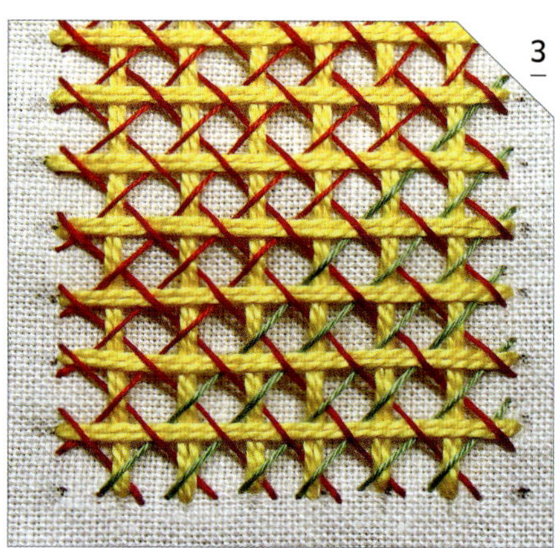

CHAIN STITCH

CHAIN STITCH – BUTTONHOLED

Also known as scalloped buttonholed chain stitch. I love the variation of this stitch, with its scallops overlapping. To create these, go down at A and up at B as shown.

CHAIN STITCH – REVERSE

The reverse chain stitch gives a very similar result to regular chain stitch (see opposite), but is worth considering for two reasons. Firstly, it is easier to make a narrower stitch line; and secondly, reverse chain stitch is useful if you are using a 'naughty' thread that twists while working loops of chain stitch.

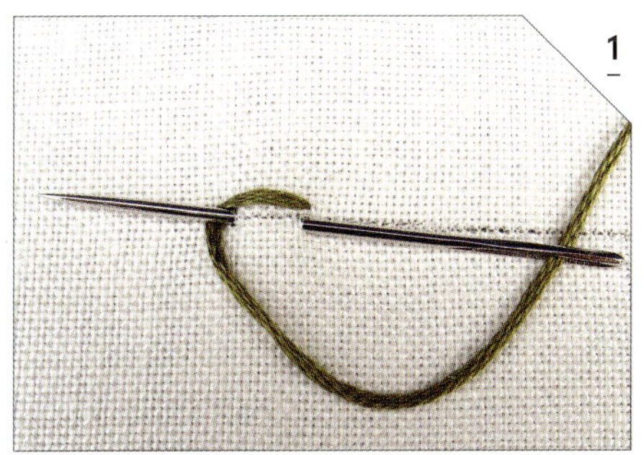

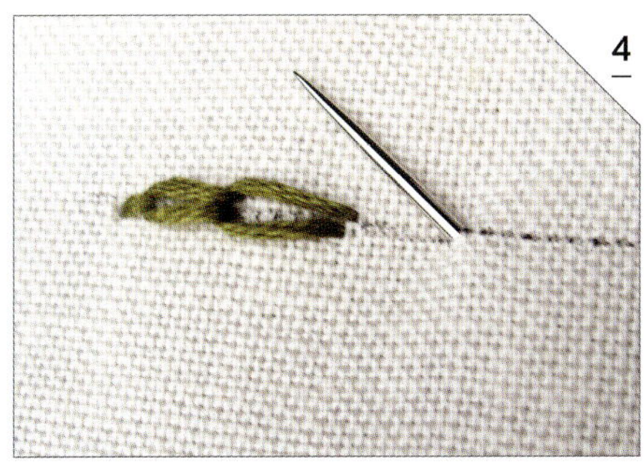

CHAIN STITCH – WHIPPED

Whipping on chain stitch can be done in two ways: over both sides of the loops (see right) or over just one side, as shown in the steps. Whipping over just one side of each loop gives a number of advantages:

- You can use contrasting threads to whip each of the two sides.
- You can whip one side in the same thread as used for the chain stitch.

Having anchored the last loop of your chain stitch, thread the needle with the thread you want to use for whipping and come up close to the first loop of the chain. When you start whipping from this end, it is important to bring the needle in from outside, while passing under the right-hand halves of the loops.

After whipping the right-hand halves of the loops, go down to the back of the fabric and come up very close. To whip the left-hand halves of the loops, bring your needle under those halves, moving it from the inside of the chain to the outer side. By following this order, you will get a nice V-shaped pattern formed with the whipping thread and following the direction of the V-shaped pattern of chain stitches.

1

2

3

4

5

Step 5 shows whipping on one side, applied to the right and to the left sides alternately, so that both of them become whipped – just in two steps.

Compare the result with the picture of chain stitch whipped on both sides in one go (see right): the look is different, and now you know why.

Whipped on both sides

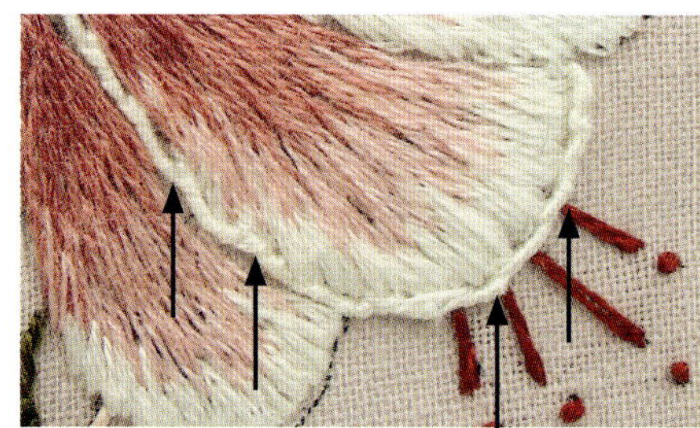

TIP

Try this stitch to outline an area for silk shading (see pages 196–197). You will get a nice rib around the silk shaded petal. Whip one side of the loops in a toning thread, then work the first row of silk shading, bringing your needle through each loop and thus covering the unwhipped part of a loop.

CORDED SINGLE BRUSSELS STITCH – 1

This is also known as corded detached buttonhole stitch. The difference between this variation and that described below is in the number of threads used for the cording.

This option uses just one thread, looping it over previous rows as shown.

Cording with one thread

The stitches are close together, and resemble a crochet pattern.

CORDED SINGLE BRUSSELS STITCH – 2

This variation of corded Brussels stitch is worked in the same way as above, but using two threads.

The question is whether to use two stitches in single thread or one stitch in double thread for this technique. When stitching in size 8 pearl cotton thread, you may use a double thread for cording, but be careful that individual threads do not intertwine. When using six strands of stranded cotton thread, it is more convenient to go there and back in a single thread, doing two straight stitches instead of one.

Cording with double thread

The texture is more sophisticated than cording with one thread. The buttonhole stitches are more spaced out, and the double thread of cording is visible through the openings.

COUCHING (THREAD)

Also known simply as couching. The couching stitches secure the underlying thread in place. They are always worked closely over the thread, and never through it.

COUCHING (TWISTED CORD)

Couching twisted cord is very similar to couching thread, except that the stitches are worked through the cord, rather than over it.

The best way is to couch at the gaps between the two threads that form the cord, as this makes the couching stitches almost invisible when worked in the same colour as the cord. Contrasting colours are used here for clarity.

You will need a needle big enough to thread the cord – a needle threader is handy for this technique, since the tip of the cord is usually very stiff and thus difficult to fit into the eye of the needle.

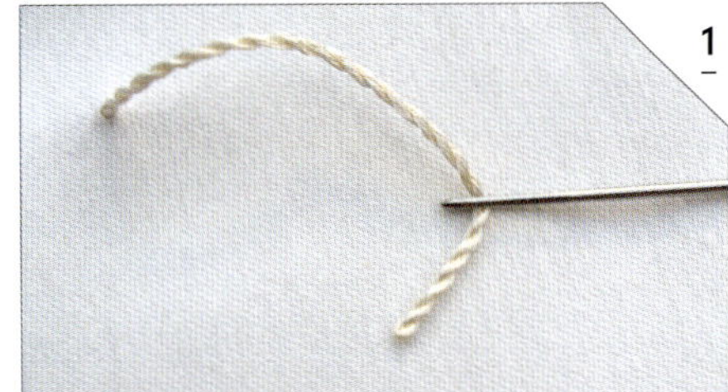

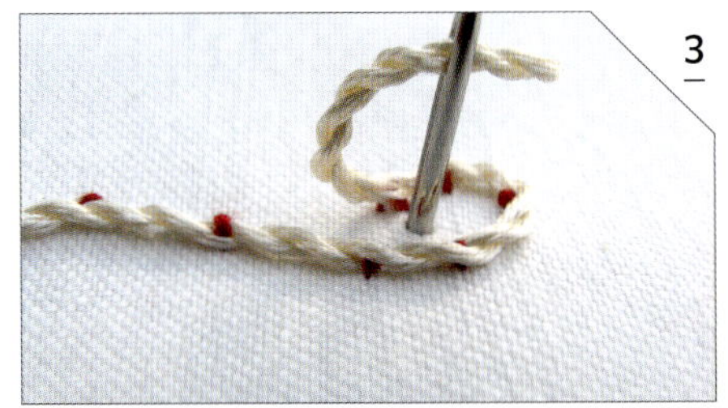

1. Bring the needle to the right side at the beginning of a stitch line.
2. Thread a second needle with single thread of the toning colour. Work small stitches through the working thread, attaching the cord along the design line.
3. Having finished, bring both needles to the back of the fabric.
4. If the remained piece of twisted cord is long enough to make a knot, anchor it with a knot. If it is too short, attach it to the stitches at the back of the fabric with couching thread.

COUCHING – GUIDED

For stitching lines which need to be more distinct, this method makes a smoother finished line – and the couching easier. Sometimes I place regular couching alongside guided couching to draw attention to the difference in their dimensions.

Before you start, work stem stitch (see page 200) along the design line using two strands of stranded cotton thread, in a colour matching the working thread. Threads of contrasting colour are used here for clarity.

1. Thread two needles: one with the working thread (e.g. six strands of stranded cotton thread) and the other with couching thread (one or two strands of toning thread). Anchor both threads as shown.
2. With the couching thread, whip both the stem stitch and the working thread.
3. Having finished the line, bring the two threads to the back of the fabric.

CRETAN STITCH LEAF and CRETAN STITCH LEAF – OPENWORK VARIATION

This is both effective and very easy way of working leaves of any shape and size. Draw or think of two lines along either side of the midrib to help guide you as you work.

1 Start at the tip and bring the needle down on the right edge of the leaf.
2 Come up a little to the right of the midrib.
3 Go down to the back of the fabric on the left edge of the leaf and come up a little to the left of the midrib.
4 Continue working the same pattern.
5 Finish with a small couching stitch. The resulting leaf will have a nice braid along the centre.

Openwork variation

This is worked in a similar way, except that the stitches are more spaced-out.

CROCHET CHAIN

DOUBLE LATTICE + 4-STITCH COUCHING

FANCY FILLING – COMPASS PATTERN

1 Work a lattice of groups of four straight stitches. The vertical and horizontal stitches should be perpendicular to each other.
2 Couch each of the crossings with two stitches.
3 Using thread of either a matching or contrasting colour, couch each line of lattice in between the intersections.
4 Continue until all the horizontal couching stitch lines are worked, then work vertical couching lines.

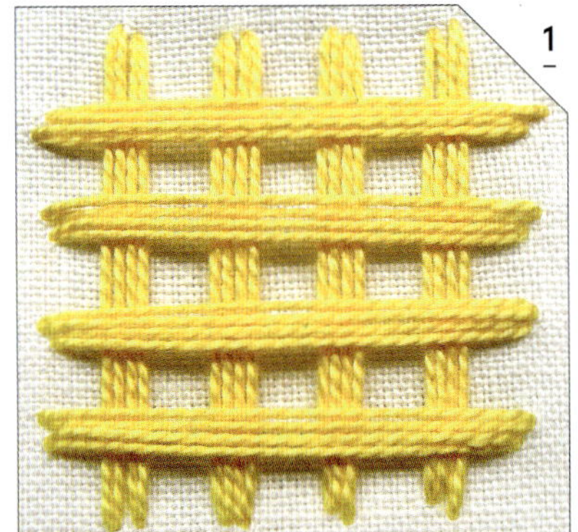

TIP

The stitch on both the vertical and horizontal parts (steps 3 and 4) resembles seeding stitch (see page 195).

FANCY FILLING – CROSS WHIPPING PATTERN

1 Work a lattice as for fancy filling – compass pattern, then use contrasting thread to start weaving around each intersection.
2 Having finished the line, do not bring the needle to the back of the fabric, but start weaving upwards.
3 Move up the first line, weaving the thread so that a small cross is formed at each intersection, then repeat for all the next lines.

FANCY FILLING – LEAF PATTERN

This is a variation on a number of other techniques within the fancy filling family. The name comes from the part of the design I first used it for: the leaf in *Queen Rose Light* (see pages 58–59).

All the steps are combined in the picture above, while the diagrams to the right show the work order. Note that the order of work may be altered. For example, you might work straight stitches in twisted cord right after stitching the lattice and before doing any couching at all.

Whatever order you choose, the lattice needs to be made first. This time it is formed by groups of four straight stitches. Think of the orientation of lattice you want to have. Then, if the stitching area is an oval shape, do the longer stitches first, then place shorter ones on top of them.

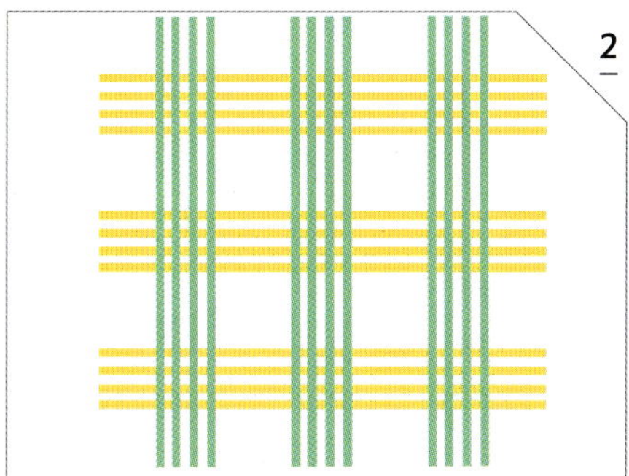

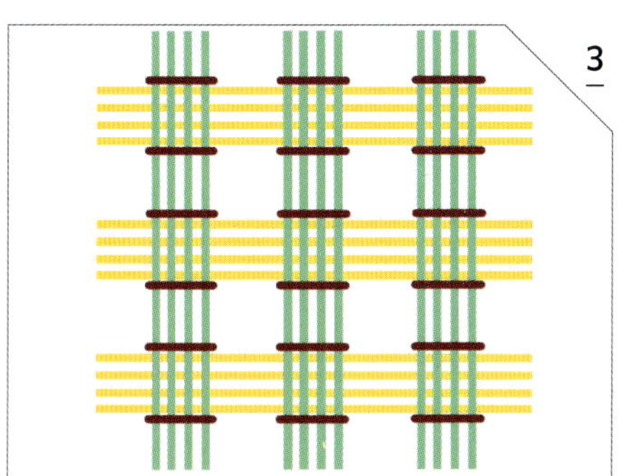

1. Work the bottom layer of the lattice using size 8 or 12 pearl cotton thread. Work straight stitches, placing them in groups of four, and leaving space between the groups a little wider than the width of each group.
2. Using the same thread, work the top layer of lattice, placing the stitches in a similar way to the previous step. Make those stitches perpendicular to the stitches of the previous layer. Do not interweave the layers.
3. Using two strands of stranded cotton thread, make couching stitches, placing them to the right and to the left of each intersection.
4. Make twisted cord, using one strand of stranded cotton thread. Work long straight stitches in the twisted cord, placing them immediately to the right and to the left of the groups of four stitches made in step 2.
5. Using either pearl cotton size 12, or silk/rayon/viscose thread of similar or finer thickness, work diagonal stitches across the intersections of lattice, couching the twisted cord. This thread both anchors the twisted cord and embellishes the pattern. Think of the colour: both toning and contrasting threads look nice but produce different effects.

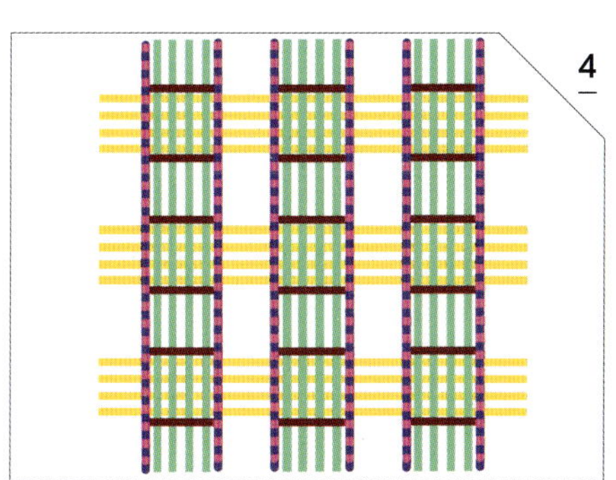

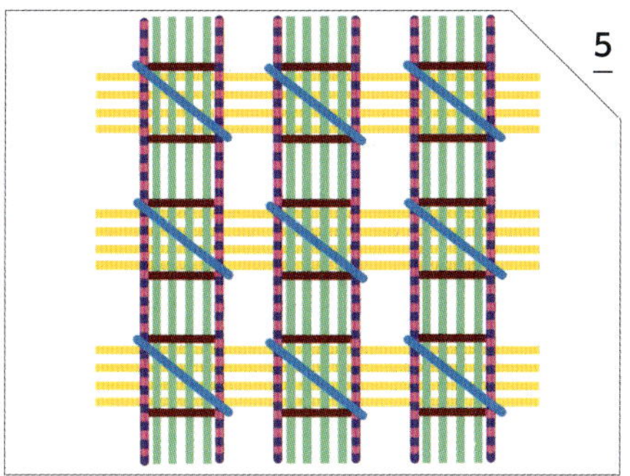

Tip
If you want the twisted cord (see step 4) to be more three-dimensional, work it using two or more strands of stranded cotton thread.

FANCY FILLING – ROSEBUD PATTERN

This is the most beautiful, and also the most complicated, of the six fancy filling techniques in this book. The look of the completed pattern will vary hugely, depending on colours used. It is used in the outer petals of the biggest flower of the *Queen Rose Light* design (see pages 56–57).

The image to the right shows the finished look of the stitch.

1 Using two to six strands of stranded cotton thread, work satin stitch – surface (see page 194), to ensure there are no long stitches on the back of the fabric.

TIP

It is more convenient to work satin stitch along the longest side of the area.

2 Using pearl cotton size 8, work groups of four straight stitches perpendicular to the direction of satin stitch, leaving gaps around three threads wide between the groups. To make the next steps easier, it is important to make these stitches loose by working them over a second needle.

3 Using the same thread as in step 2, work groups of four straight stitches perpendicular to the direction of the previous stitches. No second needle is needed here.

4 Using two threads of stranded cotton, work couching stitches, following the pattern. Use a second needle to keep the stitches loose.

TIP

Most of the square spaces inside the lattice (the 'cells') are surrounded by lattice stitches from all the four sides. Fewer cells touch the border (design outlines) and therefore one or two of the lattice stitches are missing. In the following steps, work the 'whole cells' first and then you will see how to stitch the rest.

5C

5 Using two threads of stranded cotton, bring the needle up through the centre of a whole cell. Pick up two threads of the four-thread group on the left of this cell. (the threads of the bottom layer of the lattice) (5A), then pick up two threads of the four-thread group on the right of this cell (5B). Bring the needle down through the same place in the centre of the cell (5C).

5 (cont.) You are working a loop similar to that used in couching techniques, except here the 'couched' threads are shifted from their initial places, thus forming an intricate pattern. Tighten the loop as shown.

The best thread choice for step 5 is to use two strands of cotton thread. A heavier thread is used in this example for clarity.

Having completed the stitching of the whole cells, have a look at the rest. It is now clearer what to do along the outlines of the area to make all its parts look similar.

FANCY FILLING –STRAWBERRY PATTERN

So-named simply because a strawberry was the first element I stitched using it, this filling is perfect to suggest the texture of this berry.

For clarity, the side parts of the lattice are not woven, but for a nice look of the stitched area you should fill in all the space. It is up to you whether to use a contrasting, a toning or the same colour thread for this. It looks nice in any combination, just the highlights are different.

1 Work a lattice, placing horizontal and vertical groups of four stitches perpendicular to each other, and spacing them so that only four more stitches can fit into a gap.

2 Couch each intersection with two stitches; resembling a cross-stitch.

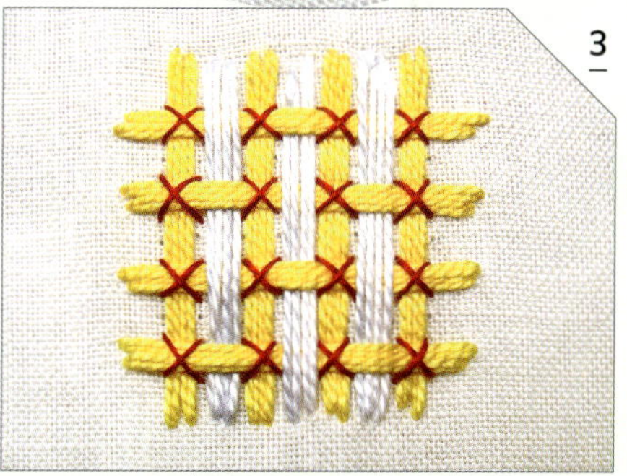

3 Coming through the spaces between the vertical stitches, weave over and under the horizontal stitches of the lattice. For a more intricate effect, change the order of weaving between even and odd columns of stitches.

FANCY FILLING – ZEBRA PATTERN

This stitch is a free-form interpretation of a number of weaving techniques and filling stitches. The threads suggested to the right and used here are just one of the numerous options, so feel free to choose your own.

Threads (all Cotton pearl DMC)

- Size 8 (colours A and B) for step 1
- Size 8 (colour C) for step 2
- Size 12 (colour D) for step 3

1 Using threads of two contrasting colours (A and B), work groups of four straight stitches (see page 201), alternating the thread colour each time you start stitching a new group. Continue until all the area is filled.

2 Change to thread C (the one used here is a lighter tone of thread B, to produce a 3D effect). Work groups of four straight stitches perpendicular to the stitches of the first layer. Place these groups at equal intervals, each about the same width as the group itself.

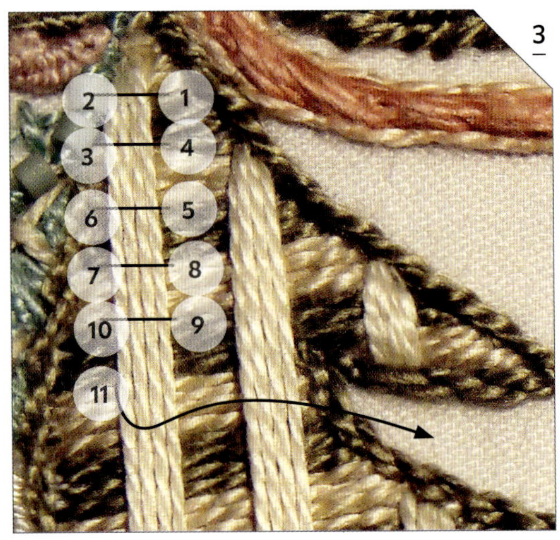

3 Couching It is important to choose a finer thread (D) for this step than in steps 1 and 2. Work straight stitches on top of and across the stitches of the second layer, following the number sequence as shown. Come up at 1, go down to the back of the fabric at 2, up again at 3 and so forth.

TIP

Note that this is supposed to be stitching, not weaving: couch the groups of four stitches down onto the fabric. The couching stitches are placed in such a way that they look like the borders of squares. These squares are in fact intersections of the two previous stitch layers.

The completed area of fancy filling.

OUTLINING FILLING STITCHES

As is often the case with filling stitches, the stitched area of these fancy filling stitches needs outlining with a border stitch for a neater look. Stem stitch or split stitch (see page 199) are both good options.

FEATHER STITCH

FERN STITCH

Start each stitch at the black dot. See page 142 for the key to the diagram.

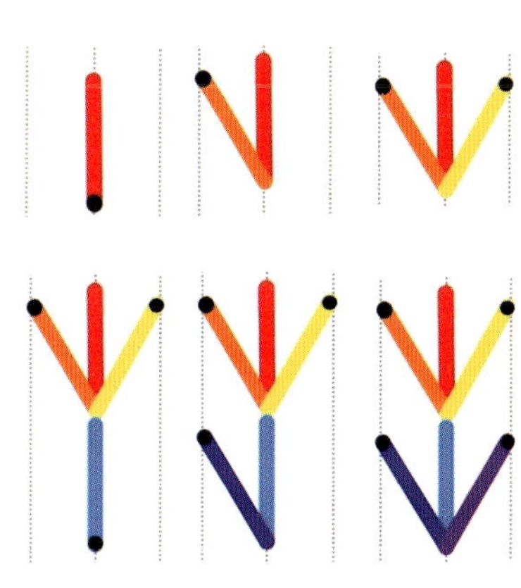

FLY STITCH

FLY STITCH – BUTTONHOLED

Work buttonhole stitches (see page 148) around the thread of a fly stitch, pulling on the thread to tighten them and push the stitches close together.

TIP

You may find it helpful to bring the thread down to the back side before working the other side of each fly stitch.

1

2

3

4

5

FLY STITCH – WHIPPED

FLY STITCH LEAF

Worked close together, a number of fly stitches can be used to create a leaf shape.

The completed stitch.

Vary the colours you use for each fly stitch for a variegated effect.

FLY STITCH LEAF – LAZY VARIATION

This is also known as lazy fly stitch leaf. While it resembles fly stitch leaf, it's made up of straight stitches worked under a line of backstitch to keep them at an angle.

The advantage of this 'lazy' variation is that contrasting colours of thread can be used to work the leaf and its midrib.

1 Work a line of backstitch, then begin working straight stitches (see page 201). Start and finish each straight stitch on the leaf outline, taking the needle under the stitches of midrib, as shown. Space them according to the length of the individual stitches of backstitch.

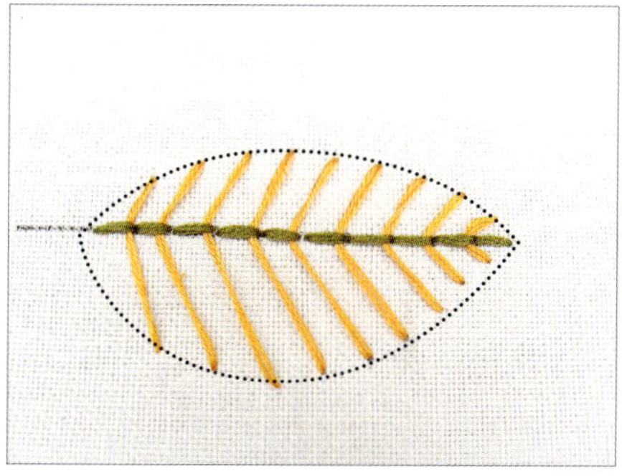

The completed stitch

As an option, you can whip the backstitch for a more distinct central vein.

FLY STITCH TRIANGLES

Also known as scattered triangle pattern. I love the look of these tiny colourful decorative elements. You can vary their size and colour shade – for the fine filigreed filling shown to the right, I suggest using one strand of stranded cotton thread. For bigger or bolder results, any other type of thread can be used. There are two ways to work this stitch.

Traditional method

Think of drawing an equilateral triangle while working the fly stitch (see page 168) in step 1. The drawback of this method is that it can leave gaps at the corners.

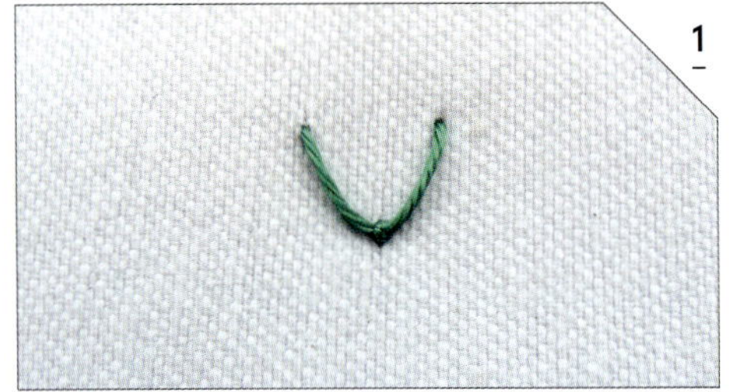

1 Work a fly stitch with a tiny couching stitch. Ensure the two 'wings' of the stitch are equal in length and placed at a 60-degree angle to each other.

2 Work a straight stitch to bridge the gap between the two tips.

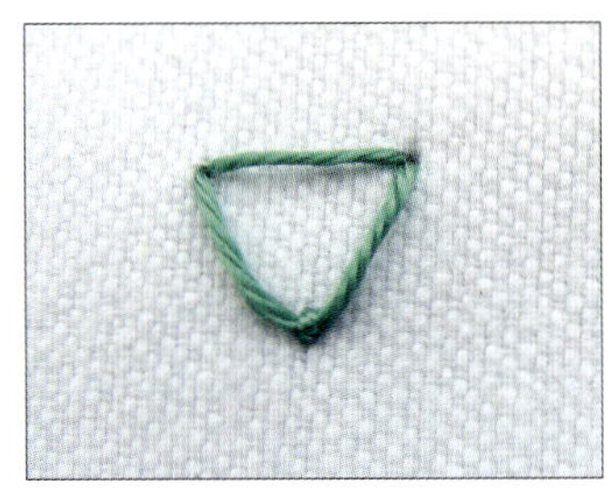

The completed stitch.

Two-needle method

I developed this way of stitching triangles to prevent any gaps appearing at the corners. While this method doesn't technically involve fly stitch, the results look similar, and so I have kept the name to make comparisons easier. Before you begin, thread one needle with a single thread, and another with a double thread, and knot each thread tail. Contrasting colours are used here for clarity.

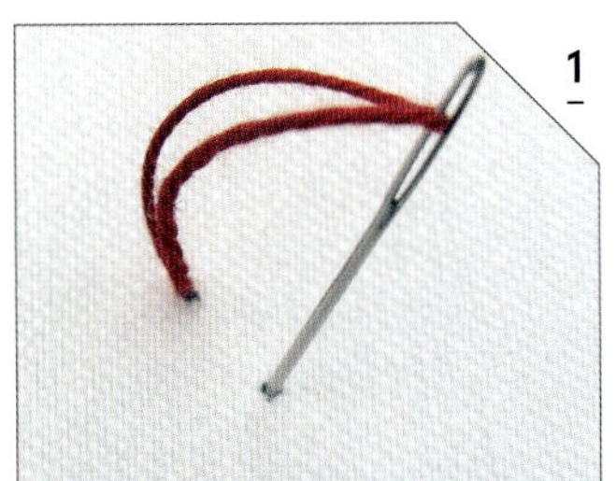

1 Work a straight stitch along one side of the triangle using the double thread (red). Do not tighten the stitch completely.

2 Pick up the single thread (green), and bring the needle between the two threads of the straight stitch.

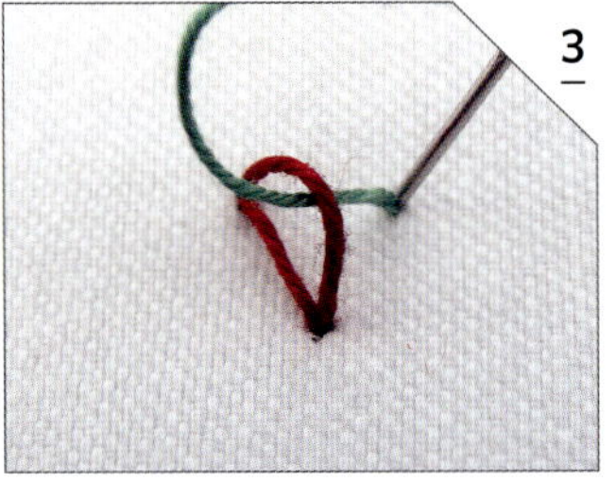

3 Couch one of them to finish the triangle. Tighten up the double thread, then anchor the thread tails at the back of the fabric or move on to work a second triangle.

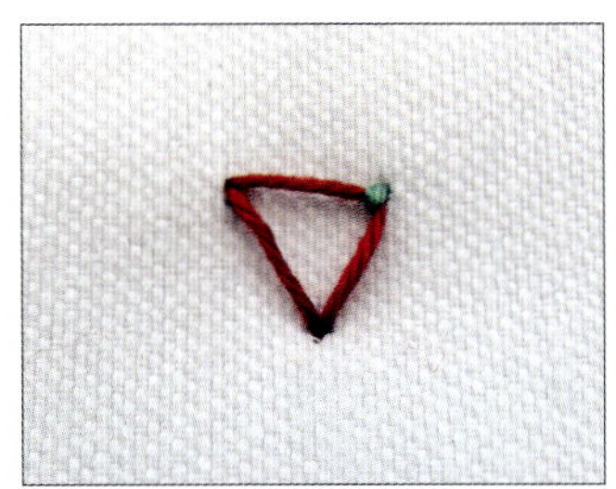

The completed stitch.

FRENCH KNOT

The number of times you wrap the thread round the needle will determine how large the resulting knot will be.

If you are doing this stitch for the first time, you may find it helpful to think of the very first step of the process as forming the letter 'T' with your thread and needle, as you can see below.

TIP

Make a blend of two or three shades of stranded cotton thread, using a few threads of each colour, then enjoy the variegated results!

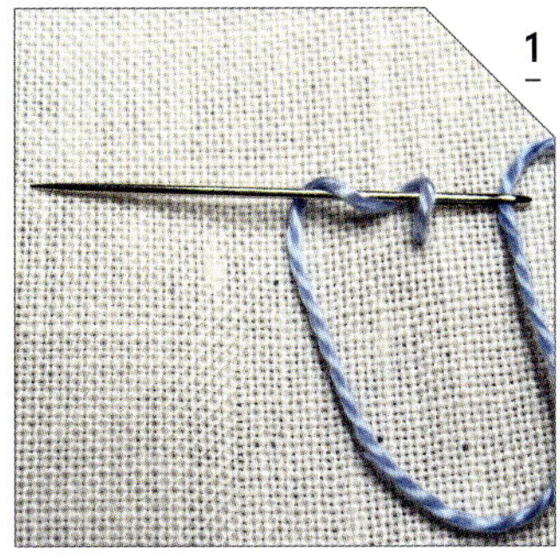

1 Wrap the thread one, two or three times around the needle.

2 Holding the wraps with your forefinger, take the needle halfway through the fabric, close to the spot where you came up.

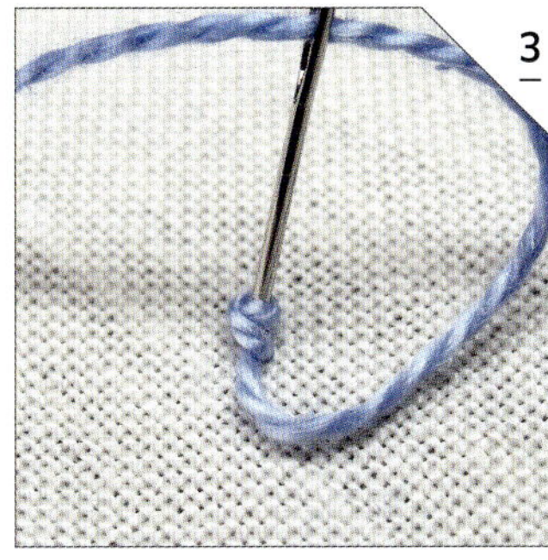

3 Tighten the loose wraps, gathering them at the base of the needle.

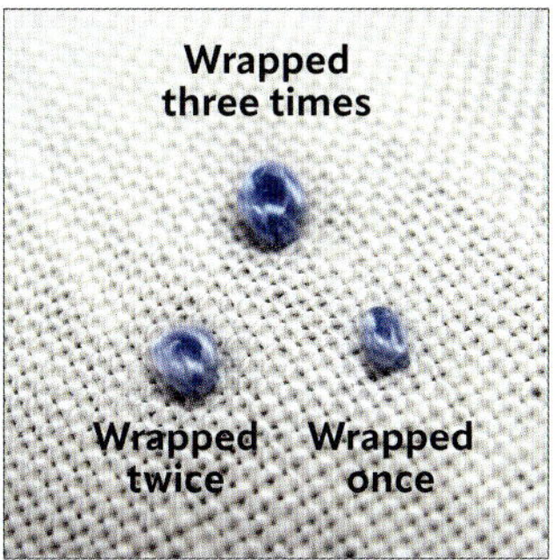

4 Bring the needle all the way down to the back of the fabric to complete the French knot.

FRENCH KNOT – LOOSE

Also known as ring knot. To get this loose variation of French knot, simply do not tighten the thread which wraps the needle before taking the needle through.

For the sake of clarity, the photographs show French knots with loops bigger than we would usually want in our stitching.

The completed stitch.

GERMAN KNOTTED BUTTONHOLE STITCH

Worked across two design lines, this stitch involves wrapping pairs of buttonhole stitches (see page 148) together.

Step 4 is a repeat of step 1. Continue working buttonhole stitches in pairs, wrapping each pair with your thread.

GORDIAN KNOT STITCH

More commonly known as braid stitch or cable plait stitch, I prefer a more unusual alternative name to help avoid confusion with all the other stitches with 'braid' or 'cable' in their names. The stitch is shown vertically here, but can be worked horizontally.

According to legend, an oracle declared that a man who unravelled the elaborate Gordian knot was destined to become ruler of all Asia. Alexander the Great simply cut it in two, reasoning that the oracle gave no restrictions on how the knot should be undone.

The completed stitch

This has been worked in variegated thread. It shows all the individual loops and twists.

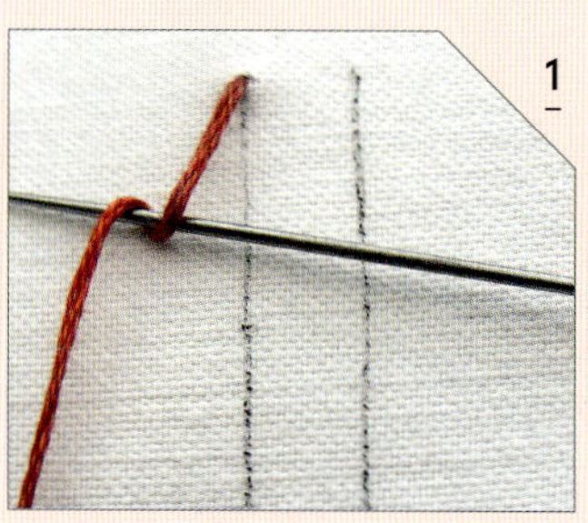

1 Draw two lines. Bring the needle up on one line and wrap the thread around the needle.

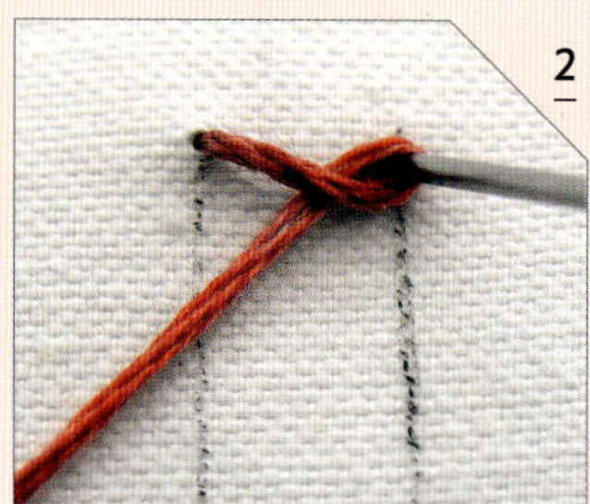

2 Bring the needle down at the other line, taking it halfway through the fabric.

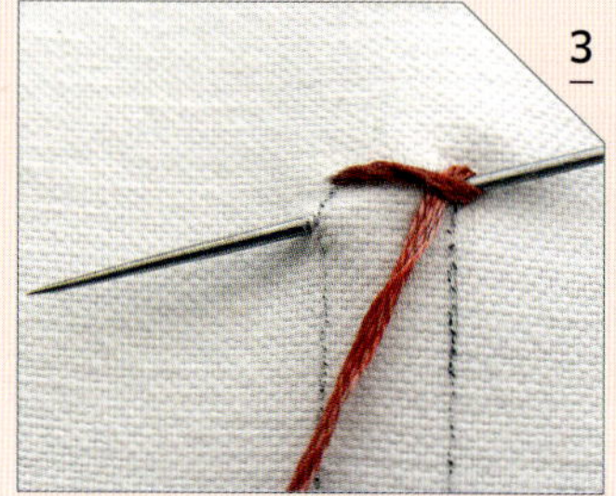

3 Bring the tip of the needle up through the other line, as if parking the needle.

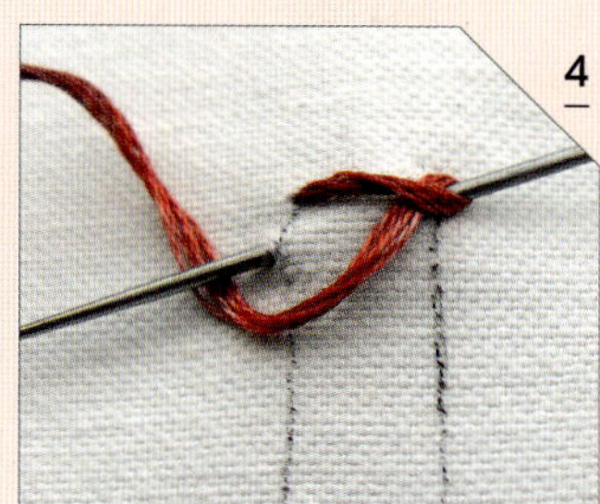

4 Work another twist by bringing the thread under the needle ...

5 ... and over the needle as shown; then draw the thread through.

6 Gently pull the thread to tighten the loop. The key to this stitch is to tighten all the loops consistently so they are the same size.

7 Repeat from step 2 to the end of the lines, then make a small anchoring stitch to secure.

GRANITOS

The key to this stitch is to bring your needle up at the black dot, and always go through the same two holes in the fabric.

The rainbow colour flow shows the sequence of stitching (see page 142): work a straight stitch first (red), then place the second stitch to the left (orange) and the third one (yellow) to the right of the first stitch. Continue alternating sides until you are happy with the size of the stitch.

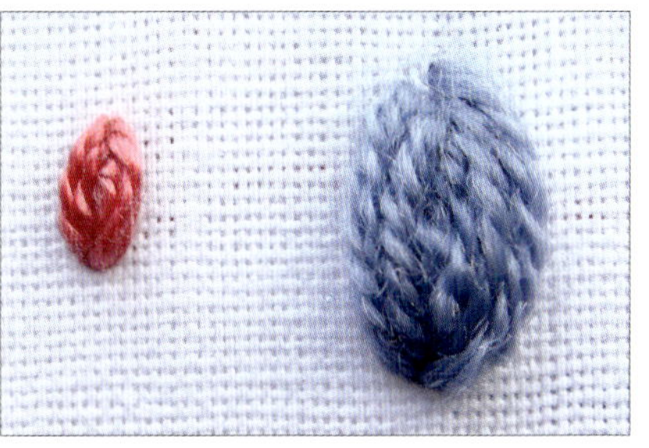

Smaller and larger finished examples.

HEAVY CHAIN STITCH

This would usually be stitched with one thread of a single colour; but I have used three threads of contrasting colours for clarity.

HERRINGBONE STITCH

The work order is shown in rainbow colour flow (see page 142).

The completed stitch.

HUNGARIAN BRAIDED CHAIN STITCH

To make each stitch more distinct, threads of three contrasting colours have been used here.

INTERLACED BAND STITCH

1 Work two parallel lines of backstitch, leaving some space between them. Bring the needle up between them.

2 Lace the backstitch lines as shown.

3 Continue to the end of the lines.

4 To finish, bring the needle to the back of the fabric, in between the lines.

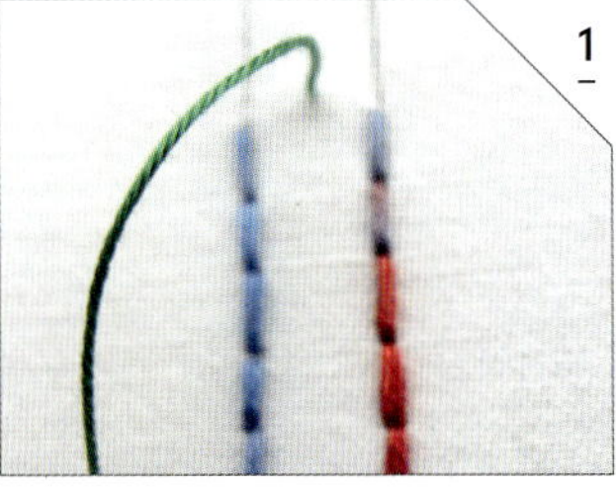

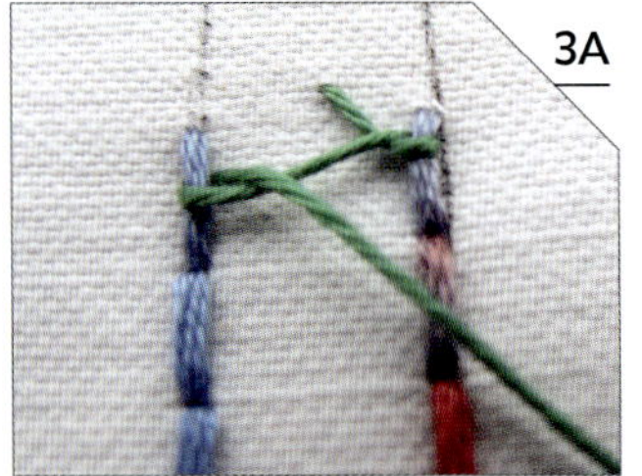

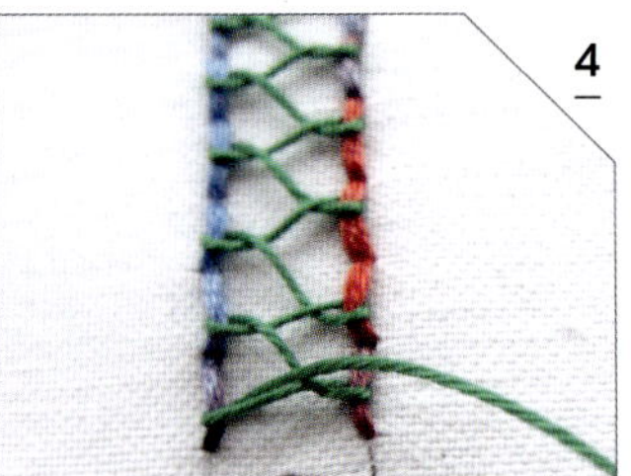

JACOBEAN STAR – PATTERN 1

Jacobean stars are combinations of different stitches, often interlacing each other. Needless to say, there is an infinite variety of options, so enjoy developing your own star with your own combination of threads.

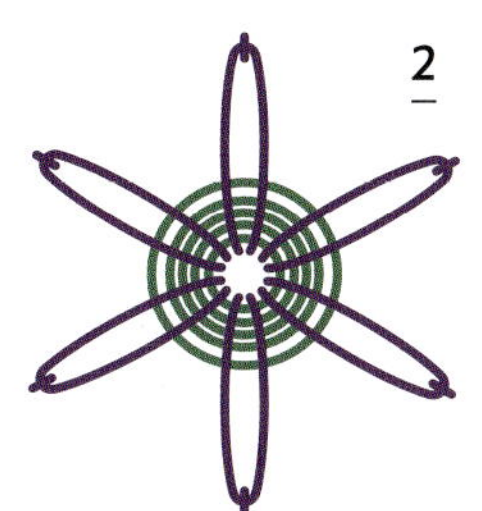

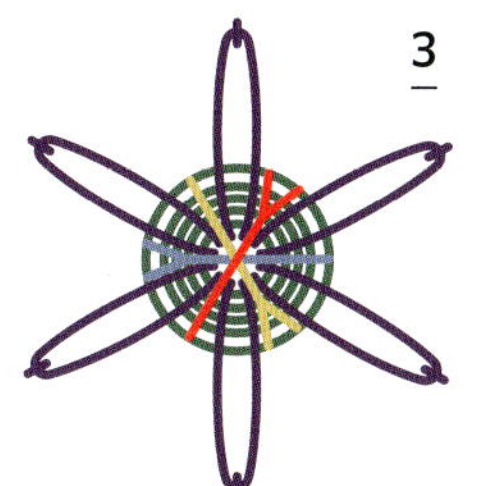

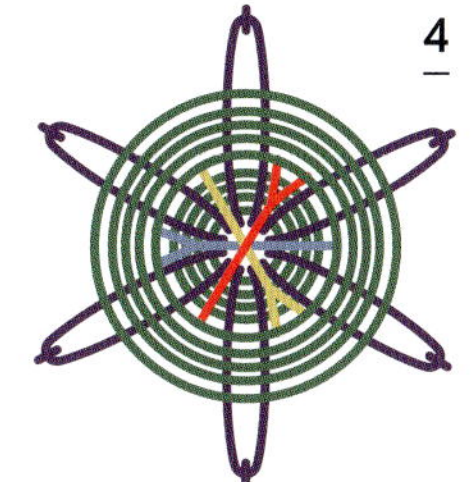

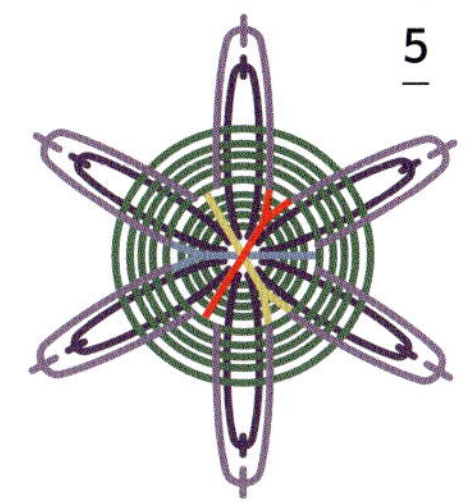

1 Work six lazy daisy stitches (see page 178) of the same length radiating from a centre point.
2 Starting in the centre, work ribbed spider web stitch (see page 189), whipping the lazy daisy 'spokes' until they are half-covered (these are marked by green circles). Add a couple of final rounds in a contrasting thread (white thread in the photograph).
3 On top of the centre, work three fly stitches (see page 168) – these are marked in red, yellow and blue.
4 Continue working ribbed spider web stitch to fill more of the spokes.
5 Work six lazy daisy stitches of open type around the upper parts of tips of spikes – marked with mauve lines in the diagram. Place these stitches on top of all the others.

JACOBEAN STAR – PATTERN 2

This is another intricate alternative to circle weaving. Try it in different colour combinations and enjoy using it for your other embroideries.

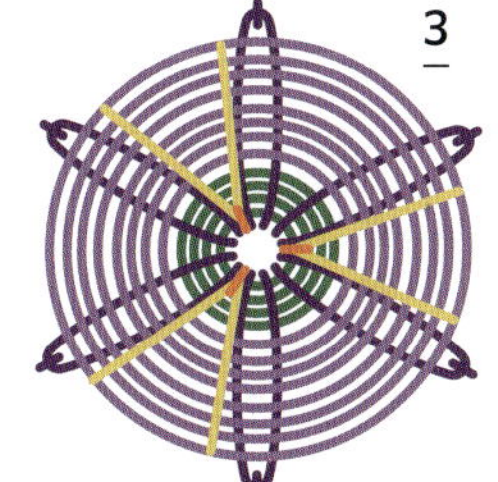

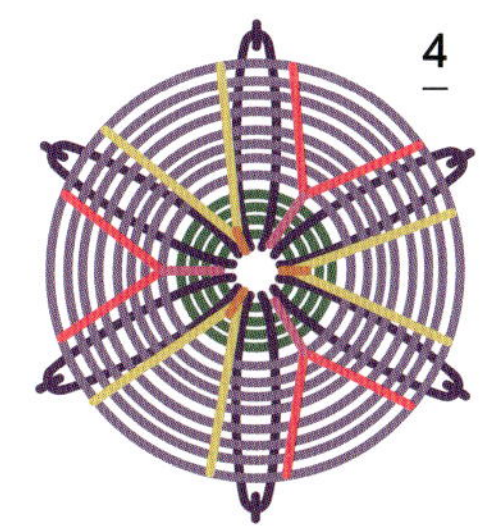

1 Work six lazy daisy stitches (see page 178) of the same length radiating from a centre point.
2 Work ribbed spider web (see page 189) weaving to cover half of the spokes, then change the thread to cover the rest. Thus you can get either a two-coloured 'button' (as in the diagram), or a contrasting colour circle inside the 'button' (as in the photograph).
3 Work fly stitches (see page 168) inside every other space between the spikes (yellow in the diagram), with tiny couching stitches (orange in the diagram).
4 Using the same thread, fill in the remaining three spaces with fly stitches too, working their couching stitches (see page 159) far bigger in proportion to the ones in the previous step. Leave these couching stitches loose, so that they remain loops.

LATTICE

Work a series of parallel diagonal stitches across the area, then work a second series at right angles to the first. Finally, couch the intersections where the stitches overlap. It is crucial to plan the angle of lattice stitches and spacing between them. To decide on the angle, place two threads crisscrossed against the stitching area and vary the angle of their crossing to see which option looks nicer to you. For spacing, put two threads on the stitching area, so that they go parallel to each other, then adjust the spacing to taste.

Here's a trick to keep the lattice lines parallel and the spacing perfect: work the first stitch of lattice, then bring the needle for the next stitch half-way through the fabric. Place the needle flat against the surface, parallel to the previous stitch, to see whether the chosen spacing is correct. If it is, bring the needle all the way up and put the thread across the area, parallel to the previous stitch, to check where to take it down. Another way to ensure you take the thread back down at the right place is to work through the thread, so you cannot shift it.

Lattice is a great filling stitch because of its openwork look, and numerous options for embellishment. Play around with thread colour and texture, and try making couching stitches very fine or more distinct. The variety of ways of couching the intersections and filling in the cells is truly amazing – as you can see in the examples above right!

You can fill in the 'cells', too. Try working lazy daisy stitch, or a French knot, or several straight stitches to fill in cells – and think of a pattern, such as filling in every second cell, for example.

LATTICE – LACY PATTERN

This is also known as lacy lattice.

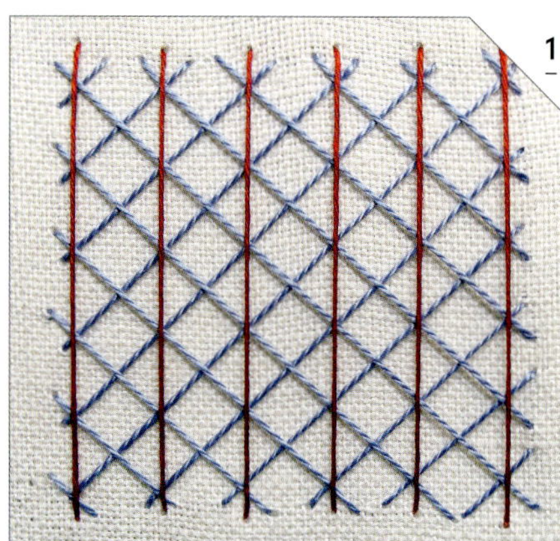

1 Work lattice stitch (described above), then make long straight stitches across the area, following the pattern shown in the picture. Work small couching stitches at each intersection of the three lines.

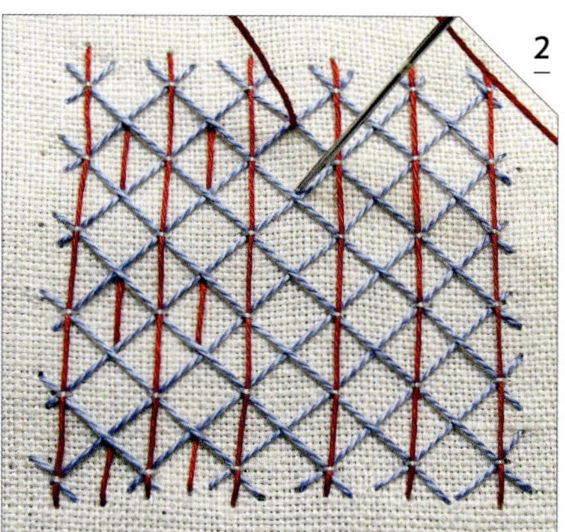

2 Work short straight stitches, filling in every other cell of the interval between the two lines. This may be done either in the manner of running stitch or of seeding stitch.

Try working all the embellishment of the lattice in toning thread, with the couching done in a slightly brighter colour.

LATTICE – MITRE PATTERN

The name for this variation derives from the particular way of joining wooden elements together. In carpentry, two wooden elements are cut at an angle, and then joined together to form the right angle. In embroidery, vertical, horizontal and diagonal lines are all gathered into one pattern.

The look of the finished stitch resembles partly worked griffin stitch.

1 Work regular lattice (see opposite), then place long vertical straight stitches (in red) across the lattice. You may find it helpful to work tiny couching stitches at each intersection of the three lines, but this is optional.

2 Work long horizontal straight stitches, using the same thread as in the previous step.

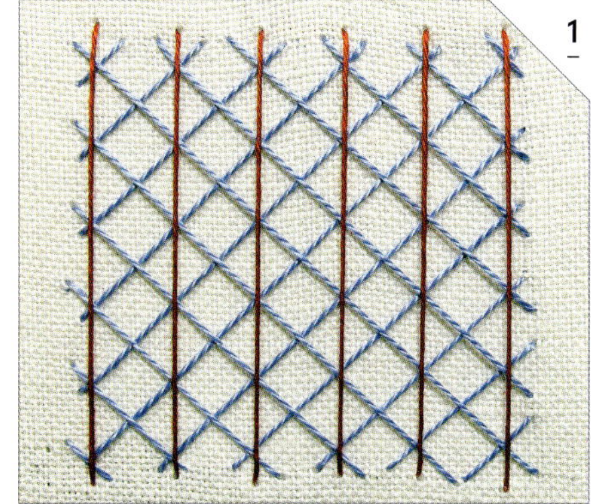

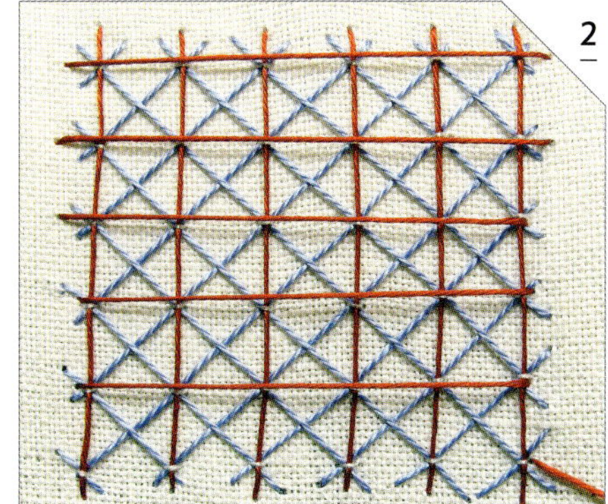

TIP

For the elaborate griffin stitch, this lattice pattern is further couched after this. Since we are not going any further for Mitre lattice, you can leave the intersections uncouched, or couch them simply – perhaps with tiny diagonal stitches going between the long straight stitches, for example.

LATTICE + WOVEN FILLING

The threads in step and step 4 should be worked in the same colour thread. They are worked in different colours here for clarity.

1 Work lattice (see opposite).

2 Couch it down by working small tying stitches at the intersections.

3 Weave with wrap (green) thread. The pink marks show the order of weaving that looks best to me.

4 Weave with weft (lilac) thread. Always go under the lattice (blue threads) and over the warp threads (green).

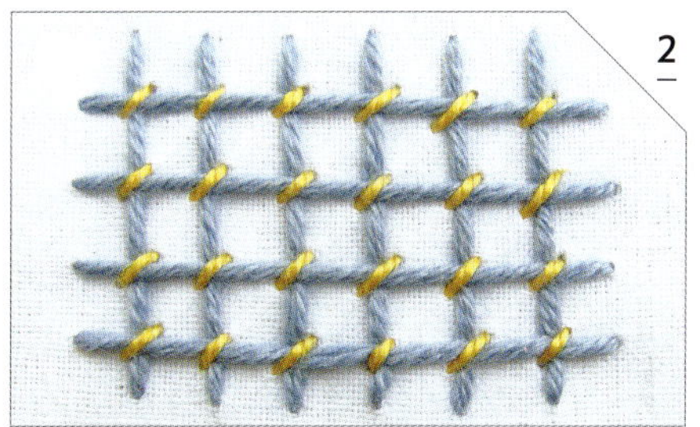

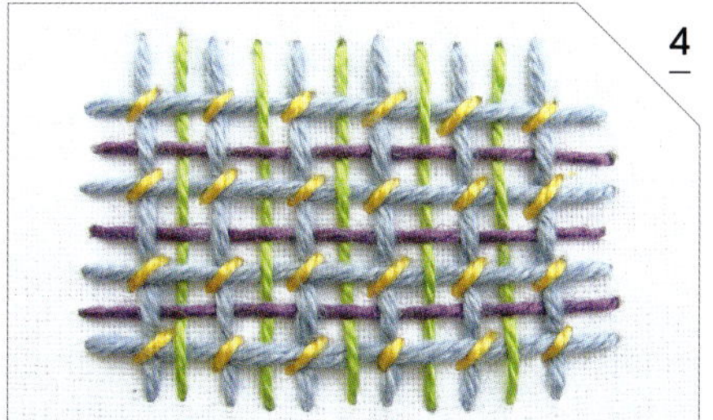

Another option for step 4

Alter the order of weaving for even and odd passings of thread. For the first and all the odd passings, work as shown above (under the blue and over the green threads); for the second and all even passings, work over the blue and under the green threads.

LAZY DAISY STITCH

This stitch has a number of variations. All are based on the basic stitch shown here:

1 Work a loop.

2 Make a small couching stitch.

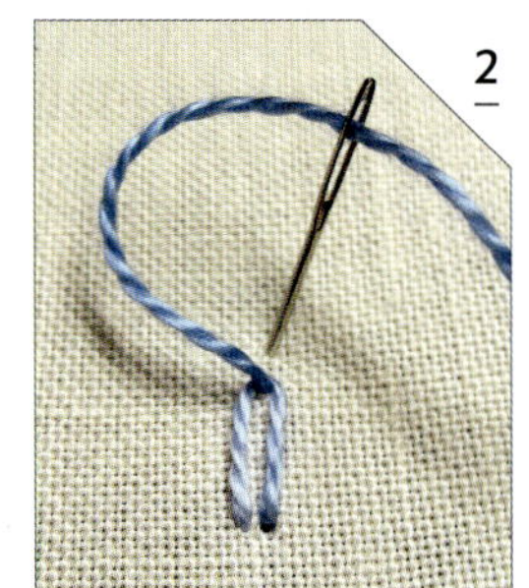

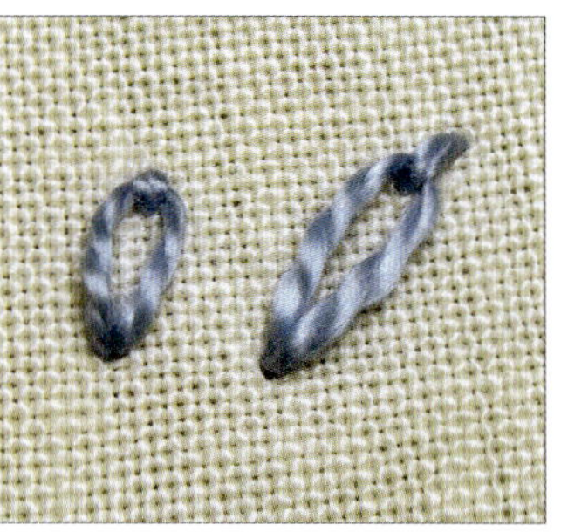

Lazy daisy stitch variations.

LAZY DAISY STITCH – BUTTONHOLED

Work a lazy daisy stitch. Using a second thread, follow the instructions for fly stitch – buttonholed (see page 168) to work over each side of the loop.

LAZY DAISY STITCH – OPEN

Work as for lazy daisy stitch, but make the loop open by leaving some space between its tips.

LAZY DAISY STITCH – OVERLAPPING

A very effective filling stitch, each row of lazy daisy slightly overlaps the previous one. Alter the thread colour for each row. Use any pearl cotton or two strands of stranded cotton.

LOOP STITCH

The completed stitch.

MOUNTMELLICK STITCH

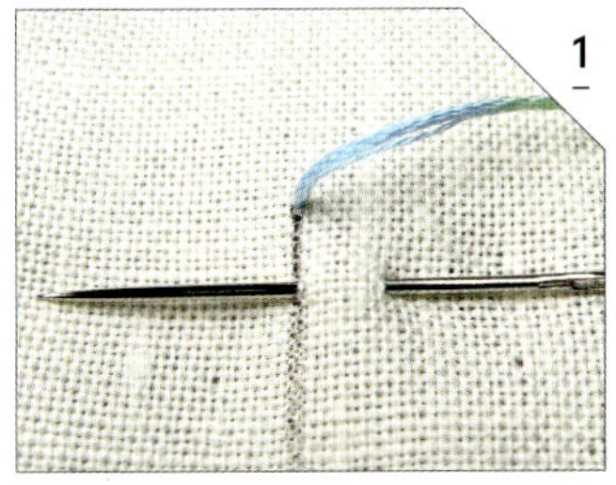

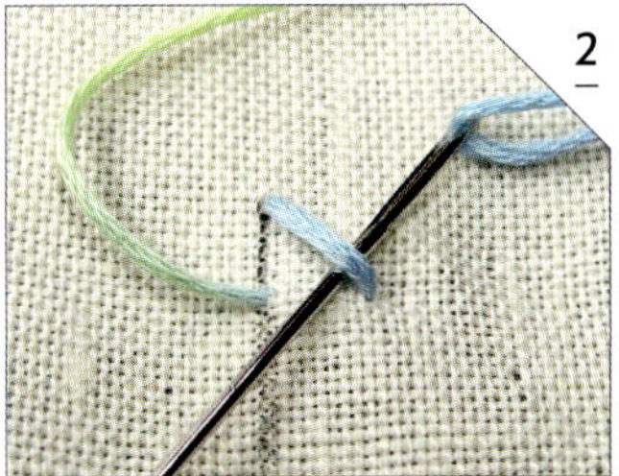

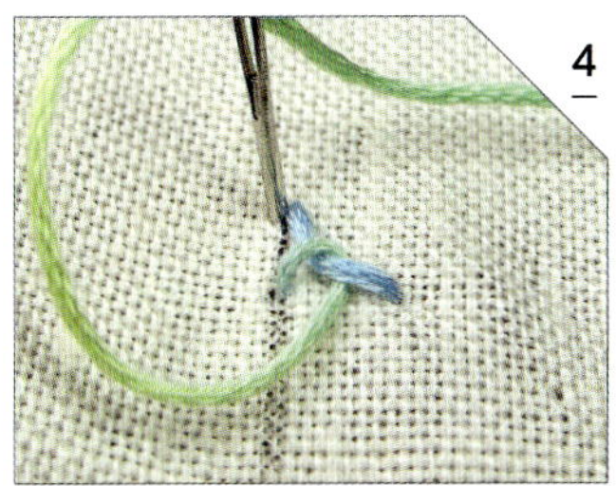

The completed stitch.

ODD FLOWER PETAL

This resembles a padded variation of open fishbone stitch (see page 181). It is a quick, simple and attractive way of stitching very small leaves or flower petals.

It looks to me like a bun with a braid along its top – very charming. Using variegated thread brings still more appeal to this stitch.

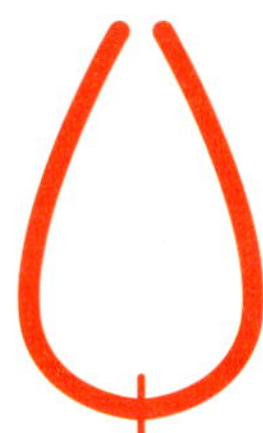

1 Using six strands of stranded cotton thread, work lazy daisy stitch (see opposite) of the size of the leaf or petal you are stitching. It will serve as padding for further stitching.

2 The black dot in the diagram indicates the beginning of a straight stitch (see page 201). Work it in two or three strands of the same thread.

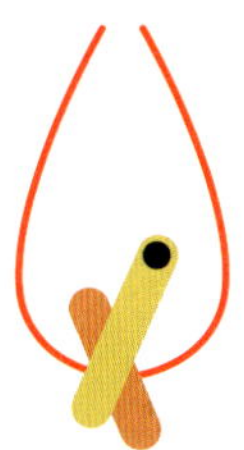

3 Continue working straight stitches, placing them diagonally, so that they overlap each other, forming a braid-like pattern.

4 Continue until the whole shape is covered.

OPEN CHAIN STITCH

This stitch is also known as ladder chain or square chain.

1 Take the needle through, following the letter sequence A–B–C–D shown. Each subsequent stitch holds the previous stitch in place.

2 To finish this stitch, work two stab stitches instead of the usual one (as indicated by the arrows).

OPEN CHAIN STITCH COUCHING

The look of this stitch resembles fish scales. I love it! It is essentially chain stitch used to couch a line of thread in place.

When planning your work, bear in mind that the whole line will become wider. The pictures here show stitches of open chain placed slightly away from the green floss being couched – that is for clarity. You can work the stitches closer to the thread that is being couched.

Straight lines

If the design line is straight or slightly curved, open chain stitch couching can be worked straight away.

Curved lines

If the line is crooked, it may be worth working some temporary stitching first (shown in blue thread), just to keep the floss in place. Unpick these stitches one by one as you progress working the open couching stitch.

OPEN CHAIN STITCH – WHIPPED

OPEN FISHBONE STITCH

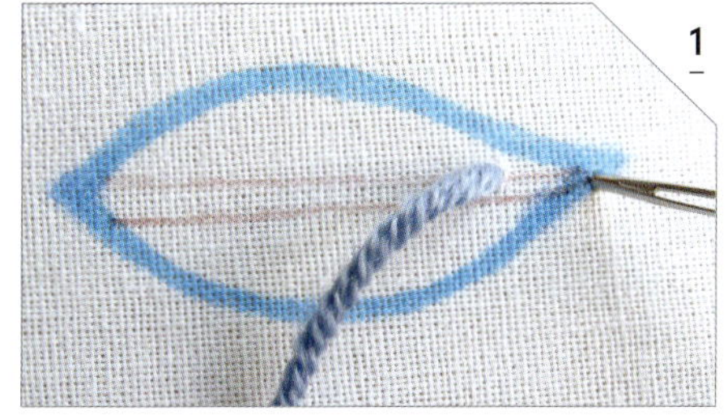

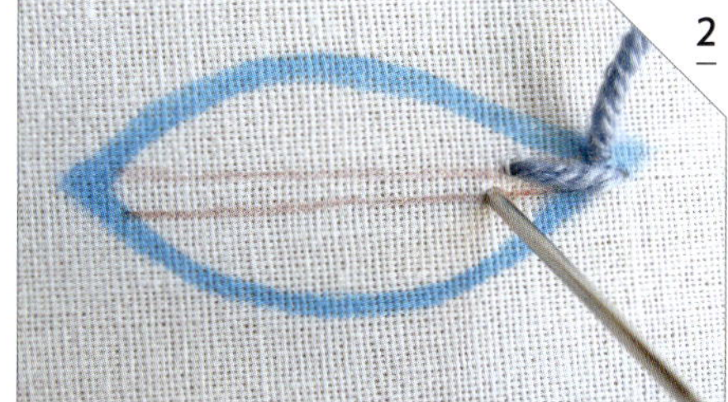

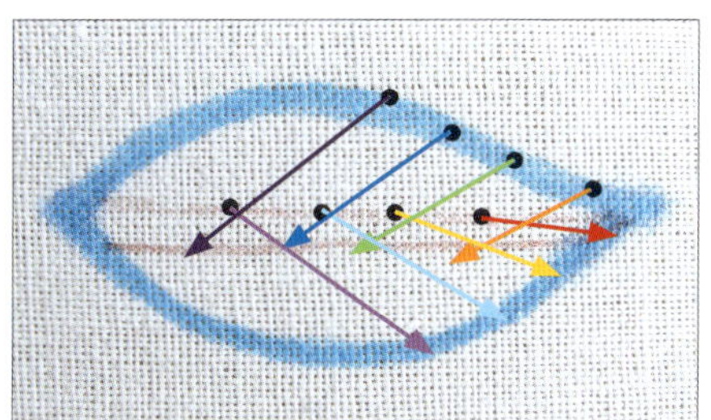

As explained on page 142, follow the rainbow colour flow, bringing the needle up at the black dots each time.

PALESTRINA STITCH

I prefer working this stitch in an asymmetrical way, which is how it appears in the designs of this book. My variation of the stitch has one side that is flat (along the blue line), and the other side notched.

1 Follow the annotated order of work to make a stitch.
2 Take the needle under as shown, ensuring that the needle tip points to the left.
3 Take the needle under the same stitch again. With the needle tip pointing down, take the needle over the thread. Tighten the loop without going down to the back of the fabric.
4 Repeat steps 1–3 to the end of the stitch line. On the final stitch, finish as shown.

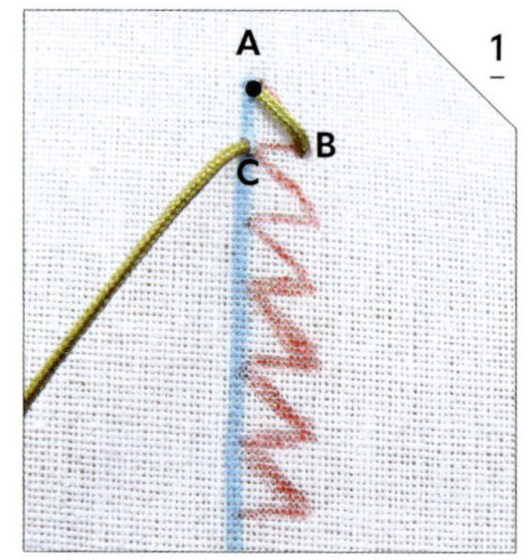

PEKINESE STITCH

This stitch is worked on a line of backstitch (see page 144).

1 Starting immediately below the first stitch of the line, bring your needle under the second stitch.

2 Draw it through to the other side of the stitch line.

3 Take the needle back underneath the first stitch of the backstitch line.

4 Draw the needle through to the other side of stitch line and tighten the twisted loop.

5 Repeat the sequence to the end of the design line. Having finished, take the needle to the back.

PISTIL STITCH

This is also known as French knot on a stalk, and involves a very similar technique to a French knot (see page 171).

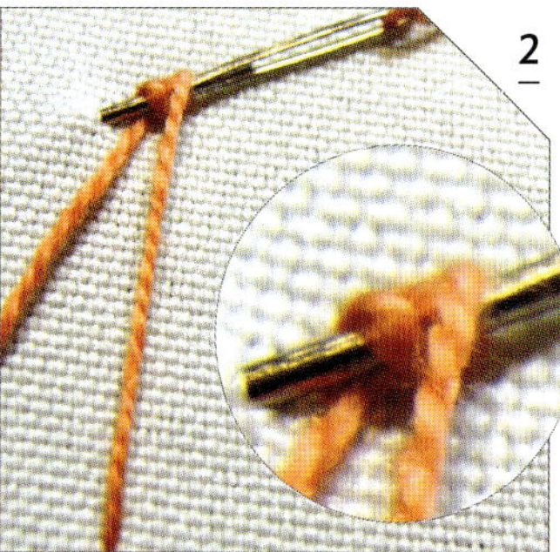

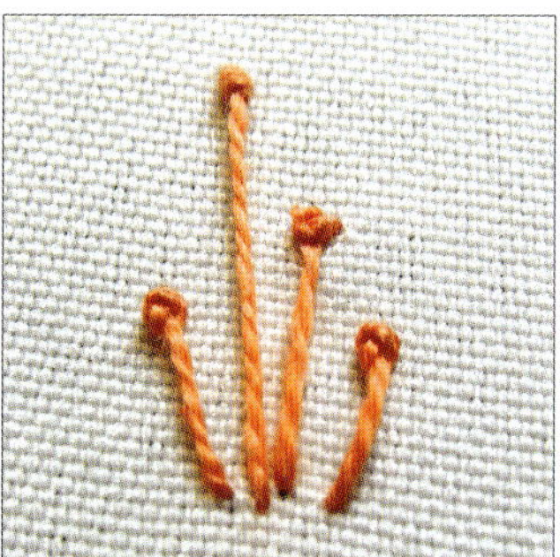

1 Wrap the thread round the needle a short distance from where you brought the needle up.

2 Keeping the thread taut, take the needle down, trapping the wrapped thread.

The length of the thread between where you bring the needle up and where you take it down determines the length of the 'stem'.

PISTIL STITCH TWIGS

The look and texture of this stitch is lovely. Have you ever heard of a knotted backstitch? Think of pistil stitch twigs as knotted stem stitch, for it resembles the technique. This stitch is ideal for working twigs and stems directly, or for outlining them.

Try the stitch in variegated thread for a more intricate effect; or work two or three lines of it, placing them side by side and slightly varying the shade of the thread colour for each line.

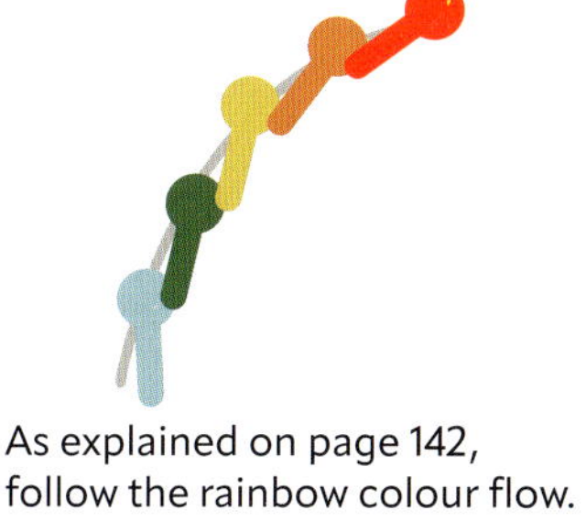

As explained on page 142, follow the rainbow colour flow.

1 Start by making a pistil stitch at the end of the tip of the stitch line.

2 Work down the twig, so the next stitch overlaps the bottom end of the previous pistil stitch.

3 Continue working down the stitch line to the end.

PORTUGUESE BORDER STITCH

First work stitches for the base and then bring the thread up. Threads of contrasting colours are used here for clarity.

1 Go under the leftmost two stitches. Repeat three times.

2 Go back under the right-hand stitch of the pair.

3 Go under the two stitches shown, but this time just once.

4 Go under the next stitch along.

5 Follow this pattern to the rightmost stitch. Go down to finish on the right-hand side of the stitch.

6 Come up for the other side. Stitch the other side then go down to finish.

PORTUGUESE KNOTTED STEM STITCH

RAISED CHAIN STITCH BAND

RAISED CHAIN STITCH BAND – STRIPED

RAISED CHAIN STITCH BAND + WOVEN FILLING

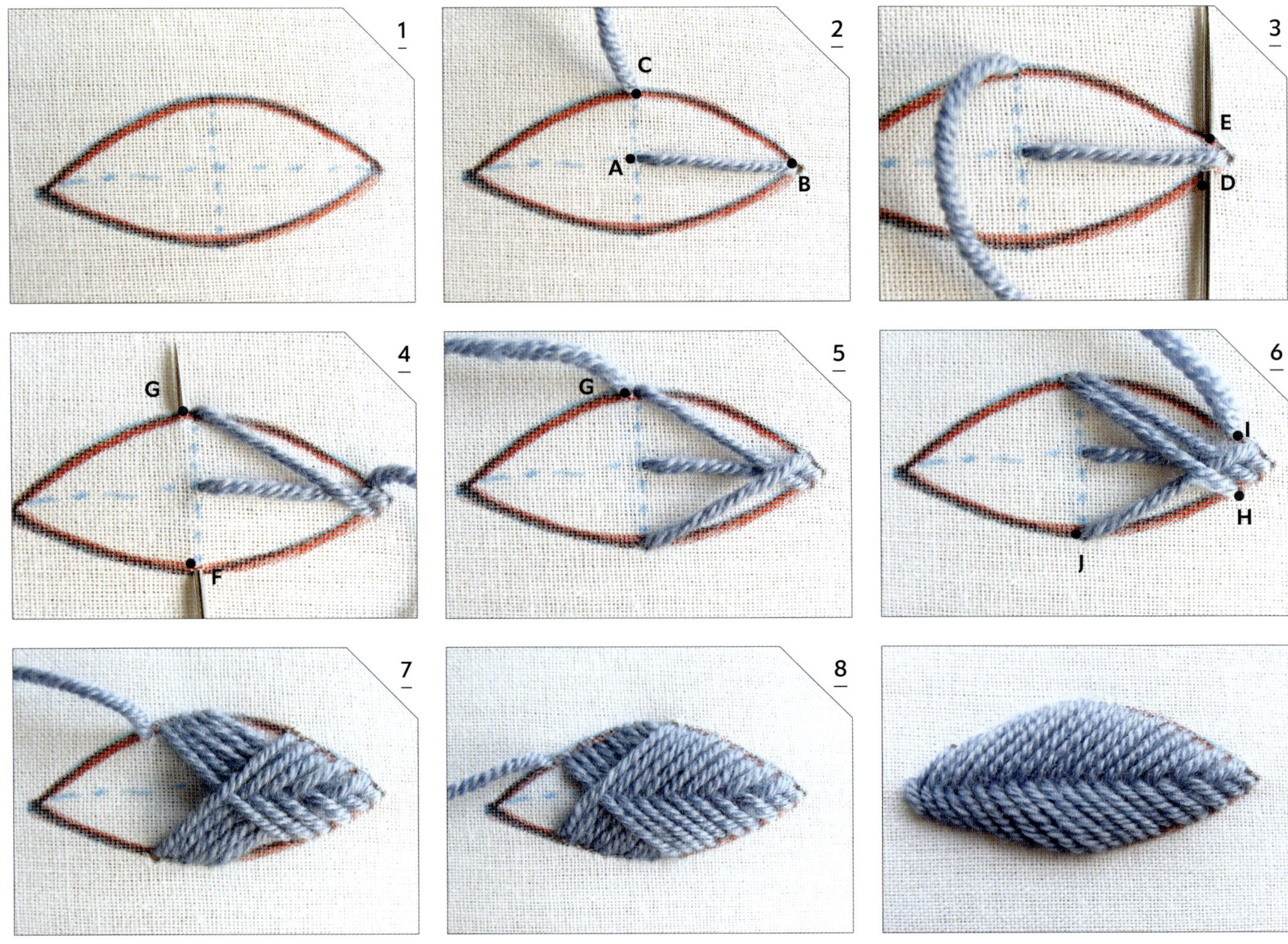

The completed stitch.

1 Draw or imagine the two lines: one is across the leaf and the other is along the leaf.

2 Make the first stitch following the order of work A–B–C.

3 Take the needle down at D, then up again at E.

4 Take it down at F and up again at G.

5 Draw the thread through to complete the sequence.

6–8 Follow the same pattern of stitching until the whole leaf is embroidered.

RAISED STEM STITCH

This is the nice way of making a smooth surface, raised above the fabric. See the striped and knit variations of this stitch overleaf for more fun.

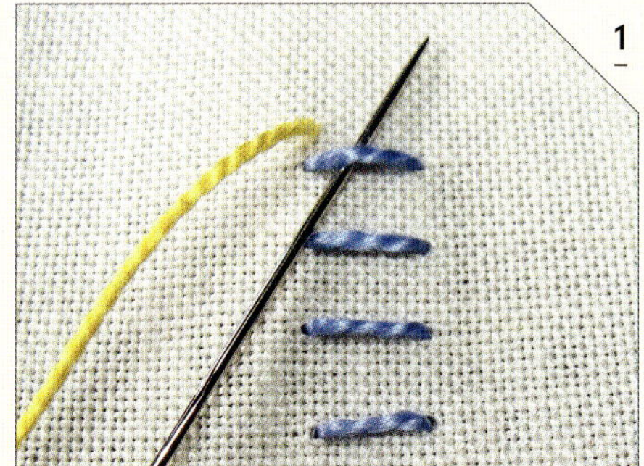

1 Work foundation stitches (shown in blue) across the area. Raised stem stitch will be worked perpendicular to this foundation.

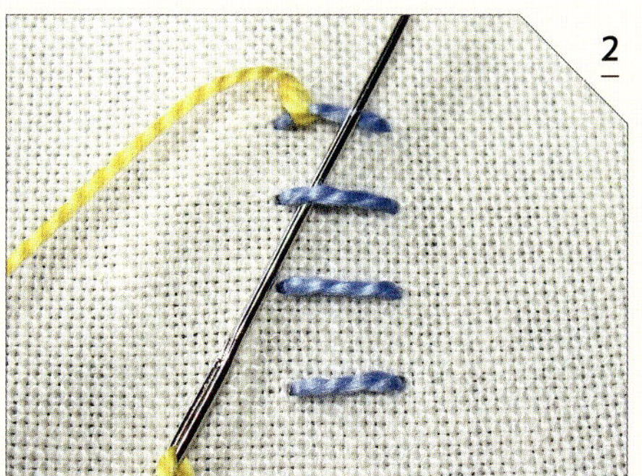

2 Change the needle to a blunt Tapestry needle and whip around the first foundation stitch, placing the thread to the left.

TIP

You can continue with your sharp needle, but you will need to turn it round and take it backwards, so that the eye end of the needle goes first.

3 Work in the same way across the other foundation stitches to create the first line of whipping. At the bottom of the foundation, bring the needle to the back of the fabric. The first line is completed.

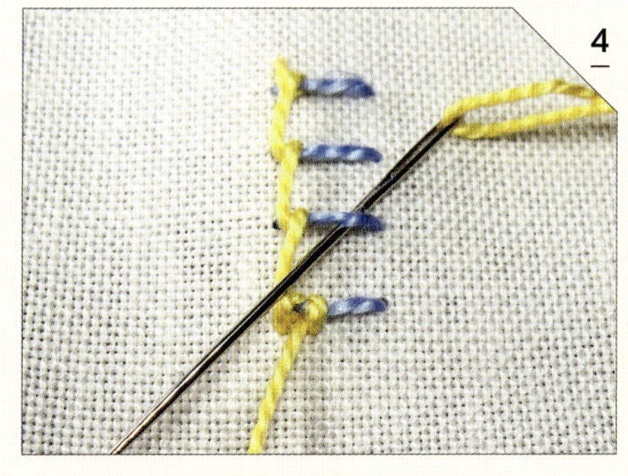

4 Come up for the second line close to where the needle went down. Progressing to the top of the foundation stitches, whip each in turn. This time, place the thread to the right of the needle. Follow this pattern every time you work upwards (i.e. for every even line).

Odd and even lines

Place the thread to the left of your stitching every time you whip downwards (i.e. on odd-numbered lines). Place the thread to the right as you work back up (i.e. on each even-numbered line).

The key thing is to alter the placement of thread for even and odd lines. This ensures all the resulting 'stitches' are inclined in the same way – otherwise, you will create the knit pattern variation overleaf: beautiful in itself, but not always what we want!

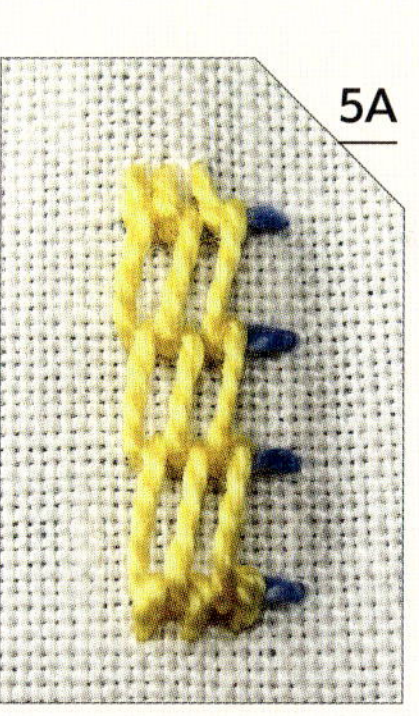

5B

5 Once a few lines are in place, the pattern reveals itself, and it starts to resemble stem stitch (see page 200). Don't worry that the individual lines look too spaced out. Continue stitching, and the lines will be pushed together as you progress.

RAISED STEM STITCH – KNIT PATTERN

See the instructions for raised stem stitch on page 187. For this variation, odd and even rows of whipping are placed mirroring each other.

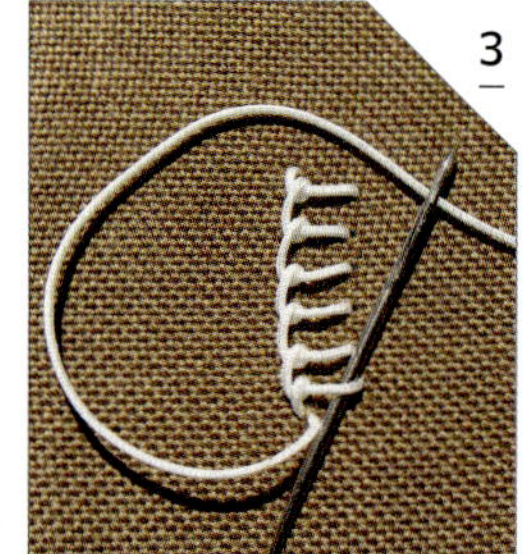

The completed stitch, alternative pattern

The odd and even rows here are marked by threads of different colour and thickness for clarity. To get this pattern, place the thread to the left of the needle all the time, for each row.

This example has been worked in six strands of stranded cotton thread.

RAISED STEM STITCH – STRIPED PATTERN

See the instructions for raised stem stitch on page 187 for the underlying technique. For this variation, alter the colour of working thread for some rows. For example, work two rows in colour A, then three rows in colour B, and so on. You can keep this pattern consistent or vary it as you progress.

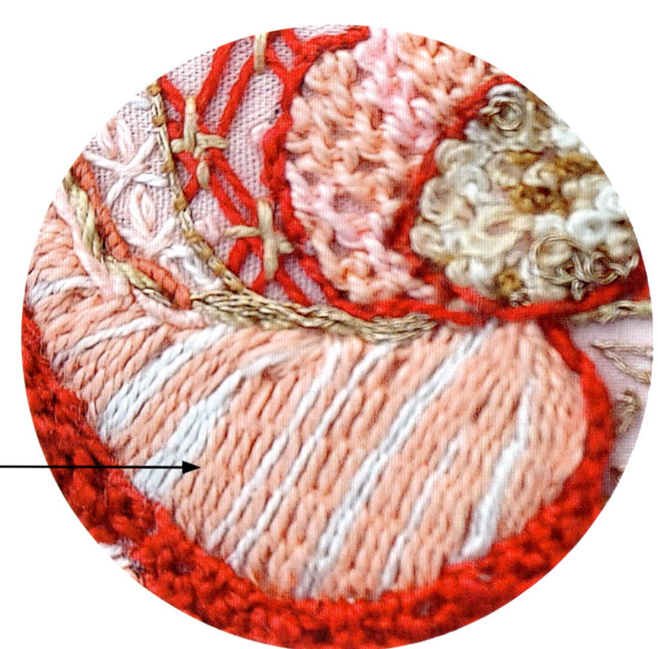

This section has been worked in striped raised stem stitch. Note how the variation in the number of rows gives stripes of varying width.

RIBBED FILLING STITCH

This is a variation of ribbed spider web stitch below.

The completed stitch.

RIBBED FILLING STITCH – FALSE LATTICE VARIATION

Having stitched the regular ribbed filling, work parallel spaced straight stitches across the area, placing them on top of the ribbed filling. The combination of the two techniques resembles lattice filling, mysteriously raised above the surface. (The image shows those stitches worked in double thread.)

RIBBED SPIDER WEB STITCH

Also known as ribbed wheel, whipped wheel, whipped spider wheel, or whipped spider wheel filling. Repeatedly follow the pattern shown in the steps to fill the area.

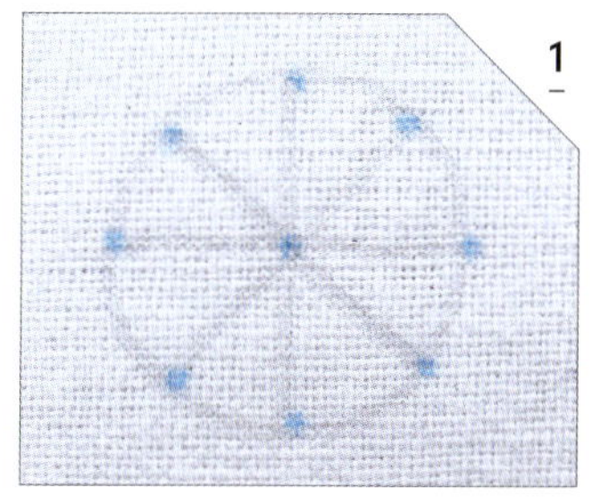

The completed stitch.

ROMANIAN LACE STAR

This star derives from the technique of lace making known under the name Romanian lace.

1 Work lazy daisy stitches (see page 178) of the same length to create six evenly-spaced spokes radiating from a central point. Weave around the centre until approximately half of each spoke's length is covered with weaving. Now the magic begins. After taking the needle under a spoke (in this example, spoke C), take it under the outer thread of the woven circle.

2 Draw the thread through. Contrasting green thread is used here for clarity, but you should use the same thread throughout.

3 Take the needle back under spoke C.

4 Draw it through, then take it under the very last thread of the weaving.

TIP

You can pick up two threads of the weaving for a sturdier effect, it all depends on the kind of thread you are using and the size of the star you are weaving.

5 Repeat steps 1–4 until the thread fills the spoke, as shown. Having finished this spoke, take the needle to the back.

6 Start each new spoke by bringing the needle up on the clockwise side of the spoke, near the edge of the original weaving. Shown here, spoke D has been completed, and we are about to begin spoke E.

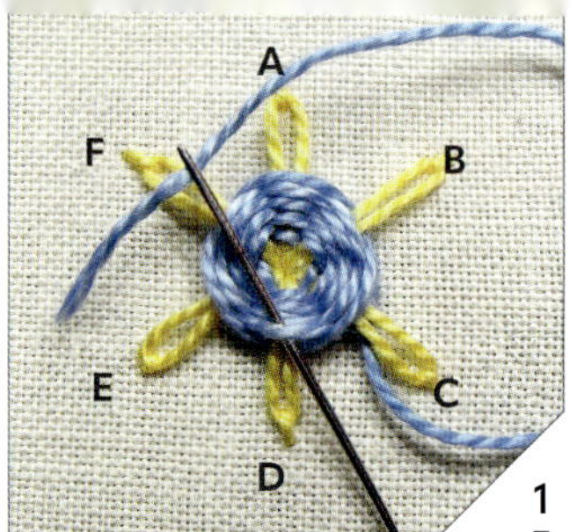

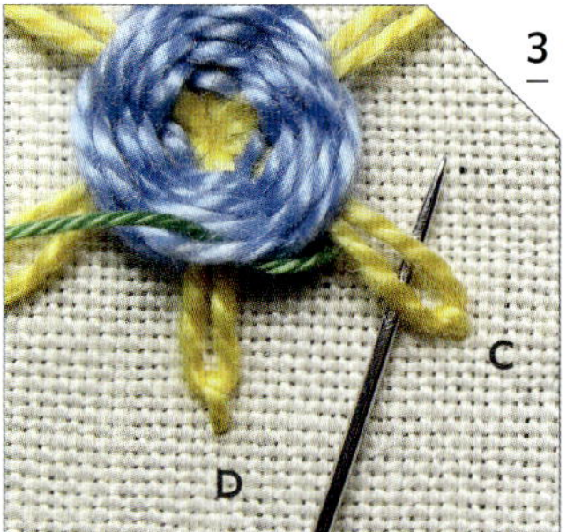

The completed stitch.

WEAVING ODD AND EVEN STARS

Weaving around a circle normally requires an odd number of spokes to create the cyclical effect. There is, however, a small trick which enables us to weave around an even number of spokes as well. It is very simple, and while perfectionists would certainly call it a mistake, it's useful to know.

Work the first circle of weaving in a regular manner, taking the needle alternately over and under each spoke in turn. Having finished the first circle, take the needle under two of the neighbouring spokes, rather than one, before continuing to weave. Repeat the process for the second and subsequent 'orbits' of the circle, taking the needle under two spokes as you start each time.

Because of the mathematics involved (and who would have thought maths would be the embroiderer's friend?), the placement of our 'mistake' moves around the circle and the surrounding threads hide it securely.

ROPE STITCH

The solid line is the design line. The dotted line running parallel to it represents where you take each stitch down – but you need only draw this while practising; just imagine it when working. For clarity, I have used six strands of stranded cotton, but any thread starting from two strands of stranded cotton will do. Working lines of rope stitch side by side will create rope stitch filling. You can use the same thread for all the stitch lines or slightly alter the colour for each line.

TIP

The twist in the loop you make in step 3 is key – remember it by looking for the fish!

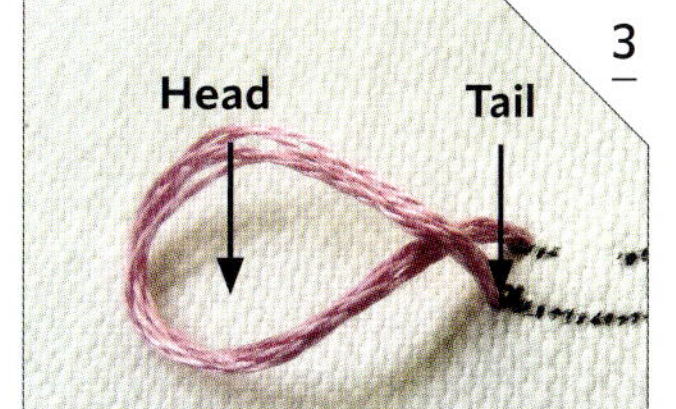

1 Bring the needle up at the beginning of the design line, then take it down at the beginning of the dotted line.
2 Draw the thread through, but do not pull it tight: leave the stitch as a loop.
3 Twist the loop as shown so that it resembles a fish (see tip above). Bring the needle up 2–6mm (⅛–¼in) further along the design line.
4 Take the needle through the fish's head and draw the thread through. Make the loop twist so the thread emerging from the dotted line lies on top of that from the design line, as shown.

TIP

Remember the pattern: the solid line is for coming up, the dotted line is for 'diving' down.

5 Take the needle back down through the dotted line just ahead of the fish's tail.
6 Repeat from step 4, taking the thread through the needle as shown. It is important to draw the needle at the angle shown as you tighten the loop.
7 To finish off, work a small couching stitch: bring the needle to the back of the fabric outside the last loop.

A NOTE ON TWISTED CHAIN STITCH

Rope stitch is the twin of twisted chain stitch (see page 191). Just as twins are not always identical, so these stitches, both worked in a similar way, have differences in spacing.

For twisted chain stitch, take the needle back down through the dotted line just above the fish's head, rather than near the tail, as shown. The resulting stitch line will be less dense than one worked in rope stitch.

ROSE LEAF STITCH – BRAZILIAN EMBROIDERY

This is truly a charming stitch, and an unusual one, for it calls for an extra bit of kit – a piece of cardboard. The size of the cardboard you need depends on the type of thread and the size of the leaf you want, but it will quickly become second nature after you try this stitch. For your first rose leaf, try using a 1 x 3cm (½ x 1¼in) cardboard rectangle and six strands of stranded cotton thread. Thread a needle, make a knot and let the magic start!

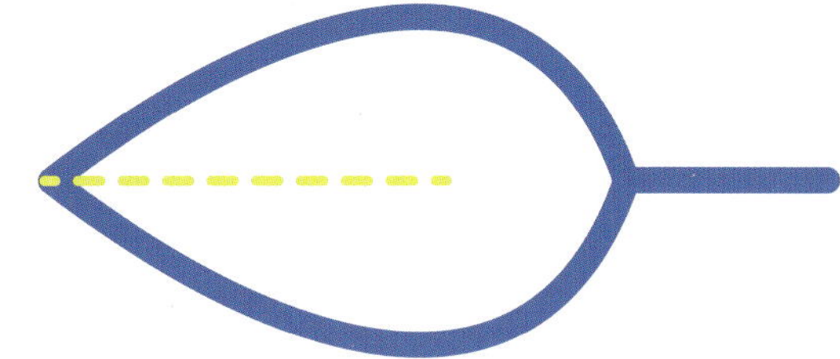

The blue outlines in the diagram show the leaf we would like to embroider. The yellow dotted line shows the actual area of stitching, which is where the needle will be passing through the fabric.

1 Bring the thread up through the working surface where you want the tip of the leaf to sit. Place the cardboard along the midrib of the leaf. Now bring the needle to the back on the other side of the cardboard. In fact, it looks like stitching a loop and inserting the cardboard inside the loop.

2 Work a second loop close to the first one, progressing along the midrib towards the petiole.

3 Continue working loops. It always depends how many of them is enough for the particular leaf. Let us do eight of them. Now bring the needle underneath the loops (3A) and draw it through (3B).

4 Carefully take the cardboard out of the loops. Now take the needle over the stitch (4A) to the back of the fabric near the base of petiole, 'inverting' the loops as shown (4B).

5 This last stitch forms the stem, and the loops lying sideways make a nice puffy leaf.

The completed stitch.

RUNNING STITCH

RUNNING STITCH – DOUBLE

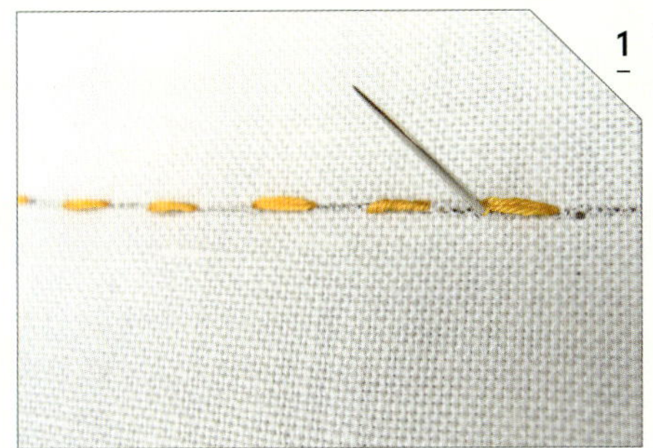

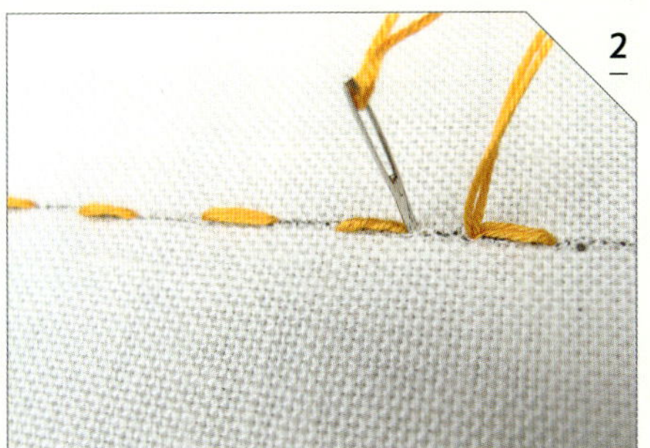

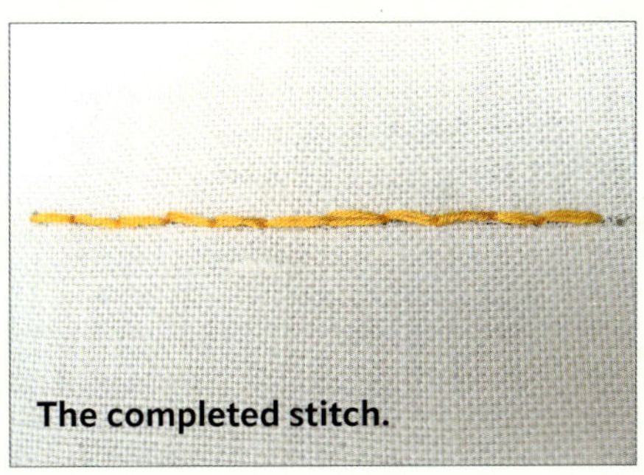

The completed stitch.

RUNNING STITCH – DOUBLE, WHIPPED

A completed line of double running stitch (above) is very similar to a line of backstitch, and so the whipping can be done in the same way – see the instructions on page 144.

RUNNING STITCH – WHIPPED

SATIN STITCH

This is the way to work regular satin stitch, which looks the same on both the right side and back of the fabric. This stitch is nice on its own and in satin stitch blocks.

It can also be used for padding, though satin stitch – surface (see below) is often used for this instead, since the surface variation does not create extra padding on the back of the fabric and therefore add unwanted toughness to the area.

SATIN STITCH – PADDED

Use one or two threads for stitching and three to six for padding.

For clarity, I have used threads in contrasting colours here.

The completed stitch.

SATIN STITCH – SURFACE

Also known as surface satin stitch. Unlike regular satin stitch, above, this variation makes all the stitching on the right side of the fabric and leaves only tiny stitches on the back. Start a new stitch on the same side of the area where the previous stitch was finished.

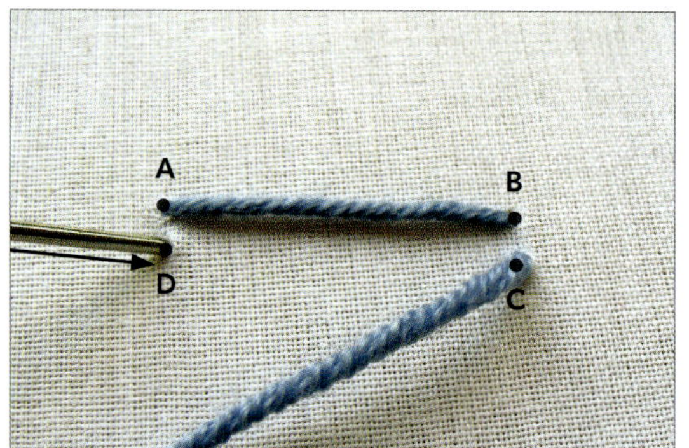

For clarity, this shows the individual stitches more spaced out than they are usually worked.

SATIN STITCH BLOCKS

Work square or diamond-shaped blocks of satin stitch (see opposite). Place neighbouring blocks at right angles to each other to create a chequerboard effect. You can play around with colour combinations.

SCROLL STITCH

The completed stitch.

SEEDING STITCH

This is similar to backstitch (see page 144), except that the stitches are smaller and spaced out, while in backstitch the individual stitches come very close to each other.

Take the needle down at the black dots and up at the blue dots.

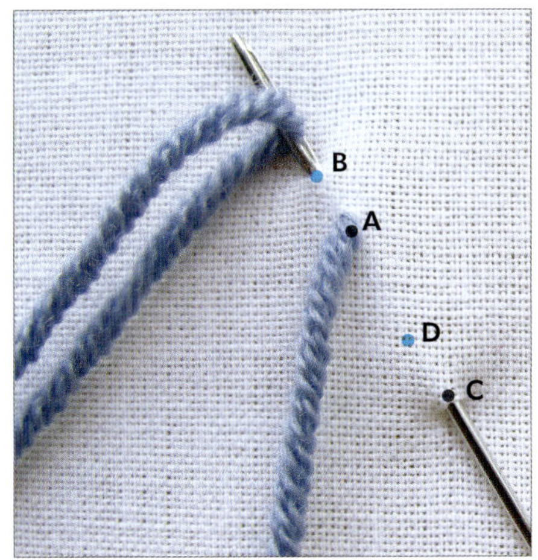

SILK SHADING

Silk shading is also known as long and short stitch shading. Traditionally, the stitches are placed side by side, coming up in a free space and going down between stitches. Here, you split the stitches of the previous row by coming up through stitches and go down in free space. This approach gives a more solid stitched area and helps to consolidate the place where stitches of neighbouring rows come together.

A trick I adopted is to place stitches at a considerable interval and then go back and fill in the gaps. See whether it helps you, too.

Though anchoring a thread with a knot never confused me, silk shading is the only case where I try to avoid knotted thread tails. For this stitch, making a waste knot (see page 18) is my favourite trick.

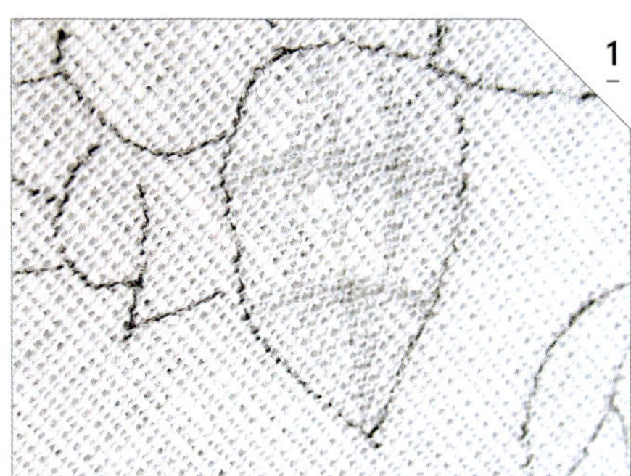

1 Draw lines along and across the area. The 'meridian' lines across the shape are there to mark zones of different shades of colour. The 'parallel' lines that run up and sown are guidelines indicating the direction of working for every stitch.

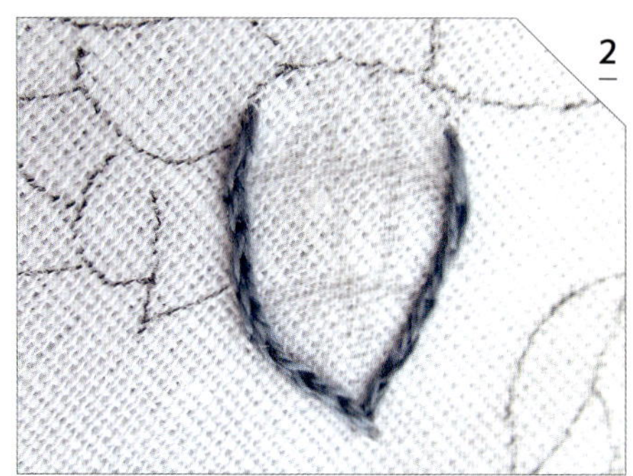

2 Work split stitch along the design line to outline it. Skip this step if you do not want edges of your silk shading to be elevated.

TIP

If you want the edges of shaded area to be smooth, try this trick. Work chain stitch (see page 156) around the outline, using two or three threads, depending on how high a rib you want to get.

Next whip one side of the chain stitch. (See the chain stitch – whipped instructions on page 158 for one-sided whipping.)

When working the first row of silk shading in step 3, bring the needle through the loops of chain stitch.

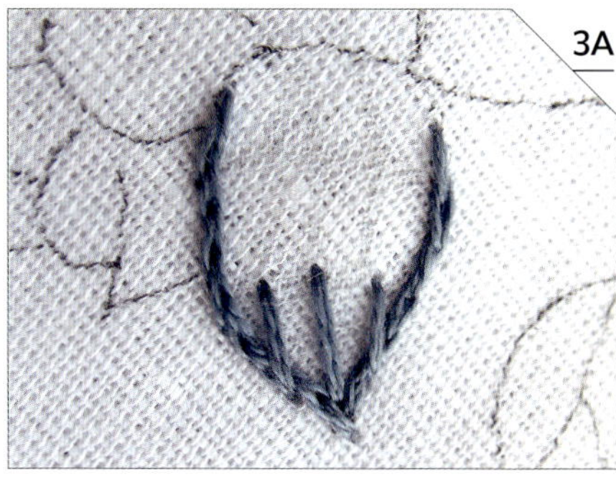

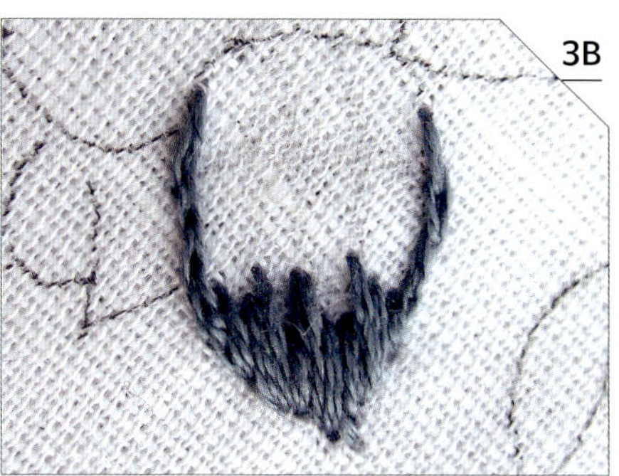

3 Work the first row of silk shading, bringing the needle through the outline stitches and down around the first meridian mark. The first row is the only one you can work in double thread. The stitches should be around 5–7mm (¼in) long, and no longer than 10mm (½in). Some should be worked directly into the meridian (3A), others should fall short or go slightly past it (3B).

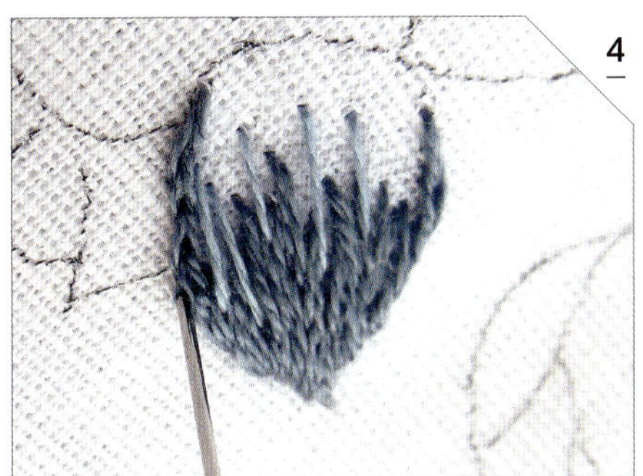

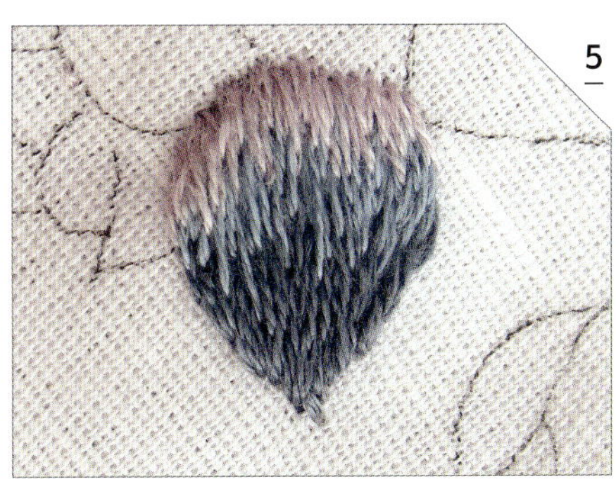

 TIP

Having finished the first row in double thread, you can use the same thread as a single thread to work more stitches – as if performing the next row. This optional alternative makes the outer part more three-dimensional – a great effect that helps the area to stand out from the surface.

4 Using a single thread of a different colour, work the second row in a similar way to the first row, from the first meridian to the second meridian. Bring the needle up through the stitches of the previous row and go to the back of the fabric in a clear area.

5 Continue working in this way. The number of rows depend on the size of the area and the number of colours of threads you are going to use.

 TIP

An attractive effect is produced when two neighbouring rows are worked using the same thread colour. This also allows you to use a small number of colours for quite a big area.

SILK SHADING – PADDED

First work the padding in satin stitch (see page 194) using two to six strands of stranded cotton and placing the stitches perpendicular to the intended direction of silk shading. Use any shade of white thread for padding.

You can also work padding in chain stitch (see page 156) using three or four strands, or simply in running stitch (see page 193) with a single thread, scattering it all over the area. The more threads are used for padding, the more dimension it will bring to silk shading.

Having finished, work the regular silk shading on top of the padded area.

This petal has been worked in silk shading – padded.

SKELETON LEAF – LARGE

The name was suggested by the likeness of the finished motif to real leaves that have lost their softer parts, leaving only the supporting veins in an intricate lacy pattern. The rainbow lines in the pictures show the sequence of stitching, as explained on page 142.

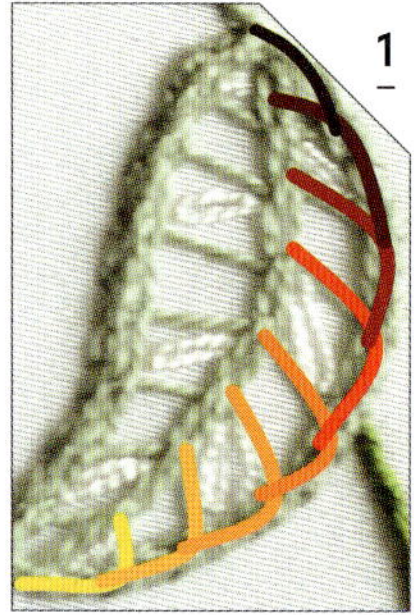

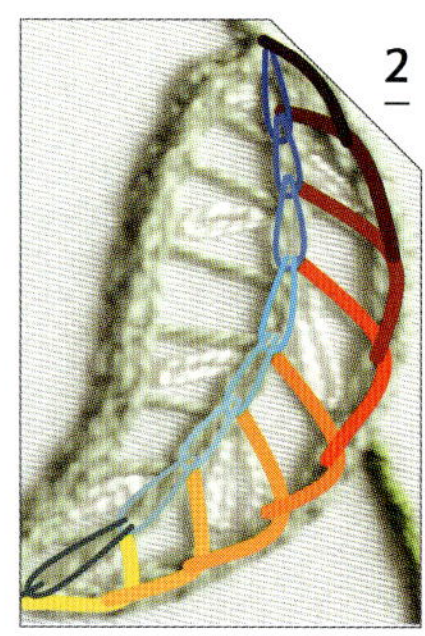

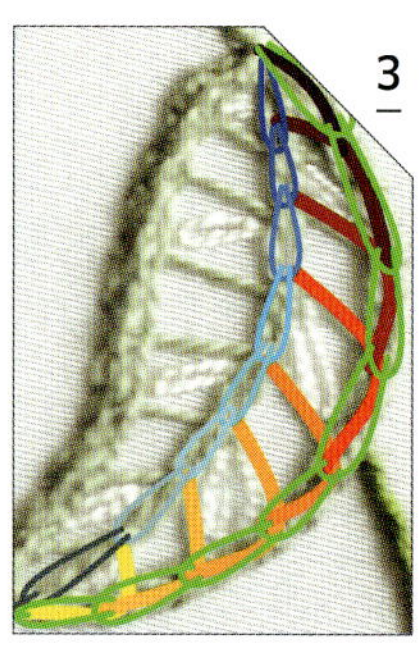

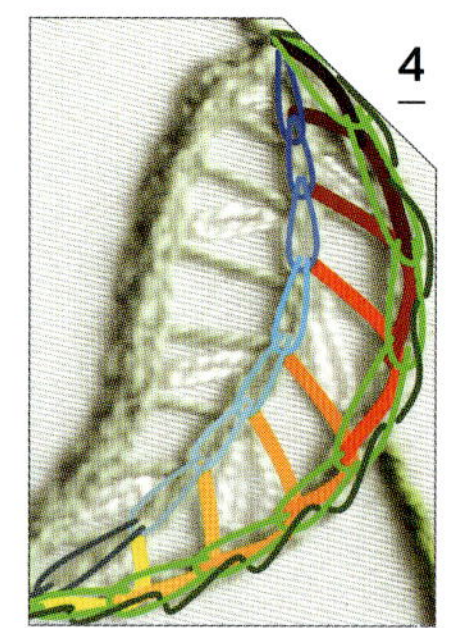

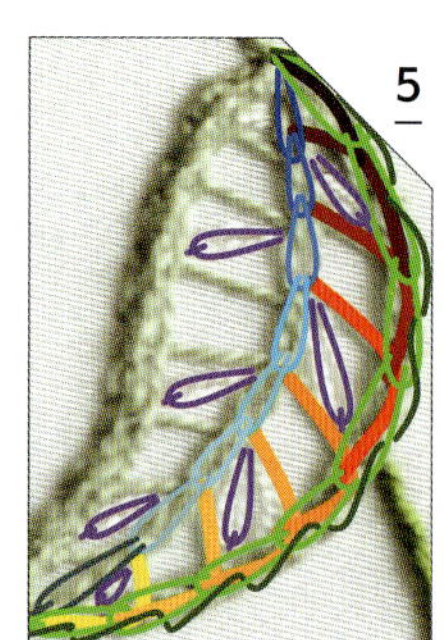

1 Work a line of blanket stitch (see page 146) along the right-hand edge of the leaf, then repeat along the left-hand edge. Make the 'spikes' of each stitch long enough to reach the midrib. Do both sides so that the spikes of the stitches meet up along the midrib.

2 Work chain stitch along the midrib. Individual stitches of the chain are worked between the two neighbouring 'meeting points' of the 'spikes'.

3 Using a finer thread, work chain stitch atop of the rib of the blanket stitch, as shown by the bright green line). The result resembles open chain stitch couching.

4 This step is optional, and marked in dark green. Whip the chain stitch (see page 158), picking up only the outer half of every loop. Repeat on the other side of the leaf.

5 Work lazy daisy stitches (see page 178) inside cells on alternate sides, as shown.

SKELETON LEAF – SMALL

This works best for smaller leaves. When choosing your thread, either use the one indicated in the instructions for a particular design, or think of your own variant.

As an option, you can outline the finished leaf with a line of stem stitch (see page 200).

1 Work chain stitch (see page 156) along the outlines.

2 With a thread of a lighter shade, work parallel straight stitches (see page 201) going across the leaf at equal intervals.

3 Work two rows of raised stem stitch, going along the midrib and facing each other, as for raised stem stitch – knit pattern on page 188. This creates a braid effect along the central vein.

Tip
Here, the straight stitches in step 2 cover the chain stitches. You can instead work through the loops of the chain stitch.

SPLIT STITCH and SPLIT BACKSTITCH

Split stitch is a very useful and popular stitch. Centuries ago it was used in ecclesiastic embroidery as a filling stitch – lines of split stitch were worked close to each other to cover the surface – much as we might use stem stitch (see page 200) for filling nowadays.

I want to emphasize the relationship between this stitch and what I call 'split backstitch' – and I have a good reason for this. While split stitch is versatile, as the name suggests, occasional splitting of the thread is almost inevitable. With double thread or any kind of soft thread all goes well. But with fine or heavily twisted threads, splitting is a problem. In these cases, split backstitch may come very handy.

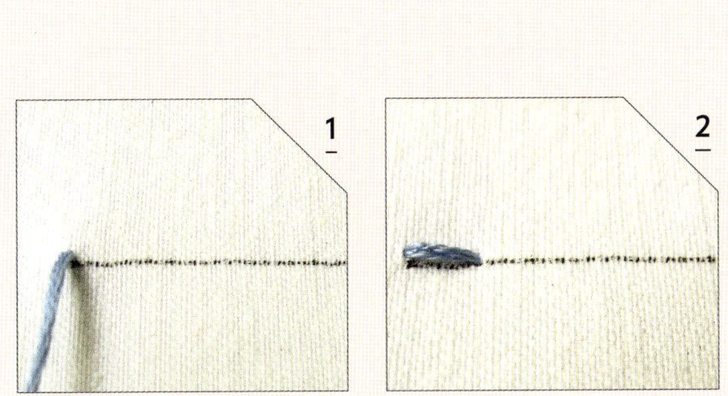

Steps 1 and 2 are common for both split stitch and split backstitch. Repeat either 3A or 3B to get either a line of split stitch or split backstitch.

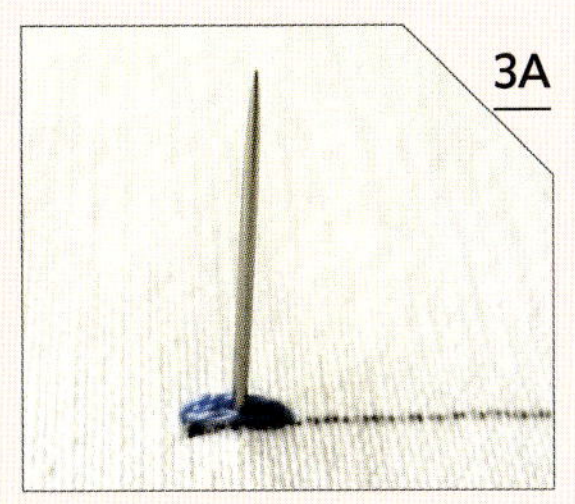

Split stitch

Go through the previous stitch of the line. The thread of the stitch is split from underneath, and it may be tricky to pick it up with the needle.

– or –

3B

Split backstitch

This is where the needle comes up for split backstitch. Can you guess what is to be done next? Sure, the needle also splits the previous stitch, but it is done from above, and therefore splitting the thread is easier. The sharp pointed tip of a needle goes through the thread effortlessly.

The completed stitches

The pattern formed is almost identical for both stitches: it resembles a very fine braid.

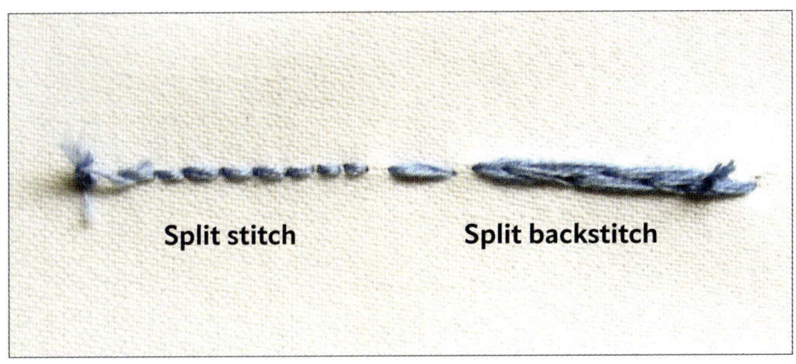

Back of the fabric

The real difference appears on the back side of the fabric and concerns the amount of thread used for stitching. Split backstitch uses more thread than split stitch, but is also much more convenient. In my opinion, that extra thread in no way diminishes the advantages of split backstitch.

STEM STITCH

Stem stitch can be worked either broad or thin. The latter variation is shown here and seems to be more popular with modern embroiderers. For the broader variation, start each individual stitch above the design line and finish it below the line. The stitches will go diagonally, thus filling in a wider space.

Outline stitch

While explaining the stem stitch, I would also like to mention its 'antagonist', the outline stitch, which makes a finer line than the former (although in my experience, any difference is there only if the threads used is manufactured with distinct twists).

Resembling a rope or a cord, a line of stem stitch is heavier and more twisted than one of outline stitch. The placement of the loop is worth remembering and observing, since mixing the two ways of stitching will only give it an untidy look.

Whichever of the two stitches you intend to make, keep the stitch pattern consistent.

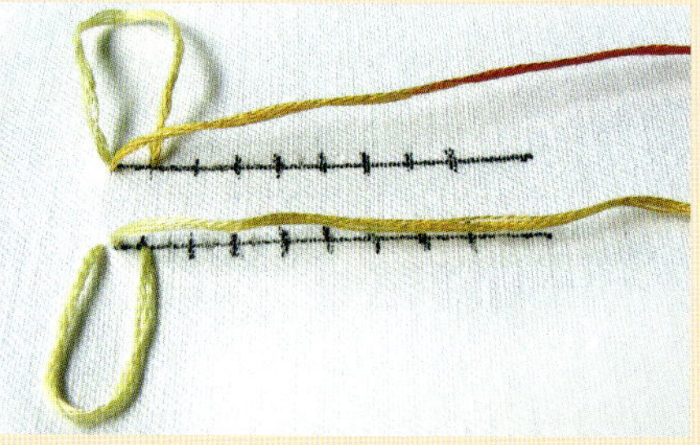

For outline stitch (top), the loop is put over the stitch line, while for stem stitch (bottom), the loop is placed under the stitch line.

Outline stitch filling is a good alternative to stem stitch filling, giving finer lines that are more raised , like fine ribs. It has a charm of its own.

TIP

Rather than using 'over' and 'under', you might like to think in terms of 'the right' or 'the left' of the stitch line. Twists and turns of a design line make it tricky to see where 'overs' and 'unders' really are, while referring to the 'right or left' means one never gets lost: just keep in mind that the right and left are in reference to the direction of stitching – like the banks of a river.

STEM STITCH – WHIPPED

While whipping, go either in the same direction as the stitches, or the opposite. Use thread of the same or a contrasting colour.

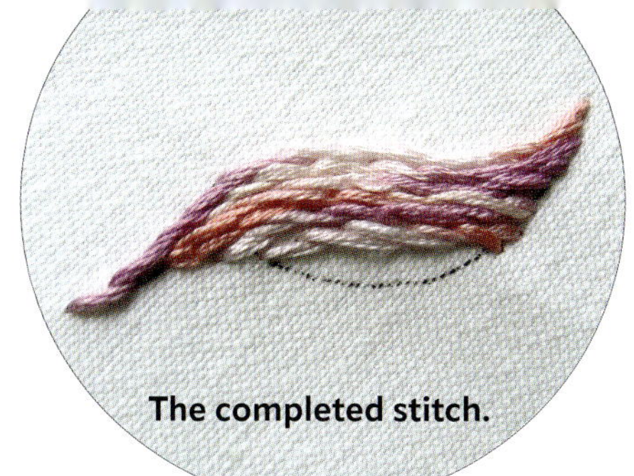
The completed stitch.

STEM STITCH FILLING

This is an easy way to get a neat stitch which resembles silk shading. Work lines of stem stitch across the area, placing them side by side.

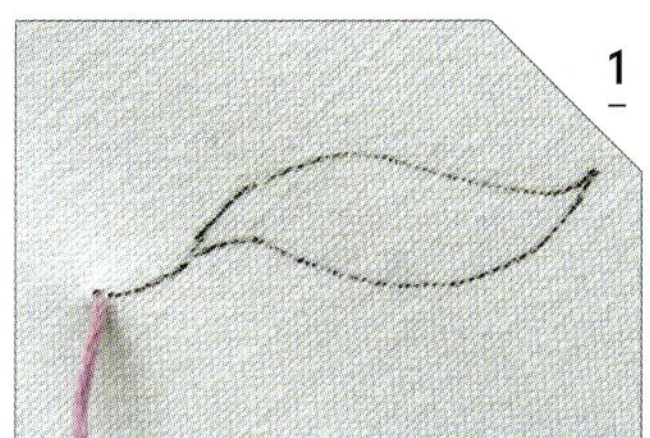

STEM STITCH ROSE

This is also known as 'rambler rose'. To produce it, work stem stitch around three French knots (see page 171) in the centre. Start at the black dots and take the needle down at the blue dots (see steps 2 and 3), then follow the pattern round.

STRAIGHT STITCH

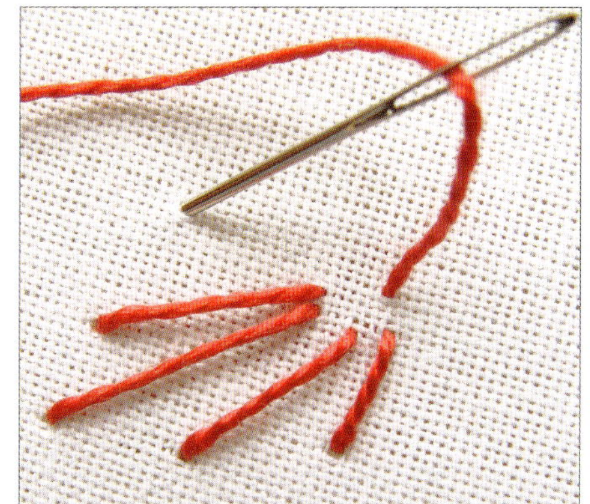

TRELLIS CUP STITCH

The name stems from the main use of this stitch: to make a tiny cup. Here this stitch is worked flat, but as 'trellis' is sometimes used as a synonym for lattice filling, I have kept the word 'cup' in the name for clarity.

As a basis, you need to work either backstitch or chain stitch along the top of the stitching area. This anchors the working thread at the beginning and the end of a stitch line. To avoid bulky sides formed by whipped backstitch, work needlelace using a sharp chenille needle instead, taking it backwards where necessary to avoid snagging the thread. With this approach, there is no problem bringing the needle through the fabric at the end of a row. Try this stitch on a spare piece of fabric first to feel the tension on the thread to form the loops of desirable size.

TIP

All self-respecting embroiderers, when they start on any of the needlelace techniques, will work a line of backstitch along the stitching area. This is because tapestry needles, which are blunt, are usually used for needlelace. Going around the backstitch is much easier than trying to bring a blunt needle through the fabric.

1 Choose the flattest side of the area as its top. Despite being worked horizontally, this stitch forms the diagonal rows. While you learn, mark the beginning and the end of each row to help keep them level, and the width of the rows consistent.

2 Bring the working thread (blue in this example) to the right side of the fabric. Make a loop, then bring the needle underneath the first base stitch, then through the loop (you can simply wrap your thread around the needle tip).

3 Pull on the thread downwards to tighten the first loop. Don't be taken aback by its odd shape – it is supposed to look like that. Repeat to work the first row.

4 Bring the needle to the back at the end of the row, then begin to work the second row in the opposite direction, couching on the loops of the first row.

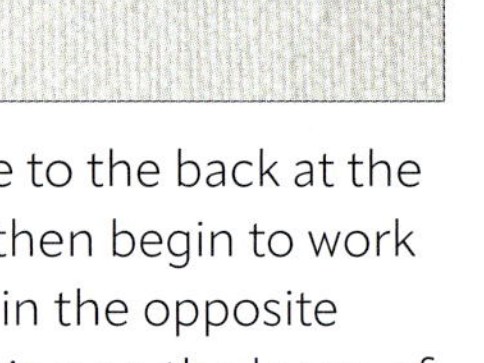

TIP

For odd rows, the shape of a loop resembles a C, while for even rows it looks like the curved part of a capital D.

5 The centre of the mesh will shrink as shown. This can interfere with our work, so make temporary couching stitches to steady the mesh. Remove these stitches once you have couched the bottom part of the trellis.

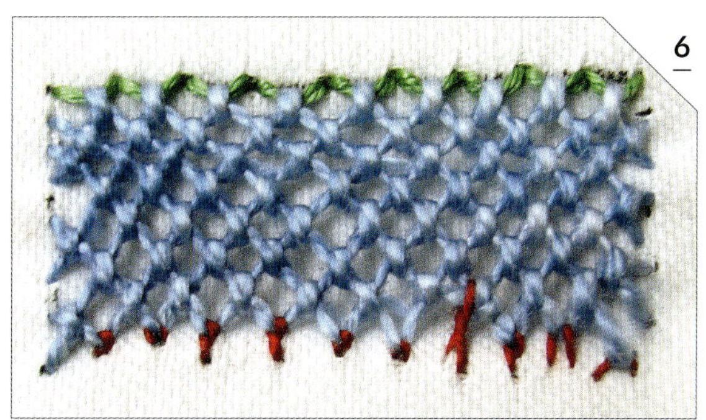

6

6 To finish off, you can work small couching stitches at each of the loops (shown in red and worked loosely for clarity). A more traditional method is to work a line of backstitch along the bottom, and couch your working thread at its individual stitches while making the last row of trellis.

TIP

Use contrasting thread for the couching stitches, so that they are easy to spot. If the trellis is long enough, you can also use sewing pins instead of temporary stitches.

TRELLIS CUP STITCH – PATTERNED

Despite its irregular look, the patterned trellis stitch makes a nice mosaic-like embellishment.

For clarity, the cells of the trellis cup stitch have been made bigger than would be usual for this type of thread (DMC size 8 pearl cotton).

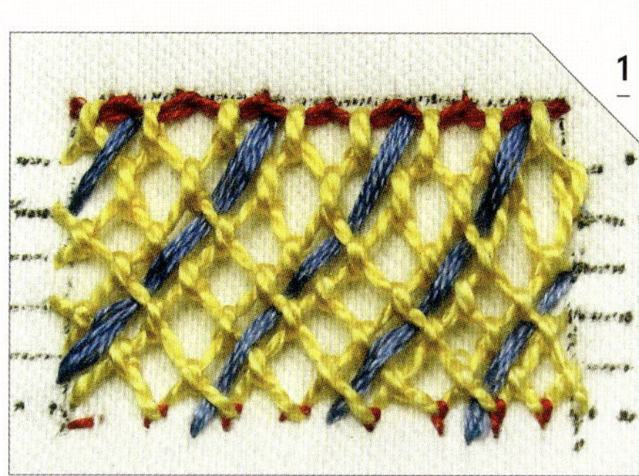

1

1 Weave every other diagonal 'corridor' of the trellis, using six strands of stranded cotton thread.

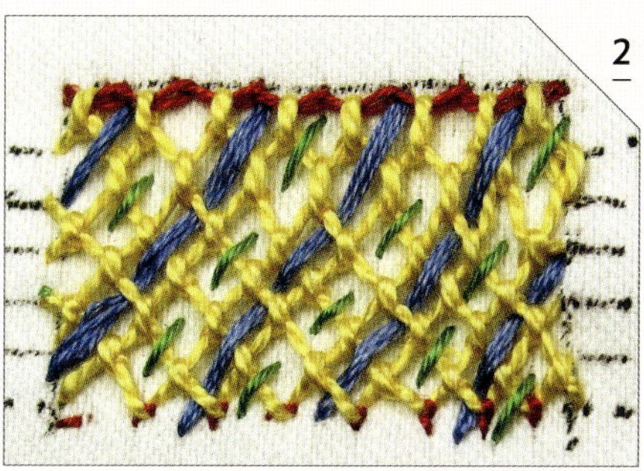

2

2 Fill in the remained 'corridors' with seeding stitch, working it over every other thread of a 'corridor'. As well as embellishing the stitch, you are also couching the trellis in place. Use any finer thread for this job.

TRELLIS CUP STITCH – WOVEN

A fine thread and big cells of trellis have been used here for clarity. The stitch looks nicer with smaller cells and the weaving worked in, for example, six strands of stranded cotton thread or similar weight thread.

1 Using contrasting thread, weave along each diagonal row. Bring your needle to the back of the fabric at the end of each row and come up for a new row.

1

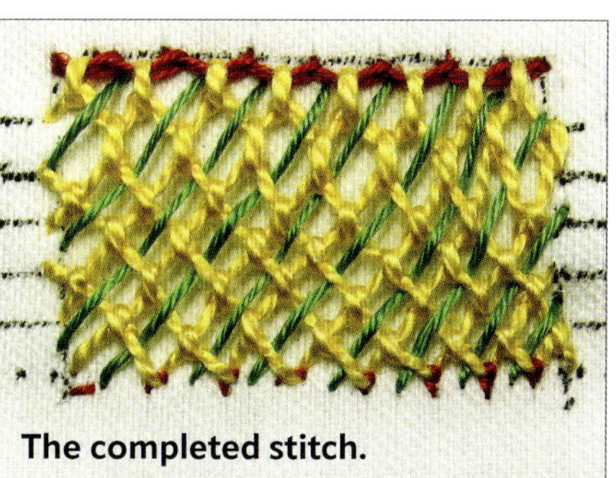

The completed stitch.

TUNING FORK STITCH

Start with a straight stitch (see page 201), then work fly stitches (see page 168) close together.

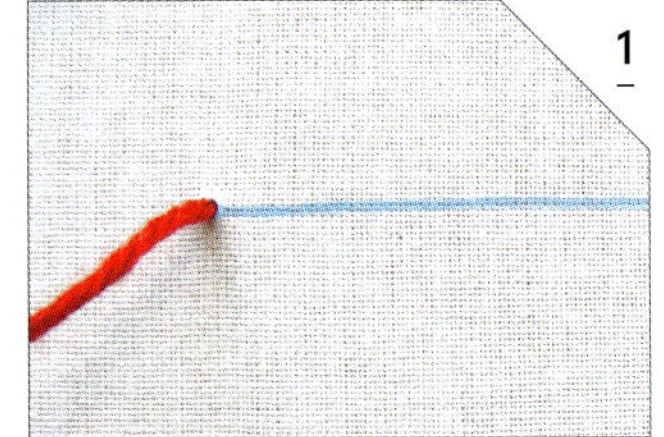

The completed stitch.

TUNING FORK STITCH – LAZY VARIATION

Also known as lazy tuning fork stitch. Work a line of backstitch (see page 144) or couched thread (see page 159) to begin.

While contrasting colours have been used here for clarity, using different colours can work well in your design.

TWISTED CHAIN STITCH

This stitch is very similar to rope stitch (see page 191). The only difference is the space left between the stitches of a chain.

1 Follow steps 1–5 for rope stitch. Bring the needle up on the design line, the length of the previous stitch further on.

2 Make a twist on the loop and bring the needle through the twisted loop.

3 Repeat steps 1–3 along the stitch line. To couch the last loop, work a small couching stitch, bringing the needle down outside the last loop.

A completed row of twisted chain stitch.

TWISTED CORD

Being worked out of embroidery thread or floss, twisted cord is not stretchable and rather hard. It may cause difficulties about threading a needle, but it looks so beautiful in embroidery that it is certainly worth trying. Twisted cord can be used for couching but also for other embroidery techniques like stem stitch, burden stitch and even silk shading.

The length of the thread and its initial softness will affect when the thread is 'finished' – that is, it will wrap around itself – so it is best to practise first.

Before you start, decide on the colour, thickness and number of threads for your cord.

1 Bring the threads together, thread a needle and make a knot (a single thread). Attach the thread to the fabric away from the design. Anchor the thread with small stitches, to prevent its tail from untwisting while you spin the other tail.

2 With the thread anchored, all is ready for twisting. Remove the needle, pinch the thread at its tip and twist it clockwise by sliding your finger along your thumb. Keep the thread stretched like a string during the whole procedure.

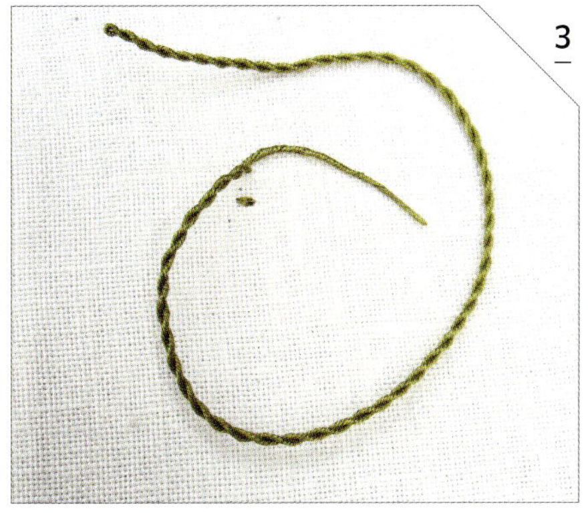

3 Making the free (unanchored) thread tail around 2.5cm (1in) longer than the anchored one, fold the twisted thread in two – the two halves will entwine.

4 Knot the tail with an invisible knot (see page 22): make a loose knot as shown, then stick a needle into the fabric inside the loop.

5 Tighten the knot around the needle: it will 'guide' the knot down to the fabric.

6 Trim off the cord. You can now thread a larger needle with the cord and use it for stitching.

TWISTED SINGLE BRUSSELS STITCH

This is also known as twisted buttonhole lace stitch.

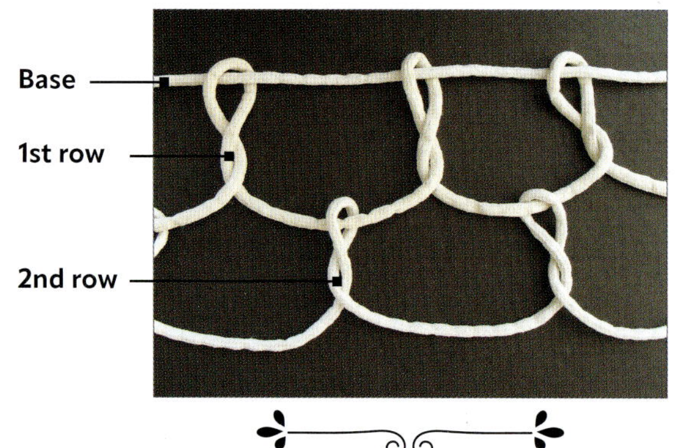

TWISTED SINGLE BRUSSELS STITCH – WHIPPED

Also known as tulle bars, this whipped variation on the stitch makes the lace firmer and therefore easier to work. My approach is slightly unusual, but easy to memorize.

Start with a base line of backstitch (the reason is explained on page 202) at the top of the area. The marks on the fabric shown here are only for clarity.

TIP

The shape at the end of step 1 is reminiscent of the gable end of a roof, where two sloping sides meet at the apex in a triangular shape.

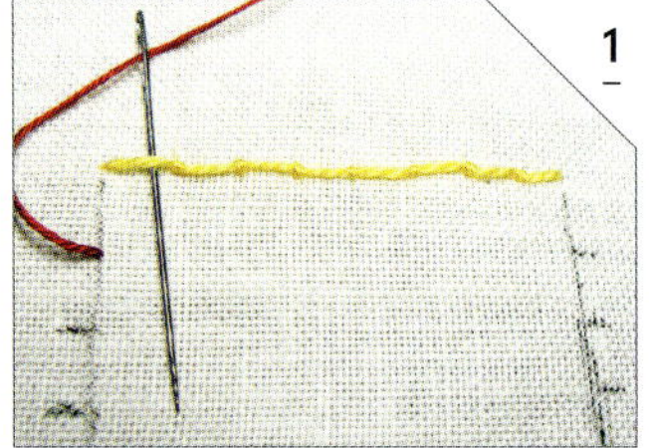

1 Bring the needle under the first stitch of the backstitch base, then draw through to tighten the thread.

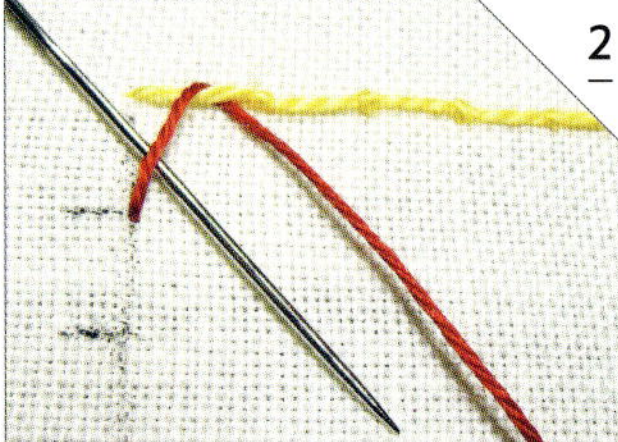

2 Bring the needle under the thread. As you draw it through, pull slightly to tighten the twist.

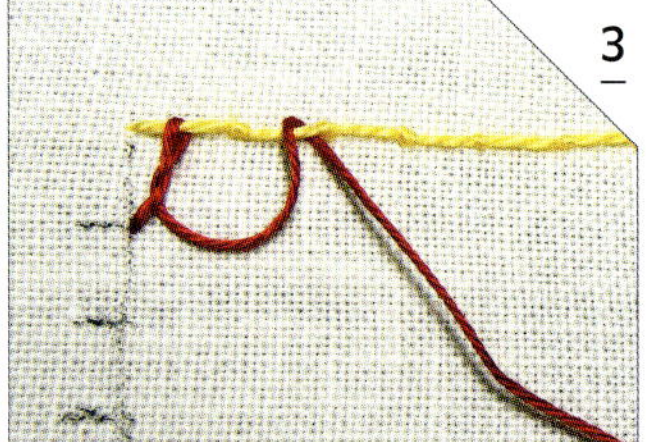

3 Come under the next stitch of the backstitch base.

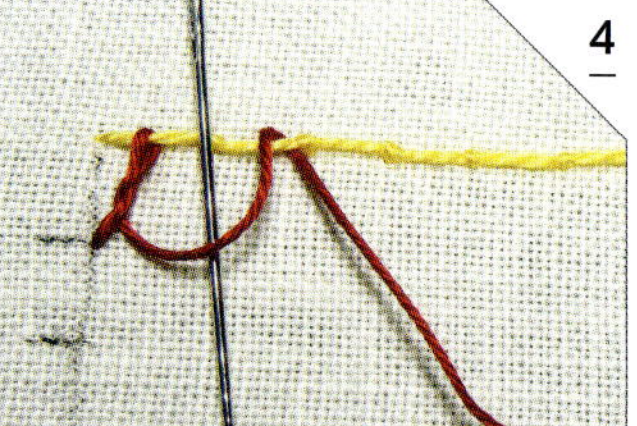

4 Repeat the trick in step 2 to produce another twist. Follow the same pattern to the end of the row.

TIP

The following steps will allow you to create the whipped variation. For the non-whipped variation, bring the needle up slightly below the first row (instead of slightly above it) in step 5, before working the second row, doing the mirror image of steps 1–4.

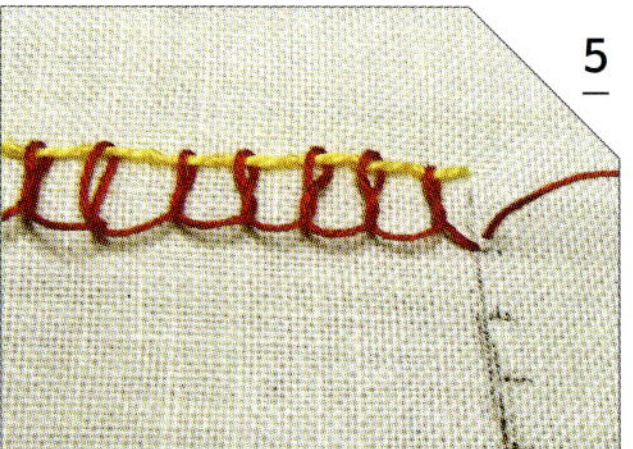

5 Bring your needle down to the back of the fabric at the end of the row, then come up level with the first row or right above it.

6 Work along the row as described in steps 1–4, taking the needle underneath each of the loops as shown.

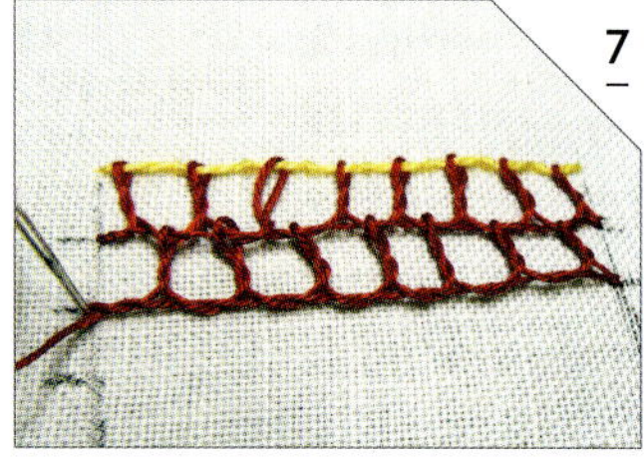

7 Go down at the end of the row, up at the beginning of the next row, and repeat until the area is filled. Couch the last row's loops to the fabric with small stitches.

VERMICELLI STITCH

The green thread meanders around within the design space, but it should not cross over itself at any point.

WHEEL SPIKE TECHNIQUE

Initially developed for stitching elements like car wheels, this technique may also be used for making flower centres and other elements of floral designs.

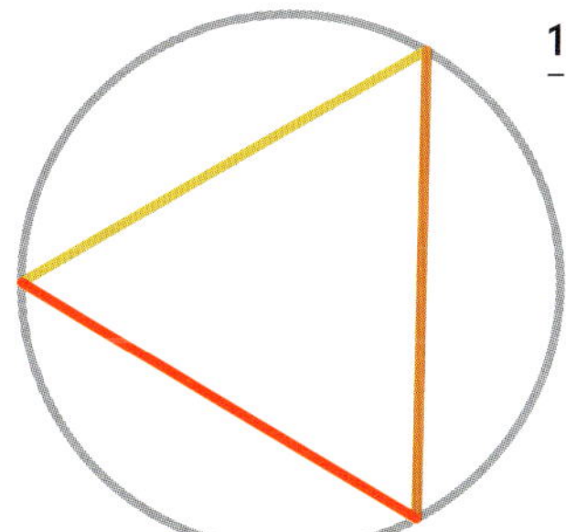

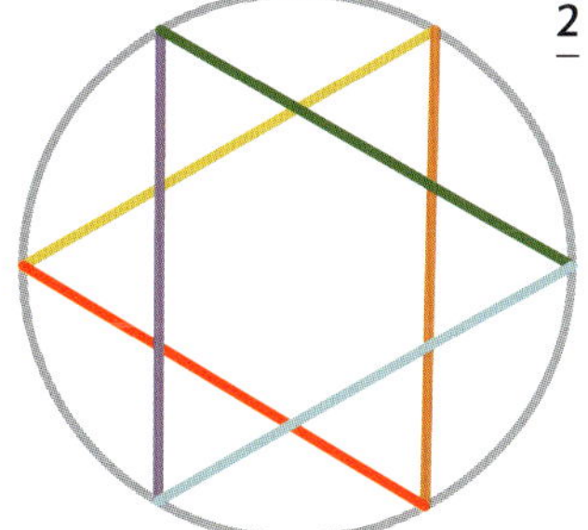

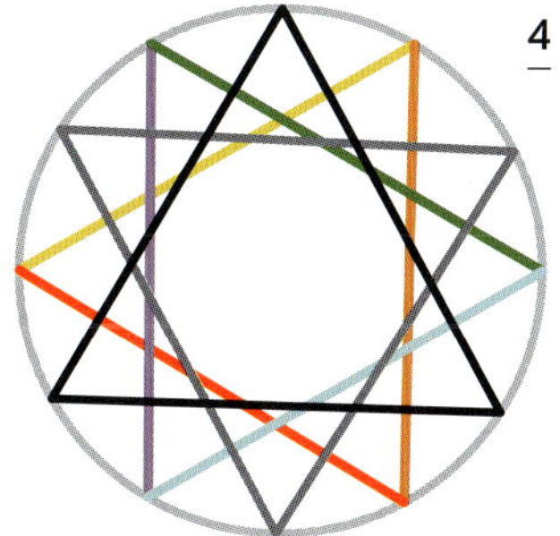

1 Draw a circle and work three straight stitches inside it, placing them to form an equilateral triangle.

2 Work a second triangle on top of the first, dividing the sections into two equal parts as shown.

3 Work a third triangle in the same way, placing it on top of the other two: no anchoring is needed.

4 Work the last (the fourth) triangle in the same manner.

WOVEN BAND

Use any number of base stitches.

1

2

3

4

5

6

7

WOVEN BAR

1

2

3

4

5

6

WOVEN BAR LEAF

Woven bar can be used for making a nicely rounded leaf. Work the base stitch loosely, then follow the steps for woven bar (see opposite).

Shown here is a semi-detached variation of the leaf. The weaving is worked in double thread over a base of triple thread, so the ribs of the leaf are distinct, but not too bulky. This approach leaves the thread coming out of the tip of the leaf at the end – hence why I call it semi-detached. The thread can be used to attach the tip of the leaf to the fabric to make the leaf slightly arched.

For a flatter result, take the thread down between an area of the weaving and trim it off.

Base stitch for a standard woven bar stitch.

Base stitch for a woven bar leaf stitch.

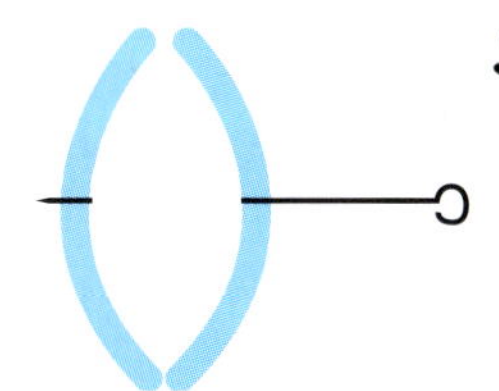

TIP

To hold the two threads of the base stitch apart, anchor them in place with a pin attached to the fabric as shown.

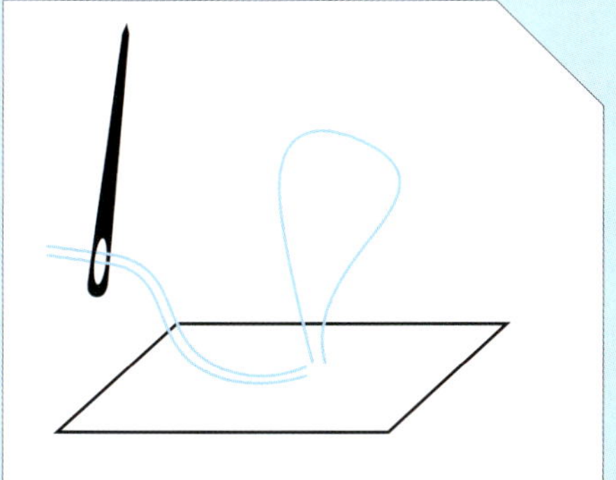

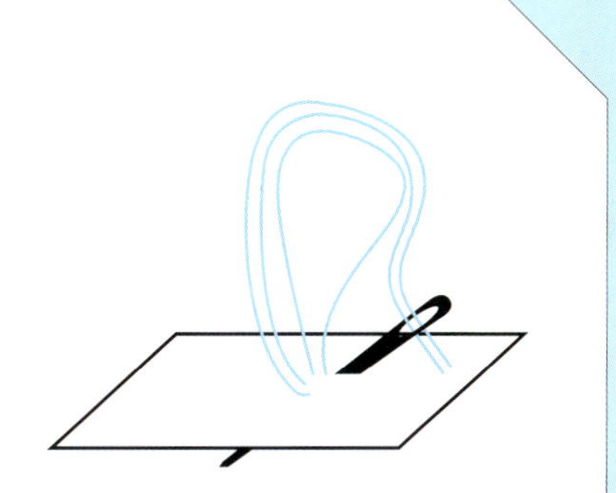

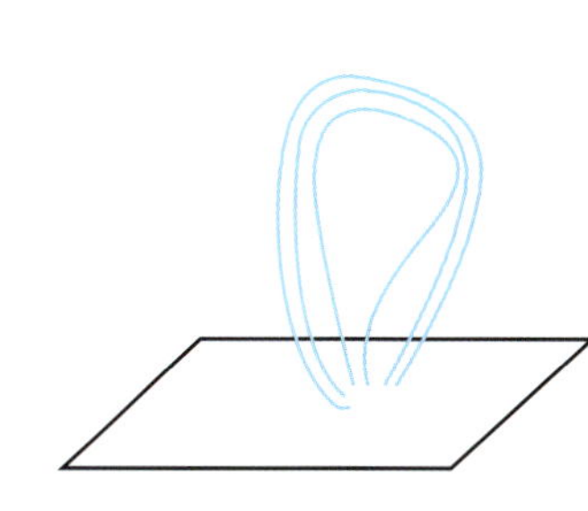

1 Bend the working thread in half. Thread the needle with the two thread tails. Now bring the threaded needle through the fabric, leaving a loop as long as the leaf you are stitching.

2 Work the second loop around the first one, using double thread this time. As a result, you get a loop worked of three strands of thread, with no knot on the back side.

TIP

You may find it helpful to anchor the loops round a pin attached to the fabric.

3 Using the same double thread, proceed to the regular weaving, tightening it more firmly at the base and the tip of the leaf, and leaving the central part looser to create the shape of a leaf.

WOVEN CIRCLE NEEDLELACE

Before you start, work parallel horizontal stitches in double thread. The distance between the stitches may vary, depending on the openwork effect you want.

TIPS

- Always pass the working thread under the double thread.
- Pull on the thread neither too tightly, nor too loosely, to get a nice woven circle without any gaps or loops.

1 Using a single thread, work the first vertical stitch over all the horizontal stitches – no weaving yet! Next, bring the needle up, take it under the topmost double stitch, and over the first vertical stitch.

2 Start weaving around the first intersection, working clockwise. Take the needle under the doubled thread (2A) on the left of the vertical stitch, then round the top and back under the doubled thread on the right (2B). Make five passes of this kind.

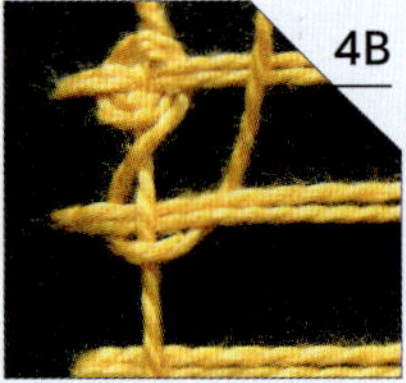

3 Take the needle under the second doubled thread, to the left of the first vertical stitch.

4 This time, the weaving goes anticlockwise (4A–C). Take the working thread round the double thread five times to form another circle (4D).

5 Repeat at each intersection to the bottom of the first vertical stitch, and then bring the needle down to the back of the fabric. To start the next line, come up at the bottom of the area, around 7mm (¼in) to the right of the first line and work a long straight vertical stitch.

TIP

The minimum space between the long stitches matches the diameter of a circle (~7mm/¼in). Working the vertical stitches this distance apart means the woven circles will be placed close enough to touch. For a more openwork effect, make the space bigger.

WOVEN FILLING – SOLID 2 × 2

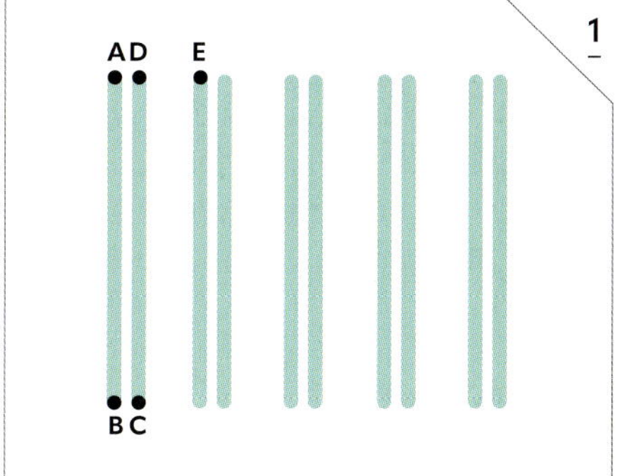

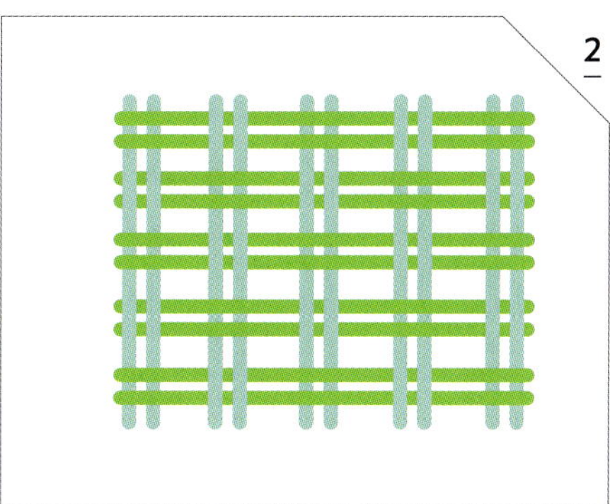

1 To make warp threads, work stitches in pairs, leaving very little space between them.

2 Weaving (weft threads). The weft stitches should also be in pairs (double stitches), so work the weaving in two steps. First weave over and under the pairs of warp stitches, using one thread only. Now go the same way with a second thread. The first double stitch is finished. Do the same for the second double stitch, going over where the first went under and vice versa.

WOVEN FILLING – SPACED BARS

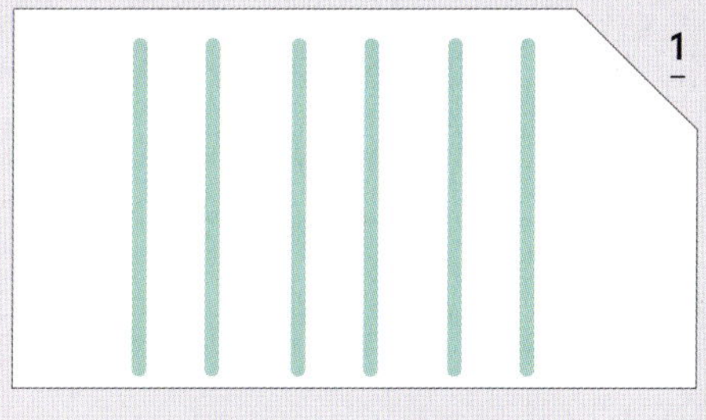

1 Work spaced stitches for warp threads.

2 Weave over and under these stitches (weft threads).

WOVEN WHEEL

TEMPLATES

I often make small additions to the designs as they occur to me, so you may spot a few differences between the finished embroideries and these templates. That is because such flashes of inspiration do not always work out for the best! These refined final versions of templates include only the best ideas.

Why do I bring attention to this? Simply because I want to invite you to follow your own flashes of inspiration, and encourage you to feel free to make your own changes to these templates. The keen-eyed will also spot small differences between some of the Light and Night versions – you are welcome to follow whichever option you prefer.

TIP

Except where noted, these templates are shown at actual size. If you need full-size or extra copies of the template, these are available to download for free from the Bookmarked Hub:

www.bookmarkedhub.com

Search for this book by title or ISBN: the files can be found under 'Book Extras'.

Membership of the Bookmarked online community is free.

Template for Doodle 4 – *Columbine* on pages 44–47.

This template is shown at three-quarters original size. Enlarge it by 133% before transferring it.

Template for Doodle 1 – *Happy Birthday* on pages 30–35.

Template for Doodle 2 – *Tiny the Snail* on pages 36–39.

Template for Doodle 3 – *Goldfish* on pages 40–43.

Template for pattern 1, used for *Queen Rose Light* on pages 52–61, and *Queen Rose Night* on pages 62–69.

Template for pattern 2, used for *Captured by Flora* on pages 72–81, and *Green Brougham* on pages 82–91.

This template is shown at three-quarters original size. Enlarge it by 133% before transferring it.

Template for pattern 3, used for *Jewel the Unicorn* on pages 94–103, and *Jewels of November* on pages 104–113.

This template is shown at half its original size. For *Jewel the Unicorn*, enlarge it to 200% before transferring it. For *Jewels of November*, enlarge it to 140% before transferring it.

Template for pattern 3, used for *Have a Nice Day* on pages 116–127, and *Good Night* on pages 128–139.

This template is shown at half original size. Enlarge it to 200% before transferring it.

STITCH INDEX

All the stitches are presented here as you might expect: in an alphabetical list. As well as allowing you to quickly find a particular stitch, you can also use this list to create your own magic stitch chart (see page 223).

Code for stitch categories

- ☐ **Line stitches** The shape of these stitches resembles a thread, a tape or a road. Ideal for stitching stems, twigs and lianas, the finest of them are also used to outline stitched areas. Stem stitch, Palestrina stitch, Gordian knot and one row of raised chain stitch band are good examples of this category, showing the variety of line width available to you.
- ◆ **Filling stitches** These are well adapted to fill in any part or area of embroidery. Lattice is a good example.
- ✪ **Isolated stitches** These are small individual stitches, such as lazy daisy stitch.
- ☙ **Leaves and circles** You may find distinguishing this type of stitch useful, as they are well-suited to fill in particular shapes. For example, raised fishbone stitch leaf is ideal to fill leaf shapes, and stem stitch rose is ideal for circles.

TIP

As with the names of stitches, the naming of categories of stitches varies, too. The divisions I suggest above are not absolute, since several rows of raised chain stitch band (for example) worked upon a broader foundation can make a nice filling stitch; and arranging lines of an outline stitch closely together will result in a new kind of filling stitch option – stem stitch filling is a perfect example.

Use these categories as starting points, and explore to your heart's content!

Your magic stitch chart

It is very handy to have the names of your favourite stitches at hand, to avoid missing any of them out. Moreover, it helps to arrange them as a table with columns headed as shown. Isolated stitches are placed between outline and filling stitches in the chart because most of these stitches can be used for these purposes. For example, French knots can be closely packed to fill an area; or worked along a design line as an outline.

If you plan to use an isolated stitch like this, draw an arrow against its name to mark its shift to the corresponding stitch group.

Make a copy of this blank magic stitch chart to use to create a list of stitches while developing your own original designs. You can also use it to help you substitute stitches of a particular kit or even – though it sounds almost heretical – to alter the designs of this book.

Outline stitches	**All the others**		**Filling stitches**
	Leaves and circles	*Isolated stitch*	

TIP

There is more than one way of organizing stitches into groups. Rather than grouping them into outline, filling and so forth, you might create your own categories – or simply use the magic stitch chart to highlight and keep track of your favourite stitches, so you know where best to use them in a design.

First published in 2025
Search Press Limited
Wellwood, North Farm Road,
Tunbridge Wells, Kent TN2 3DR

Printed in China.

ISBN: 978-1-80092-271-6
ebook ISBN: 978-1-80093-270-8

Suppliers
If you have difficulty in obtaining any of the materials and equipment mentioned in this book, then please visit the Search Press website for details of suppliers: www.searchpress.com

Extra full-size copies of the templates are also available to download free from the Bookmarked Hub. Search for this book by title or ISBN: the files can be found under 'Book Extras'. Membership of the Bookmarked online community is free:
www.bookmarkedhub.com

You are invited to visit the author's website:
www.owl-crafts.com

Publishers' note
All the step-by-step photographs in this book feature the author, Tatiana Popova, demonstrating how to embroider. No models have been used.

The projects in this book have been made using metric measurements. The imperial equivalents are rounded to the nearest ⅛in. Always use either metric or imperial measurements, not a combination of both.

ACKNOWLEDGEMENTS

'Thank you, WORLD!' These are the only words I am able to utter. It was early 2022: winter chills were almost gone and spring was in the air. Snow had melted in the streets of Kiev, the capital of Ukraine, and tender pussy willows were beginning to bloom here and there. We were looking forward to the joys of a new spring and sunshine. My husband and two sons were expecting progression in their jobs; my new website was about to be made public; and I was adding the finishing touches to the manuscript for this book and anticipating the usual 'will-they-won't-they' game with my nice publishers. We all felt so happy.

Then suddenly we realized… it was the time when all Ukrainians had to confront a horrible drama.

It is impossible to mention all the kind-hearted people who cared for, supported, prayed for, donated to, and placed orders to help me raise funds for my family, invited me to stay with them, and then assisted and supported us again. People from all walks of life and from all parts of the globe reached out to ask whether I was safe and how they could help me. I will never be able to list their names, for that list would beat the length of the 260-metre-long 'Monster Petition' of Victoria. Besides, some people prefer to remain anonymous. Their unanimity in kindness was so touching and their support so priceless – it literally helped us all to survive.

Humane kindness. We all need it, just to stay human.

Now I am safe and sound in my new UK home. While writing these lines, the delicious aroma of fragrant white jasmine blooms is drifting into my studio through the open windows – just as it did in my home city. I am safe and comfortable, and able to work again. Thank you, the far country, for letting me in! Thank you, kind Englishmen who helped me in. Thank you everybody, who assisted in my relocation.

And as a modern writer had it: 'I'm made up of everyone who has changed the way I think.'

THANK YOU, WORLD!

BIBLIOGRAPHY

Encyclopedia of Needlework by Thérèse de Dillmont, Bracken Books, new edition 1987

Encyclopedia of Victorian Needlework by Sophia Frances Anne Caulfeild, Dover Publications, 1972

Three-Dimensional Embroidery Stitches by Pat Trott, Search Press, 2005

Crewel Twists by Hazel Blomkamp, Search Press, 2012

Jacobean Crewel Work and Traditional Designs by Penelope, Wm. Briggs & Co. 1950.